The Philosophy of Xunzi

The Philosophy of Xunzi

A Reconstruction

Kurtis Hagen

OPEN COURT

Chicago and La Salle, Illinois

To order books from Open Court, call 1-800-815-2280 or visit
www.opencourtbooks.com.

Open Court Publishing Company is a division of Carus Publishing Company.

© 2007 by Carus Publishing Company

First printing 2007

Printed and bound in the United States of America.

Library of Congress Cataloging-in-Publication Data

Hagen, Kurtis.
  The philosophy of Xunzi : a reconstruction / Kurtis Hagen.
    p. cm.
    Summary: "Gives a new interpretation of Chinese philosopher Xunzi's ideas,
  which were central to Confucianism for over a thousand years. Xunzi is not
  absolutist or insistent upon conformity, but rather sees social roles as contingent
  and context-sensitive"—Provided by publisher.
  Includes bibliographical references and index.
  ISBN-13: 978-0-8126-9597-7 (alk. paper)
  ISBN-10: 0-8126-9597-6 (alk. paper)
  1. Xunzi, 340-245 B.C. Xunzi. 2. Philosophy, Chinese–To 221 B.C. I. Title.
  B128.H7H34 2007
    181'.112—dc22
                                                    2006037185

—To my parents—

Contents

Preface

English Translations and
Recent Commentary on Xunzi

Currently there are four substantial English translations of the Xunzi,[1] John Knoblock's three-volume set completed in 1994 being the only complete one. Burton Watson and Homer Dubs both offer translations of what they consider the most important chapters. Dubs's was first in 1928, and Watson followed in 1963, covering nearly the same material as Dubs. Most recently (2001), Eric Hutton has translated important sections from several chapters, though this is substantially shorter than the translations of Dubs and Watson.

Most texts on the history or philosophy of China devote a section or chapter to Xunzi, but this is usually confined to a handful of pages. Books on Chinese philosophy, such as A. C. Graham's *Disputers of the Dao*, and Chad Hansen's *Daoist Theory of Chinese Philosophy*, and David Nivison's *The Ways of Confucianism*, also deal with Xunzi to some extent, but until recently there were relatively few books exclusively devoted to Xunzi's philosophy, although there are numerous articles addressing specific aspects of his thought.

Until the last decade, the scholarship devoted to Confucius or Laozi dwarfed that focused on Xunzi. Mencius and Zhuangzi had likewise enjoyed more scholarly attention. Although the difference was less drastic, it did seem out of proportion with the importance of this thinker in the development of Chinese philosophy and culture. He is clearly among ancient China's seven most important thinkers, and offers us the most closely argued text of that period. To study Confucius but not Xunzi would be like studying sayings attributed to Socrates while ignoring Aristotle.

It is appropriate, then, that there has recently been a sudden increase of interest in Xunzi's thought. Before Paul Goldin's 1999 *Rituals of the Way* there were only three books in English (excluding translations) devoted entirely to Xunzi's thought (Dubs's 1927 *Hsüntze: The Moulder of Ancient Confucianism*; A. S. Cua's 1985 *Ethical Argumentation: A Study in Hsün Tzu's Moral*

---

1. There are also various chapters, sections, as well as bits and pieces published here and there. See, for example, Eno 1990, Machle 1993, Mei 1951, Duyvendak 1924, and Chan 1963. While some chapters ("A Discourse on Heaven," "The Rectification of Names," and "Man's Nature is Evil") have been translated many times, for the majority of the text there is only one published English translation, Knoblock's.

Epistemology, and Edward Machle's 1993 *Nature and Heaven in the Xunzi: A Study of the Tian Lun*). Goldin's book was the first since Dubs's to offer an interpretation of most of the major themes in the *Xunzi*. It was followed in 2000 by a collection of essays edited by P. J. Ivanhoe and T. C. Kline, *Virtue, Nature, and Moral Agency in the Xunzi*. Kline has put together a second collection, *Ritual and Religion in the Xunzi*, which was published as I was completing this book. In addition, a huge volume on Xunzi came out in 2003: *The Confucian Quest for Order: The Origin and Formation of the Political Thought of Xunzi*, by Masayuki Sato. Further, Janghee Lee, a former classmate, has written *Xunzi and Early Chinese Naturalism*, which has just recently been released. And, finally, A. S. Cua published another book on Xunzi in 2005, *Human Nature, Ritual, and History: Studies in Xunzi and Chinese Philosophy*.

The book you are reading is different in the degree to which it is in conversation with other works on Xunzi. In particular, I directly challenge the interpretations of a number of scholars regarding Xunzi's fundamental worldview. I also introduce the views of several Chinese and Japanese scholars, whose works are available only in Chinese or Japanese. In addition, I provide the original text for those quotations, as well as for quotations from classical Chinese sources. In the case of Xunzi, I also provide references to both Knoblock's translation and Watson's translation. Further, though it is certainly about Xunzi on one level, this book is more importantly about a set of interrelated philosophical ideas, and thus may be of interest to students, scholars, or anyone else with a serious interest ethics, political theory, or the philosophy of language, as well as Chinese thought.

Regarding My Purpose and Approach

Throughout this book, I highlight dozens of statements made by a number of scholars that are at least suggestive of views that I argue are problematic and unjustified as interpretations of Xunzi. In some cases I may appear to be oversensitive, as my position, in the end, may not be so different from that of at least some of those I have criticized. However, it is precisely because of the prevalence of what I will call the "realist" interpretation of Xunzi in the English-language literature that it is important to be extra careful not to even inadvertently suggest this view with the language we choose.

Although my approach may seem polemical, it is not my objective to *demonstrate* anything. Indeed, final demonstration is incongruent with the constructivist view I am trying to encourage. Rather, my goal is to *call into question* certain views, and to articulate an alternative. At times, when Xunzi does not provide a concise statement that would clearly support my position, I fill in the gap with an interpretation based on a more holistic understanding.

In such cases, I often quote some other scholar—whether Western or East Asian[2]—who has expressed a similar view on the particular point. This is not to prove that I am right, but to establish that the interpretation I am offering is at least plausible, as well as to add more voices to the conversation. The strategy is to construct an interpretation that hangs together better than the realist one. While the parts need to support the whole, in the end it is the whole that vindicates the parts.

Though do I offer a positive, "constructivist" interpretation of Xunzi's major themes, my project is most fundamentally a critical one. Given my purpose, to challenge realist interpretations, one should not expect to find balance in terms of praise and criticism. Specifically, one should not infer from my relentless critique that I disagree on every point with those I am challenging, or that my criticisms, even when judged to be convincing, discredit or even diminish the importance of the works in which I have found some fault.

On the contrary, one would be right to assume that, for those whom I have taken issue with in these pages, in every case, I have done so precisely because I take them to be serious and competent scholars who are at least potentially influential. Rather than anything like an attempt to discredit their work, this critique should be viewed as an encouragement to read their interpretations, but to do so with a critical eye with respect to the several issues I have focused on. It is my sincere hope that I have offered a corrective that, when considered together with arguments from the other side, will facilitate the working out of a still more adequate account.

As for my positive account, I do not distinguish interpretive reconstructions from what may be considered "accurate descriptions." However, this is not a feature peculiar to my interpretation. Pretense otherwise notwithstanding,[3] *all* good interpretations involve an inseparable mix of both. Indeed, transmission mixed with constructive innovation has been the lifeblood of Confucianism. That having been said, I have endeavored to provide a textually grounded interpretation, which strives to be loyal to not only to Xunzi, and to the text that bears his name, but to sensibilities that I understand as characteristic of the early Confucian tradition generally.

---

2. While there are significant differences between interpretations of Xunzi found in the English language literature and those found in the East Asian literature, it is beyond the scope of this project to assess the latter comprehensively. Nevertheless, in reviewing Japanese and Chinese secondary sources, when I find statements in support of positions I have taken, I do not hesitate to cite these. I have also written a short summary of the first three chapters of this book in Japanese, which I plan to publish in Japan. In these ways I hope to make each side a little more aware of the other.

3. Aaron Stalnaker opines, "An accurate analysis of Xunzi's own position should be the basis for any construction of a neo-Xunzian position for our time, and these two related goals should always be kept distinct" (2002, 296).

Notes and Conventions

Earlier versions of each chapter were published as follows:

Chapter 1: "A Critical Review of Ivanhoe on Xunzi," *Journal of Chinese Philosophy* 27.3 (September 2000): 361–73.

Chapter 2: "The Concepts of *Li* and *Lei* in the *Xunzi*: Constructive Patterning of Categories," *International Philosophical Quarterly* 41.2 (June 2001): 183–97.

Chapter 3: "Xunzi's Use of *Zhengming*: Naming as a Constructive Project," *Asian Philosophy* 12.1 (March 2002): 35–51.

Chapter 4: "Xunzi and the Nature of Confucian Ritual," *Journal of the American Academy of Religion* 71.2 (June 2003): 371–403.

Chapter 5: "Artifice and Virtue in the Xunzi," *Dao: A Journal of Comparative Philosophy* 3.1 (Winter 2003): 85–107.

I have significantly revised each chapter (chapter 2 receiving the lightest revisions). Chapter 1, in particular, is quite different from the original article. While it contains most of the material from that article, it is twice as long, and the argument no longer focuses on just P. J. Ivanhoe. Significantly, I have added support from Chinese and Japanese sources (of the original articles, only the last one contained quotations from these sources). In addition, this version provides the Chinese and Japanese text for quotations translated into English.

Chinese terms occurring in quotations, if romanized by any system other than pinyin, have been converted to pinyin, and "Xunzi" is written as one word. Also, for the sake of uniformity, simplified Chinese characters have been converted to traditional ones.

Unless otherwise indicated, translations are my own. References to the Chinese text of the *Xunzi* are to *A Concordance to the Hsün Tzu*. References to Knoblock's translation, as well as Watson's translation (when there is one), and occasionally others, are provided for comparison. I have used the following conventions to abbreviate citations:

pp/cc/ll	page/chapter/line number, in *A Concordance to the Hsün Tzu*
K: 12.3a	chapter 12 section 3a in Knoblock's translation
W 123	page 123 in Watson's translation (*Hsün-tzu: Basic Writings*)
H 123	page 123 in Hutton's translation
D 123	page 123 in Dubs's translation
GSR: 123a	character number 123a in Karlgren's *Grammata Serica Recensa*

Acknowledgments

This project had two sources of inspiration. One was my encounter with John Searle's *The Construction of Social Reality* in a directed reading with Kenneth Kipnis, as a graduate student at the University of Hawaii. The other involved recognizing certain problems with Burton Watson's translation of the *Xunzi*, while comparing it to the classical Chinese text in preparation for one of Roger Ames's seminars. Reconsidering key passages with Searle's ideas still fresh in my head, an alternative interpretation, which I labeled "constructivism," began to take form. The more passages I considered, the more confident I became that a constructivist interpretation was not only possible, but had significant advantages over the realist view that I was finding in much of the secondary literature on Xunzi.

As I worked out this interpretation over the next several years I accrued many debts. I am grateful, first of all, for my dissertation committee's patience and for the latitude they afforded me in developing my views, as well as for their skillful balance of encouragement and critical review. Especially noteworthy are the comments I received from Jim Tiles—detailed and helpful constructive criticisms, encouragements, and suggestions of the nature his students have come, by habit, to expect from him. Of my chairman, Roger Ames, suffice it to say here that he was an inspiration, both personally and philosophically, from long before this project took form. His insights into the nature of early Chinese thought shown like beacons guiding my search for a more adequate account of Xunzi.

Kakuko Shoji, of the East-Asian Languages and Literature department at UH, is to be commended for her willingness to provide directed readings, not only for myself, but for any serious student who needed training in reading advanced Japanese, even when not a member of her department. This was enormously helpful. Further, David McCraw's skillful introduction to classical Chinese followed by a string of translation courses offered by professor Ames were godsends.

My experience working as a teaching assistant for Thomas Jackson, a.k.a. "Dr. J," (in the Philosophy for Children program), and later with Graham Parkes, substantially influenced my thinking leading up to my dissertation proposal, and during the initial phases of writing. In addition, I profited from innumerable discussions with classmates, and especially those with Steve Coutinho who served as an invaluable sounding board at the critical stages just before my project began to take form. In later stages, Kwong-loi Shun (from whom I received my first introduction to Chinese philosophy eleven years earlier) was kind enough to advise me on appropriate Chinese secondary sources, and Jinmei Yuan cheerfully assisted me regarding tedious details of translation (any errors, or course, are mine alone). I also benefited from constructive comments and suggestions from Peter Manicus, David McCraw, Chung-ying Cheng, Bryan

Van Norden, and several anonymous reviewers, as well as a correspondence with Eric Hutton. One reviewer of the book manuscript, Paul Goldin, is no longer anonymous. His critical comments and suggestions (though I did not follow all of them) were of great assistance as well.

Also, I am grateful for having received a Monbusho scholarship from the Japanese government, and for the support of Professor Ikeda Tomohisa, which together made possible my first extended stay in Japan. In addition, my "tutor" at the University of Tokyo, Hirose Kunio, was of enormous help for his critical evaluation of my translations (again, any errors are mine alone). I am also thankful for the support of the Japan Society for the Promotion of Science which providing me with an opportunity for a second extended stay in Japan, during which I was able to complete extensive revisions of earlier versions of each chapter, and better integrate them.

Finally, I would be remiss not to note a special kind of gratitude owed to the late John Knoblock, who has furnished the only complete English translation of the *Xunzi*, and to P. J. Ivanhoe, as well as all the others whose views I have in these pages criticized. Were it not for their pioneering work, this project would not have even been thinkable. I hope, humbly, that I have at least helped create a space, a not yet clearly articulated domain between the views advocated and those criticized, wherein a more adequate account may continue to be worked out.

Introduction

Xunzi's Context and Influence

Xunzi lived during the Warring States period, shortly before the unification of China in 221 BCE under Qin Shi Huangdi, the so-called first emperor (whose unearthed army of terracotta warriors may be seen in Xi'an). At this time, the various states that composed China were engaged in a mortal struggle, either vying for supremacy or else fighting for their lives. It was a time of great upheaval. It was a time rich in philosophy.

Xunzi is sometimes said to occupy in the history of Chinese philosophy the place of Aristotle in the Western philosophic tradition, appearing at the end of the heyday of the classical period (see Knoblock 1988, vol. 1, vii). He is chronologically third of the three great Confucian thinkers of that period—the first being Confucius himself, who lived from about 551 to 479 BCE. Since Confucius's ideas left ample room for interpretation, Mencius (fourth century BCE) provided a more determinate account of key doctrines. Xunzi (fl. 298–38 BCE) arrived on the philosophical scene shortly after Mencius. Two of Xunzi's pupils, Li Si and Han Feizi, played roles in the formation of the legalist philosophy adopted by the first emperor. The Qin dynasty was short lived, however, and Confucianism was adopted as the orthodox philosophy of the Han dynasty, which followed—lasting four hundred years, from 206 BCE to 220 CE. Several of Xunzi's students were instrumental in editing and transmitting Confucian classics, ensuring Xunzi's indirect influence on the development of Confucian thinking throughout the Han period and beyond. Xunzi's direct influence during the Han was also substantial. For example, as Dubs notes, "The greatest scholar of the period, Dong Zhongshu, was profoundly influenced by Xunzi" (1966a, 136).

Xunzi revered Confucius, but was sharply critical of Mencius, at least with respect to one important doctrine: the evaluation of *xing* 性 (which for Xunzi meant the dispositions we are born with, but for Mencius was something which could grow and develop). The dispute led to the question of who was the legitimate transmitter of the Confucian way. Though Xunzi's ideas informed Confucian thinking for centuries, by the time Zhu Xi (twelfth century CE) compiled the "Four Books"—the *Analects* of Confucius, the *Mencius*, the *Daxue* (Great Learning), and the *Zhongyong* (Doctrine of the Mean)—which served as the basis for the examination system that qualified aspiring civil servants for political office, it was clearly Mencius who was dubbed "orthodox," and Xunzi was marginalized. However, as Dubs also notes, "The fact that Xunzi was later condemned because of his teachings about human nature does not alter his influence upon Confucianism, for at the time when that judgment was finally passed by Zhu Xi, Xunzi's teaching had already passed into the orthodox stream of thought and even Zhu Xi himself had been influenced by it" (1966a, 136). Further, strains of Xunzi's philosophy are even more apparent in the works of Confucian critics of Zhu Xi, such as Zhu Xi's contemporary Chen Liang, and the Qing dynasty's Dai Zhen, as well as Tokugawa Japan's Ogyū Sorai.

While a host of commentaries on the great thinkers of the Zhou dynasty were authored during the Han,[1] the earliest extant commentary on the *Xunzi* (by Yang Liang) dates back only to 818 CE. By then a thousand years had passed. Dynasties had risen and fallen, and Buddhism had entered China and mingled with Daoist sensibilities for at least 500–700 years. The gulf that separated the first known commentator on the *Xunzi* from his subject matter is nearly as wide as the gulf that separates us from the text today.

The history of ideas is important, in part, because there is continuity between how people conceive the world and how their intellectual ancestors did. In addition, the way people conceive the world influences the way they endeavor to manage their way though it. Though Westerners are not the intellectual heirs of the ancient Chinese philosophers, our world is becoming smaller, and we are increasingly in contact with those who are. Whether this contact is a collision or a constructive collaboration will depend in part on the adequacy of our mutual understanding. Understanding Xunzi, to some degree, contributes to the understanding of Chinese thought and culture. Further, while this type of justification would hold for any historical figure, its force is particularly great for Xunzi and our topic.

Xunzi is arguably the single most brilliant philosopher of the rich classical Chinese tradition, with the possible exception of Zhuangzi. Further, it is not adequately acknowledged that Xunzi fully understood and appreciated the significance of Zhuangzi's fundamental insight into the conventionality of language and social norms.[2] However, he saw this insight as a something that could be useful to Confucianism, not as a refutation of it.

On one interpretation, Xunzi claims that the sages of old "gave birth" to a language that truly and uniquely describes the world and our roles and reciprocal obligations in it. On this view, the ritual patterns embodied by the sages are uniquely appropriate, and universally and eternally so. Moral categories expressed in language are real, and alternative interpretations are necessarily false and thus pernicious. There is no room for discussion, unorthodox doctrines are

---

1. During this period, sometime after 26 CE, Liu Xiang compiled, edited, and arranged some 322 manuscripts of the *Xunzi* (mostly duplicates) down to the 32 chapter-length books we have now. The present sequential order of the books, however, is a result of changes made by Yang Liang.

2. As exceptions, see Yearley 1980, and also Nivison 2000.

to be silenced, and the crooked are to be pressed straight in conformity with the true standard. No one person has stated all of this position so baldly. It is a composite. Nevertheless, its various aspects are stated or implied by a number of scholars, and the overall picture seems to guide many interpretations and translations.

I seek to establish that the text supports a different—and more reasonable—interpretation. The moral categories and roles and responsibilities that go along with them, which were articulated and put into practice by the sage kings, serve as a model for achieving the order necessary for a flourishing community. There is a significant difference, however, between saying they serve as an exemplary model, and saying they serve as an absolute standard. The sages over time and through trial and error developed a workable set of social institutions. This does not entail that it is the only, or even absolutely best, set of institutions, or that it is final, complete, universal, or timeless. Rather, institutions are social constructs designed to facilitate peace and social harmony. As circumstances change, the institutions may also change.

For Whom Are Xunzi's Teachings?

In 2003, Masayuki Sato published the most extensive study of the formation of Xunzi's thought yet available in English. Therein, he suggests that Xunzi's teachings were directed solely at rulers. He sets the tone in his preface, writing: "Xunzi's theory is . . . offered exclusively to conductors[3] [i.e., rulers], not to all the participating performers" (xiii). Making a related point, he also writes, "[O]nly a ruler in the imagery of Xunzi's thought is exclusively allowed to speculate on the meaning and significance of the social norms" (xiii).[4] While it is clear that Xunzi's theory *is* meant for rulers, to say that it is exclusively so is problematic. While some of his teachings may be directed mainly toward rulers, such as "Kingly Regulations," most are ambiguously directed, at least in part aimed at the intellectual elite of various levels. His "Encouraging Learning" and "Improving Oneself" could be for anyone.

While the early Confucians certainly made efforts to influence rulers, they would generally teach anyone who made a concerted effort to learn. This is most obvious in the *Analects.* When asked what more could be done for people who were already flourishing, Confucius answers succinctly, "Teach them (教之)"

---

3. The full metaphor on which the idea of the ruler as conductor is based is as follows: "The composer is an ancient sage king, musical scores are the rituals and social norms (which were believed to have been institutionalized by the sage kings), the conductor is the ruler, the members of the orchestra and choir are the people living in a society, and the perfect performance of the music is the peace and order which Xunzi aimed to attain with his theory" (Sato 2003, xiii).

4. Sato sums up the paragraph: "In short, the *Book of Xunzi* is a manual for aspirants on how to become the top leader in society" (2003, xiv). This is also too narrow an interpretation. The *Xunzi* would be better described as a manual for anyone aspiring to make constructive contributions to the instantiation of *dao* in the world.

(*Analects* 13.9). Of himself, he remarked, "I have never yet failed to provide instruction to anyone who has come to me of their own initiative [even though they could afford no more than] a gift of dried meat."[5] As a general statement, Confucius says, "In teaching, there are no [social] classes."[6]

There are no such pithy sayings to be found in the *Xunzi*. And, indeed, much of the content of the *Xunzi* concerns how to govern effectively. Nevertheless, Xunzi's first rule of good governance is to promote good people. Where are these people to come from? Theoretically at least, even for Xunzi, they can come from any class. Xunzi writes, "Although one may be a descendent of commoners, if one accumulates culture and learning, is upright in personal conduct, and is able to devotedly apply oneself to the observance of ritual propriety with a sense of appropriateness, such a person should be brought up to the status of chief minister or high official."[7]

In addition, regarding whether it was possible for any person to become an equal of the sage king Yu, Xunzi writes: "Yu became a sage through his practice of *ren* 仁 (comprehensive virtue) and *yi* 義 (appropriateness), by following a model (*fa* 法), and being morally upright (*zheng* 正).[8] That being the case, *ren*, *yi*, *fa*, and *zheng* have a reasonableness (*li* 理) that is understandable and enabling. Everybody, even an ordinary person, has what it takes to understand the basic substance of *ren*, *yi*, *fa*, and *zheng*; everybody has the wherewithal to develop these abilities (*ju* 具)."[9]

Further, the passage goes on to assert that if one exerts oneself over a long period, even an ordinary person could "form a triad[10] with *tian* 天 and *di* 地 (the forces of nature)."[11] That is, anyone who has sufficiently developed his or her moral character and intellect can contribute to the ongoing creation and

---

5. 自行束脩以上，吾未嘗無誨焉。 (*Analects* 7.7). Indeed, Confucius's favorite student, Yan Hui, was in continuous poverty.

6. 有教無類。 *Analects* 15.39.

7. 雖庶人之子孫也。積文學。正身行。能屬於禮義。則歸之卿相士大夫。 (9/26/3; K:9.1; W 33). Cf. *Analects* 12.22.

8. *Zheng* means "upright" or "straight," and in ethical contexts has the sense of "proper conduct," "moral rectitude," or "just" in the sense of "unbiased." See the glossary of key terms for descriptions of *ren*, *yi*, and *fa*. Also, notice that *ju* 具, in addition to "talent," more basically means "tool," "utensil," or "implement." *Ren*, *yi*, *fa*, and *zheng* are thought of as developed talents that are akin to tools. See chapter 5 for the relation between artifice and virtue.

9. 凡禹之所以為禹者。以其為仁義法正也。然則仁義法正有可知可能之理。然而塗之人也皆有可以知仁義法正之質。皆有可以能仁義法正之具。 (89/23/61–62; K: 23.5a; W 166).

10. The *Huangdi* expresses what forming a triad with *tian* and *di* amounts to: "The activities that form a triad with *tian* and *di* are called cultural patterns (*wen* 文)" (動靜參天地謂之文). It also says, "Forming a triad with *tian* and *di* involves uniting with the heart-mind of the common people" (參於天地，合於民心) (*Huangdi, Sidu*, chap. 1.5). One must not ignore the role of the common people in the formation of culture. Strictly top-down interpretations of Confucianism are too simplistic. See section 3.4 for the roles of different classes in the process of naming. (See also Sato 2003, 318–19, for his translations of the above passages, in which he interprets the ruler as the focus).

11. 89/23/69; K: 23.5a; W 167 (see next note for Chinese text); cf. K: 3.5, 8.11, 9.15, 13.9, and 17.2a.

renewal of culture, for that is the role of people in relation to nature and the human predicament. Sato translates this part of the passage as follows: "Suppose that a man in the street observes the teachings of [Confucian moral] practice and makes them the curriculum of his learning, concentrates his mind/heart and will on learning, and considers and examines things carefully. If he continues his efforts over a long period of time and accumulates good acts without repose, then he will master miraculous [transformation] and illuminating intelligence, and form a trinity with Heaven and Earth."[12] At this point, Sato concedes, "Xunzi transformed the unrealistic goal of forming a trinity into an *attainable aim* for any individual who diligently practices moral cultivation" (Sato 2003, 323; emphasis his).

It would be hard indeed to reconcile the idea that the teachings of Confucian moral practices can be taken up by a so-called man in the street, but that Xunzi's theory is only for rulers. Xunzi's teachings have as their goal the facilitation of moral development, namely, to help people become *junzi* 君子 (exemplary people), and even, possibly, sages. While Xunzi's philosophy may be especially important for rulers, it is also for any ordinary person who has taken on the daunting challenge of becoming extraordinary. In order to cultivate oneself, however, Xunzi insists repeatedly that a teacher and model are of the utmost importance. "In learning, nothing is as useful as drawing near to the proper people. Rituals and music may be taken as models but they do not offer explanations."[13] Rituals are not enough; one needs a competent teacher. And, indeed, Xunzi was such a teacher.[14]

* * *

A central theme in the *Xunzi* is the advocacy of becoming a *junzi* 君子, which I will translate "exemplary person."[15] Sato's insistence that Xunzi's theory is only for rulers is likely a result of another questionable view that he emphasizes repeatedly: that the term *junzi* refers simply to rulers.[16] He claims that the terms *shengren* 聖人 (sages)[17] and *shi* 士 (which he translates as

---

12. Sato 2003, 322, brackets are his; cf. p. 397, where his translation is a bit different. 今使塗之人者以其可以知之質可以能之具。本夫仁義之可知之理可能之具。然則其可以為禹明矣。今使塗之人伏術為學。專心一志。思索孰察。加日縣久。積善而不息。則通於神明參於天地矣。(89/23/67–69; K: 23.5a; W 167). See K: 8.11 for a similar theme.

13. 學莫便乎近其人。禮樂法而不說。(2/1/34; K: 1.10; W 20).

14. We only know about a handful of Xunzi's students (see Sato 2003, 57–60), and while most were politically active, at least one of them, Fuqiu Bo, did not seem to have had an interest in being directly involved in politics, but rather choose the path of scholarship and teaching.

15. See the glossary of key terms.

16. Note that the opening passage of the *Analects* suggests that it was possible for one's worth to go unnoticed and still be a *junzi*. Confucius says, "To be unappreciated yet not resentful, is this not characteristic of a *junzi*?" 人不知而不慍，不亦君子乎？(*Analects* 1.1). Cf. *Analects* 15.7, 15.19, 15.20.

17. Sato writes, "[T]he status of sage is interchangeable with that of the rulers of a country" (2003, 332). On the contrary, "sage," like *junzi*, is foremost a moral and intellectual category, rather

"officer-aspirants"[18]) also indicate rulers[19] (although in the latter case it could be one of modest scope).[20]

In one case Sato even takes *ren* 人 (person) to indicate a ruler, translating a passage: "Man (ruler) maintains [social] order" (2003, 318). I read this passage, "People have their orderly government,"[21] which I take to mean it is the province of people, as opposed to the some natural or mysterious force, to create order. The passage occurs, after all, in the general context of distinguishing the "different roles for *tian* (nature) and *ren* (people)."[22] If Xunzi had wanted to clearly indicate that it was exclusively rulers he was referring to, he could have easily done so, but he did not.

In any case, even if what Xunzi meant here when he used the term *ren* is ruler (which I would admit is not entirely implausible), still, no one would say that the word *ren means* ruler. Neither does *shi* or *junzi*.[23] There are cases where Xunzi uses the word *junzi* to unambiguously refer to a ruler. However, for Xunzi, as for Confucius, *junzi* was primarily a moral category, and did not correspond to the actual holding of office, but rather to possessing those developed moral and intellectual traits that qualify one as worthy of holding such a position. Xunzi writes, "*Junzi* are able to act in ways that are praiseworthy, but they are not necessarily able to make others appreciate them. They can act in ways that are useful, but they cannot necessarily make others employ them."[24] He also writes, "*Junzi* are born no different [from anybody else], but they are adept at availing themselves of things [i.e., Confucian teachings]."[25]

Sato does admit that *shi*, *junzi*, and *shengren* are, at least in part, moral terms, and he recognizes that the worthy might not always hold office. He writes, for example, "Xunzi says that the significance of learning starts with behaving oneself as a '*shi* 士'. . . . Xunzi had conceived of his own groupings on these three levels [i.e., *shi*, *junzi*, and *shengren*] according to the accomplishment of

---

than a political one—although it does entail large-scale accomplishments, which only a ruler is typically able to provide. Thus, sages are generally rulers, but rulers are not generally sages.

18. I approve of this translation, and would note that it undermines the idea that *shi* are rulers. Rather, officer-aspirants are people who *aspire* to be of service.

19. Sato writes, "[S]*hengren* 聖人, *junzi* 君子 and *shi* 士 all belong to the rank of rulers or high administrators" (2003, 417–18).

20. Sato writes, "It should be noted that in the *Xunzi*, terms [such] as *shi* 士 and *junzi* 君子 also [in addition to *renren* 仁人 ('the man of benevolence')] denote a governor of, at least, a municipal level in the modern sense" (2003, 268 n64; cf. 96 n64).

21. 人有其治。(62/17/7; K: 17.2a ; W 80; Sato 2003, 318).

22. 天人之分。(62/17/5; K: 17.1; W 79–80).

23. In fairness, Sato never goes so far as to say that *junzi means* ruler, but merely that Xunzi uses the term in *reference* to rulers. Indeed, as the discussion below reveals, he seemed to take the category *junzi* to imply both moral as well as political status. My concern is one of emphasis. Repeatedly stressing that *junzi* refers to rulers, and implying that it does so consistently and exclusively, has the effect of—and I think this was the intent—reinforcing the view that Xunzi's philosophy is (only) for rulers.

24. 君子能為可貴。不能使人必貴己。能為可用。不能使人必用己。(101/27/134–35; K: 27.114).

25. 君子生非異也。善假於物也。(1/1/8–9; K: 1.3; W 16).

morality as the result of one's 'learning.' . . . In Xunzi's categorical framework, *shi* were those who *should be* appointed at least a governor 邑宰 of a town or higher. So were *junzi*" (2003, 404; emphasis his). However, he then stresses, "In this conception of *shi*, when a person was appointed the governor in a local government, that meant that he stood *at the top of all the people there*. This would seem to indicate that 'learning' was the affair of a very small percentage of the people of the society" (2003, 404; emphasis his).

Sato argues, "[T]he ability to *read* the text of *Li* naturally required a high level of literacy; the learning of *Li* was a privilege thus reserved for a very small part of the population" (Sato 2003, 404). Fair enough. Still, one cannot equate literacy with rulership. There was a whole class of literati, and it was largely the most worthy among them that the ruler was encouraged to promote to office. Such "officer-aspirants" and exemplary people became worthy by reading the classics and following *li*, preferably under the guidance of a teacher and exemplary model. Surely Xunzi's philosophy was, to some degree, intended for such people, that is, for people who took on the task of self-cultivation. Indeed, the process starts even before one qualifies as a *shi*. Sato's own translation reveals that, in the beginning, "learning has as its purpose *becoming* an officer-aspirant."[26]

Further, Sato himself writes, "[T]he early Confucians were convinced that they were worthy because they practiced moral values which had been ignored by the ruling class. Seeing themselves in this light, Confucians took it for granted that they should be treated as mentors of the royal family and

---

26. 始乎為士。 (2/1/26; K: 1.8; W 19; Sato 2003, 403; emphasis added). See *Analects* 13.20 for Confucius's moral criteria for being called a *shi*, such as "conducting themselves with a sense of shame" (行己有恥), and note how it contrasts with his attitude toward the "worthless" officials of his day.

In addition, a story told near the end of the *Xunzi* confirms that *shi*, like *junzi*, is a moral rather than political category. In response to a direct question from Duke Ai, Confucius responds: "Those who are called *shi*, although they are not able to fully exhaust the methods of the way, they do necessarily have standards to which they conform (率). Although they cannot be admirable and effective in everything they do, they definitely have places (in which they excel). . . . Thus, neither riches nor high rank can improve them; neither poverty nor humble circumstances can diminish them. Such a person can be called a *shi*." 所謂士者。雖不能盡道術。必有率也。雖不能偏美善。必有處也。 . . . 故富貴不足以益也。卑賤不足以損也。如此則可謂士矣。 (106/31/9–12; K: 31.2).

The meaning of the character 率 is complex and interesting. Yang Liang interprets 率 as 循 (*xun*, to follow, abide by). Similarly, Kanaya Osamu understands this as *shitagau* (to follow, obey). In a note, he paraphrases the passage as follows: "While they cannot completely exhaust the methods of the way (道術), they take them as their standard and abide by them." 道術を完全に尽くすことはできないが、それに準拠して従っているということ。 (see Kanya 1974, 397–401). In fact, the character 率 (*lü, shuai*) has a number of meanings that are appropriate in this context. First of all, it means not only "to follow" or "abide by," but also its opposite: "to lead" (as well as "general" or "key person"). Thus, *shi* are simultaneously leading and following. In addition, it means "standards" or "norms," which I worked into the translation. However, this passage also suggests the meaning "more or less," or "on the whole." This meaning fits the contrast with the previous clause, and completes the parallelism with the following sentence. The "officer-aspirant" is not yet exemplary in the fullest sense, but is more or less proficient. There is no English word or phrase that will do all this work.

aristocracy of the time" (2003, 254). It is to these moral elite that the term *junzi* is meant to apply. Of course, Xunzi would like rulers to be more like *junzi*, and for these *junzi* to be promoted to positions of authority. Nevertheless, the important thing to stress is that since the category *junzi* was primarily moral, rather than political, anybody who diligently applied themselves could become one.

An Overview of the Argument

There is a sense of realism that maintains not merely that there is a reality independent of our thoughts about it, but that there is a privileged description of this reality, that concepts can and should mirror it, and that there is a uniquely correct way of being in it. In particular, properly chosen moral concepts capture eternal truths revealing the one true way. In most recent interpretations, and implicit in existing English translations, Xunzi[27] is taken to be a realist in this strong sense. He is thought to claim that the sage is able to perceive the way the world really is and thus is able to make *the* uniquely correct distinctions. This is an undeserved impoverishment of Xunzi's philosophy. It is philosophically problematic on its own, and it fails to provide the most coherent interpretation of the *Xunzi*. Further, the realist interpretation masks many subtle and philosophically compelling aspects of Xunzi's thought.

As an alternative, I will offer a "constructivist" reading of Xunzi's philosophy, that is, one that stresses the importance of formulating constructive social constructs. The distinctions made by the sages have no absolute status. Rather, categories are judged according to values, such as harmony and social stability, which are in turn justified by their critical role in facilitating the satisfaction of a substantial number of our desires. Given that we humans are constituted the way we are, some sets of conceptions and social structures work better than others for providing what we find (or can find) satisfying. However, Xunzi's underlying worldview—informing everything from his philosophy of language to his understanding of the role of ritual propriety—suggests that there may be more than one way to achieve success in constructing a moral world.[28] In

---

27. I use the personal name "Xunzi" as a convenience to refer to the text bearing that name, and to the ideas presented in it, which I take to be at least inspired by, if not mostly written by, the philosopher himself—though my main concern is articulating a compelling interpretation of the received text.

28. This view has resonance with certain later Confucian thinkers, for example Chen Liang, a twelfth-century Confucian scholar famous for his debate with Zhu Xi. Chen, who was strongly influenced by Xunzi, conceived of *dao* as both plural and ever-changing. As Hoyt Cleveland Tillman explains, "[Chen's] willingness to consider the Dao plural in number and ever-changing in nature contrasts significantly with the insistence of philosophers like Zhu Xi who maintained that the Dao was one and constant" (1994, 24). Moreover, "Chen held that laws, ritual, and the Dao evolved as inherent aspects of the process of history, as situations changed with the times. He suggested that laws should accord with the times and declared that we should 'make rules based on situations.' . . . [H]e told Zhu Xi that the Dao of Confucius 'was based on arriving at the public interest

other words, on the constructivist view there is no privileged description of the world—concepts, categories, and norms, as social constructs, help us effectively manage our way through the world rather than reveal or express univocal knowledge of it.

More than twenty years ago, Lee H. Yearley published an insightful paper entitled "Hsün Tzu on the Mind: His Attempted Synthesis of Confucianism and Taoism," which came close to anticipating the need for this study (though the bulk of the literature I address was written *after* Yearley's paper). His paper pointed the way toward a constructivist understanding of Xunzi,[29] and is worth quoting at length:

> Xunzi cannot argue that people should become Confucians on the grounds that Confucianism represents the one eternally true way, the only way that reflects what people really are and what the universe really is. (Yearley 1980, 479)[30]

> He denies both that language's distinctions have an intrinsic appropriateness and that they convey some stable reality. But he joins those denials with the ideas that language is necessary and that some forms of language, given certain situations, are better than other forms of language for the creation of an orderly society and orderly people. . . .

> Xunzi does sometimes write as if moral judgments are universally applicable, and almost all interpretations of him focus on this strand in his work. He appears to assert that the problems humans face are so similar that a single resolution—that resolution represented by the rules of at least the later sage-kings—should bind all people. The extraordinary insight of the sage-kings gave people the only rules that work, no matter how apparently different the present social situation is from that of their time.

> Xunzi may waver between varying positions, but it seems more likely that he espouses this universalist position only in exoteric writings aimed to affect the unsophisticated. His relativistic position is more basic, as we can see when we focus on how he emphasizes the need to apply all abstract judgments to particular situations, chooses which sages to follow on the pragmatic grounds of available information about them, hints at the way changing circumstances may modify certain sage-like judgments, and argues for a position on language that necessitates maintaining at least the possibility that judgments may change. (Yearley 1980, 476)

---

in accordance with the times.' In essence, Chen had found a manner of reconciling two demands: that rites and social norms change, but not in an arbitrary manner" (1994, 32).

29. Chad Hansen articulates a position seemingly similar to Yearley's. However, the similarities here are superficial. Though Hansen is credited as having a "conventionalist" interpretation of Xunzi, we will see that he interprets Xunzi to be incoherently both conventionalist and absolutist, but with absolutism being primary. In the end, Xunzi is not viewed as a synthesizer of Confucianism and Daoism, but rather Xunzi's philosophy fails, by Hansen's lights, because it is not Daoist.

30. A longer version of this quotation can be found in section 4.6.

I will take the argument a step further. Rather than dismissing seemingly problematic passages, I attempt to rethink those passages to see if they truly imply a "universalist position" or some such similar interpretation, or whether, on the contrary, they are compatible with constructivism. I will argue that even if Xunzi is at some points addressing "the unsophisticated," as Yearley suggests, his statements do not contradict his basic constructivist outlook.

I begin with the general concept of *dao* (way), and argue that while Xunzi sees a practical problem in having competing moral doctrines, his worldview allows for the possibility of pluralism. Further, his *dao* is positively processional, contextual, and contingent. There is no assumption of any singular ultimate or transcendently fixed *Way*. The *dao* is constantly being made and remade by the conscious efforts of exemplary people making the most of the situations they confront. The second chapter goes straight to the core of the problem, which is a misunderstanding of Xunzi's conception of the nature of *li* (patterns). *Li* are not fixed in nature as givens. Rather, while *li* address regularities in the world of nature and human nature, *li* also necessarily involve interpretations of those regularities.

Then I turn to the issue of naming, which serves the function of formalizing particular patterns (or ways of patterning) in language. That is, naming not only assigns a label to a pattern, but also establishes particular patternings as significant. The character *ming*, generally translated as "name," includes both the idea of name as *label*, as well as the idea of *concept*. For Xunzi, naming is both labeling and making judgments about what patterns should be thereby sanctioned. This can be done well or poorly, but there is no predetermined or privileged set of patterns waiting to be discerned and then labeled. While this applies to names generally, the Confucian emphasis on *zhengming*, or attunement of language, centers primarily on concepts of moral significance, "father" and "son" for example, and the patterns of roles and responsibilities that go with those name-concepts. Thus, the construction of language, for Xunzi, is a task with great ethical significance.

Like naming, ritual propriety, which is central to Confucian self-cultivation, involves a kind of patterning. In this case, norms of appropriate behavior are patterned through the habit-forming practice of ritualized conduct, rather than through language. After discussing ritual propriety as the means of self-cultivation, I turn finally to the *goal* of that cultivation: virtuous character. I argue that, for Xunzi, there is not just one way to be virtuous, and neither is the project of developing oneself ever complete. Thus, Xunzi's conception of virtue as contingent and evolving is consistent with his conception of language and ritual propriety. This completes the circle, for it is the virtuous person (*junzi*), cultivated through ritual practice, who in turn sets the standards for that practice, and for an appropriate patterning of language to go along with it.

Sages (*shengren*) and *junzi* are both the product and the source of the various constructs of which the way is composed. Thus, on the one hand, *dao* is defined as the path of *junzi*.[31] When one has developed sufficiently to serve as a model of appropriate conduct, one may be called "exemplary." It is ritualized exemplary conduct that expresses the way. Norms of ritual propriety (*li* 禮), as the embodiment of *dao*, are, in this way, products of exemplary people and sages.[32] At the same time, it is these norms that provide guidance for novices, who are inspired by the model of exemplars to develop compelling characters themselves. Considered in this light, the translation "exemplary person" is a fitting one for the concept of *junzi*. In addition to their role as interpreters of ritual propriety, it is necessary for exemplary people to participate in the patterning, categorizing and naming process—the attuning of names—even as the category of *junzi* itself is attuned.

---

31. "'The way' is not the way of *tian* 天, neither is it the way of the earth. It is that by which the people are lead; it is the path of exemplary people." 道者非天之道。非地之道。人之所以道也。君子之所道也。 (20/8/24; K: 8.3).

32. "Ritual propriety and a sense of appropriateness (*liyi*) are the products of sages." 禮義者。聖人之所生也。 (87/23/11; K: 23.1c; W 158; H 285).

Constructing the Way

1

1.1. The Role of People and the Role of "Heaven"

In his recent book, *The Ambivalence of Creation*, Michael Puett offers a sweeping and rhetorically persuasive account of the concept of innovation in early China. He fits Xunzi neatly into a compelling narrative that contrasts conservative Confucians with Mohists who advocate continued reinventing of culture[1] and Daoists who reject cultural artifice altogether. Rather than truly creating or innovating, on Puett's reading of Confucius and Mencius, sages simply "bring patterns from Heaven [*tian*[2] 天] to humanity" (2001, 57). Puett sees Xunzi, ultimately, as holding a similar position. Indeed, Puett is on sound footing when he holds, for example, that for Xunzi *liyi* 禮義 (understood by Puett as "ritual and morality") is "in no sense an arbitrary creation" (70). However, he goes too far when he claims, "In fact, the production of culture [defined in terms of ritual and morality] did not involve acts of *zuo* [作 (creation)] at all. . . . [C]ulture is . . . the teleological (if not immediate) product of Heaven[3]" (70). This is a point he stresses.[4] Indeed, regarding Xunzi, it is his main point.

Puett's interpretation here represents a departure from mainstream Chinese interpretations. For example, Chen Daqi writes:

> The standards of ritual and propriety for ordering a country and cultivating oneself originate from exemplary people and are produced by sages. It is people themselves who invent and establish them; they do not exist naturally. Because *tian* cannot be

---

1. Xunzi criticizes Mozi for focusing too narrowly on utility and stressing uniformity, while opposing ritual and music. He uses forward-looking consequentialist reasoning to suggest that Mozi's strategies are not going to be effective. He does not criticize Mozi for innovation itself, but for suggesting *misguided* innovations (see K: 10.8; K: 17.12, W 87; K: 19. 1d, W 91; K: 21.4, W 125; and book 20, *yuelun pian*).

2. Puett consistently translates *tian* as "Heaven" with a capital "H," without giving any description of what it means for Xunzi. This is very misleading. For Xunzi, *tian* is something very close to nature, and it is morally neutral. See the glossary at the end of this book.

3 Rejecting Puett's position, Eric Hutton aptly points out, "we do not attribute the cause of a person's actions to his mother, even though she brought him into this world" (2003, 7).

4. Puett writes, "Heaven thus gives man the faculties which, if used properly, will guide his actions. In order to further highlight the implicit teleology here, Xunzi refers to the final stage of this process of cultivation as 'knowing Heaven'. . . . For Xunzi, the crucial things that were produced in the past were ritual and morality, and these were not created but rather generated from the Heaven-given mind" (2001, 68, 70).

patterned after, people must establish [*liyi*] themselves. Xunzi does not establish the way of people (*rendao* 人道) based on the way of *tian* (*tiandao* 天道). This is one of the great distinguishing characteristics of Xunzi's theory. The way of people is what people create. This view can be called artificial-ism (人為主義).[5]

Similarly, Jiang Shangxian explains:

> So-called *liyi fadu* 禮義法度 (ritual and propriety, models and norms)[6] for cultivating oneself, governing one's family, ordering a country, and pacifying the whole world begin with exemplary people and are produced by sages. They are not things that exist naturally in the cosmos, but are rather things that we human beings, on account of our own intelligence and abilities, as well as our needs, come to invent and create. Just because *tian* lacks what can be patterned after, and cannot show people concrete examples, there is no alternative but [for these things to come] from us human beings on account of our own intelligence and abilities, as well as our needs, what we come to invent and create. Xunzi did not base his idea of *rendao* on the concept of *tiandao*, he advocated "different roles for *tian* and people" (*tian ren zhi fen* 天人之分). This is the most distinctive expression in his thought.[7]

Jiang also suggests that Xunzi believed people should seek to further improve the human condition (求人類生活的進步。1966, 32), and that Xunzi himself broadened the way (31).

The theme running through an essay on Xunzi by Lin Lizhen is *tian sheng ren cheng* (天生人成, *tian* generates, people complete).[8] Lin takes *tian* as nature

---

5. 國修身的禮義法度，始自君子，生於聖人，是人們自己所發明而創設的，不是自然存在的。正因為天是無可取法，所以祇好由人們自己來創設。荀子不依據天道以建立人道，是荀子學說的一大特色。人道是人所造，此一見解，可稱之為人為主義。(Chen 1954, 5). Similarly, Chen also writes, "*Tian* is something which cannot be patterned after, thus *dao* does not emerge from *tian*. Human nature is bad, thus *dao* also does not come out of human nature. *Dao* does not develop and exist naturally, it is something formulated by the intelligence of sages. *Dao* is what sages formulate, thus *dao* is entrusted to sages, and sages become the concrete expression of *dao*. So if you want to follow the *dao* all you have to do is imitate the sages." 天是無可取法的，故道不出於天。人性是惡的，故道亦不出於人性。道不是自然生存的，是聖人的理智所創制的。道為聖人所創制，故道寄托於聖人，而聖人成了道的具體表現，所以要想有合於道，祇須師法聖人。(1954, 8). Note that to truly follow the sages, ultimately, is to become a sage oneself. Xunzi says that any ordinary person can become a sage, (K: 8.11 & K: 23.5a; W 166–67) and indeed, he encourages learning with this end in mind (K: 1.8; W 19). The implied continuing need for sages suggests that the process of formulating structures to help mold good people is an ever-ongoing one.

6. This phrase occurs twice in a passage in Xunzi's *xing e pian* (87/23/24–28; K: 23.2a; W 160).

7. 所謂修身，齊家，治國，平天下的禮義法度，始自君子，生於聖人，不是宇宙中自然存在的，而是我們人類憑藉自己的智能與需要，而來發明創造的。正因為天是無可取法的，不能示人典型的，所以只好由我們人類憑藉自己的智能與需要，而來發明創造的。荀子不依據天道觀念以建立人道的思想，主張天人之分，是他思想中最為獨特的表現。(Jiang 1966, 31). The importance of *tian ren zhi fen* in Xunzi's thought is commonly noted in the Japanese literature as well, for example, Kanaya Osamu and Ikeda Tomohisa both assert it to be Xunzi's most fundamental idea (see Kanaya 1970, 1, and Ikeda 1966, 5).

8. Xunzi quotes a saying: "Nature (*tiandi*) produces it, sages complete it." 天地生之。聖人

(*ziran* 自然) and holds *xing* 性 (original human nature) to be closely related, that is, *xing* is produced by *tian* and is in many ways analogous to it. Now, Xunzi clearly says that *liyi* does *not* come from *xing*. "Ritual and propriety (*liyi*) are produced by the conscious activity (*wei* 偽) of sages. They are not products of people's original nature (*xing*)."[9] So, Lin strongly implies, *liyi* likewise cannot be thought of as coming from *tian*. Lin writes:

> [Xunzi's] theory of *tian* takes *tian* as nature (*ziran*), opposes the idea of a moral *tian*, and advocates rule brought about by people. His theory of *xing*, [original human nature] likewise takes *xing* as lacking sprouts of goodness, opposes the idea of a moral *xing*, and advocates man-made artifice. His theory of people does not stress intuitive knowledge or abilities of pure consciousness, but rather has the characteristic mark of an intelligent heart-mind (*xin* 心) which elects (*ju* 舉) appropriate distinctions and is capable of forming groups.[10]

As Lin observes, the standard (標準 *biaozhun*) for making distinctions is using one's "public mind" (*yi gong xin bian* 以公心辨), that is, with concern for the common welfare (see Lin 1978, 66).

Tian cannot be responsible for the formation of culture because, as Xu Fuguan notes, "[Xunzi] considered the functions and regularities of nature (*tian*) not to contain intention or purpose."[11] Most Chinese and Japanese scholars agree.[12] Indeed, it is pretty clear from the opening lines of the *tianlun* chapter:

> Nature's course has regularities, which don't exist for the sage Yao and then disappear for the tyrant Jie. Responding to them with orderly government is auspicious, while responding to them with chaos is inauspicious. If you strengthen the fundamentals and moderate expenditures, nature cannot make you poor. If you are well nourished and act according to the seasons, then nature cannot make you sick. If you follow *dao* and are not of two minds, nature cannot bring you to ruin.[13]

Tian, having no purposes of its own, or at least no ability to intervene, merely provides us with a starting point, a natural world with regularities in which to

---

成之。(33/10/39; K: 10.6). Knoblock notes that the saying does not occur elsewhere (although Xunzi repeats it in book 27, K: 27.41).

9. 凡禮義者。是生於聖人之偽。非故生於人之性也。(87/23/22–23; K: 23.2a; W 160).

10. 他之論天，乃以天為自然，反對天之道德義，而主張人治；他之論性，亦以性無善端，反對性之道德義，而主張人為。他之論人，亦不強調靈明自覺的良知良能，而特標舉義辨與能群的理智之心。(Lin 1978, 22).

11. 但他認為天的功用與法則，不含有意志，目的在裡面。(Xu 1963, 227).

12. See Kodama 1992, 93–95, for a long list of similar positions taken by both Chinese and Japanese scholars, followed by his own dissenting opinion. For a similar dissent in English, see Machle 1976. In this matter, I follow the majority.

13. 天行有常。不為堯存。不為桀亡。應之以治則吉。應之以亂則凶。彊本而節用則天不能貧。養備而動時則天不能病。脩道而不貳則天不能禍。(62/17/1–2; K: 17.1; W 79; H 260).

operate. It is up to people to bring about (*cheng* 成) a workable social structure. And, this structure is not latently waiting to be discovered. Xunzi goes as far as to say, "If there were no exemplary people, nature and the earth would not be patterned."[14] People have, in other words, at least some degree of independence in the process of ordering the human world. Kanaya Osamu observes, "The division of *tian* and people certainly means the division between the natural and the human, and it established an independent standpoint. However, at the same time, it limited the work of humans to the world of humans as humans—this is also the human world of which Xunzi concerned himself."[15] That is to say, in the realm of human affairs, of which Xunzi was primarily concerned, it is the role of people, from a standpoint in some sense independent of *tian*, to establish an effective social order.

Kanaya also perceives a subjective element in the decisions of the heart-mind (*xin* 心). "Xunzi's distinction between *tian* and people establishes a human subjectivity independent from nature. By finishing off with 'artifice' based on this subjective activity of the 'heart-mind,' he stresses the positive activity of humans, who form a 'triad' with *tian* and earth."[16] In a similar vein, Lao Siguang writes, "The 'heart-mind' is regarded as the source of culture, and at the same time also expresses a moral will (since it is capable of making choices). . . . Xunzi understands 'heart-mind' as 'subjectivity.'"[17] What is meant by "subjectivity" here is just the degree of independence from *tian* that entails personal responsibility for the creation of culture.

If people are responsible for constructing a moral system, and proper use of their natural faculties is insufficient to fully determine the specifics of such a system, then at least some degree of innovation would seem to be required. This innovation, however, would not at all be radically free or unbounded. It would still be restrained by the proper use of our natural faculties—as Puett rightly points out. According to Xunzi, Puett explains, "the sage can create new names only after he has correctly used his Heaven-given faculties" (2001, 71), for Xunzi "has limited the arbitrariness of such conscious activity by defining it normatively as the process of correctly using one's Heaven-given faculties" (72).[18] However, these "faculties" are just the senses, combined with intelligence. Properly using one's faculties simply does not imply teleology, as Puett suggests it does. Intelligent use of sensory input is under-determinant for imposing

---

14. 無君子則天地不理。(28/9/66; K: 9.15; W 44–45).

15. 天人の分は、確かに自然と人と分別して人間の主体的立場を確立したものではあるが、同時に人間の働きを人間としての世界—それも荀子の考えた人間の世界—に限定した。(Kanaya 1970, 7).

16. 荀子の天人の分は、自然から独立した人間の主体性を確立し、その主体的能動性を「心」にもとづく「偽」によってうち出すことによって、天地と「参」になる人間の積極的な活動を強調するものであった。(Kanaya 1970, 13).

17. 此「心」即視為文化之根源，同時亦表道德意志(因能作選擇)。...荀子以「心」為「主體性」。(Lao 1968, 262).

18. Puett's position is discussed further in section 2.1 below.

categories on the natural world,[19] and even more so with respect to the social and moral world. This is evident from the fact that different languages construe concepts differently. Xunzi may, indeed, look to nature and the heavens for inspiration and analogy, but we need not infer that he assumes there to be a determinate grounding for morality.

On the contrary, according to Xunzi's philosophy, people are supposed to complete (*cheng*) what is provided for by nature (*tiandi*). They are supposed to beautify and ornament their nature, and produce an effective social system so that desires, appropriately shaped, can be largely satisfied. He believes that rituals are the best way to achieve the transformations necessary to do this. But it is fundamentally a human task, using our senses and intelligence—yes, provide by *tian*. Further, while we may also seek metaphors in the natural world, ultimately, for Xunzi, people are the masters of *tian*, not the other way around. As A. C. Graham has succinctly put it, "Man creates morality and manipulates for moral ends the resources (including his own natural endowment) which Heaven has put at his disposal" (1990, 56).

1.2. Uniqueness Interpretations (Realism)

Many Western scholars have approached the *Xunzi* with an attitude similar to Puett's. Xunzi has been characterized variously as a realist, an objectivist, an intellectualist, and an absolutist.[20] For example, Robert Eno claims, "*Xunzi*'s theory of language is realist. Although individual words are initially chosen arbitrarily, their consistent use and syntactic relations in language create a perfect correspondence between the elements and structure of language and the objects of the world and their relations" (272 n65; see also sections 2.1, 2.3, and 3.2). Bryan Van Norden writes: "Xunzi held what might be described as an 'intellectualist' position: Confucianism can be justified with almost mathematical certainty, and knowledge guarantees right action" (1996, 3). Paul Goldin describes Xunzi's position as "uncompromising objectivism" (1999, 99). And, Chad Hansen refers to Xunzi's view as an "absolutist account of discovery of the single correct *dao*" (1992, 342).

For the purposes of this chapter, I will sort and discuss various positions as a group of general themes. A commonality among these themes is the thesis that Xunzi holds the sage to have a uniquely correct conception of reality, both physical and moral. Often what underlies "uniqueness" claims is a conception of *li* (理 pattern) which is fixed and singular. As a convenience, I will sometimes refer to these theories collectively under the heading "realism," since this

---

19. See Lakoff 1987(esp. pp. 118–21 and 185–95), and Stephen Jay Gould's "What, If Anything, Is a Zebra?"

20. Hansen even uses most of these terms in a single sentence: "Objective or absolute justification of 'realist' traditionalism are available by making maximizing survival and effectiveness the test of *the correct* system of names (*dao*)" (1983, 182; emphasis in original).

conception of a fixed and singular *li* seems to operate as the foundation of a "real" determinate order that underwrites uniqueness claims. I will elaborate on this in the next chapter; for the present I will just address the surface features of these views.

While not all interpreters have adopted a uniqueness interpretation, the list of those who, in one form or another, propound it with seemingly great confidence includes an impressive array of top scholars in the field. It includes the following interpreters: P. J. Ivanhoe, Donald Munro, Chad Hansen, Benjamin Schwartz, and David Nivison—to name only those whom I will discuss in this chapter. In addition, this view is assumed in the most often cited translations of Xunzi's works, those by Burton Watson and by John Knoblock. Of course, this is not to say that these interpreters and translators share the same, or even compatible, interpretations of all aspects of Xunzi's philosophy.

1.2.1. Strong Fixed Uniqueness

In a footnote to a discussion on Xunzi's position, Ivanhoe states, "Xunzi believed that the society worked out by the former sages provided the one and only way to a happy and flourishing world" (2000, 247 n8). This seems to follow from his claim, "The Confucian rituals provide a way to realize an orderly design inherent in the world" (240). If the world has a singular order that the sage is privy to, and rites are essentially a social mapping of the real and singular relations in nature, then there can be only one legitimate social construction. At least, this is how Ivanhoe's reading seems to have it.

Elsewhere Ivanhoe goes further, suggesting that not only is there just one legitimate *dao*, but that it is fixed and changeless. "This is the key to understanding how Xunzi justified the Confucian rites as the 'unalterable patterns' for human beings to follow. The rites alone provide for universal harmony and the common flourishing of heaven, earth and human beings. Only the *dao* offers the possibility of this *happy symmetry*" (1991, 321). Let's call this type of position "Strong Fixed Uniqueness" (SFU), where "strong" indicates that it is a fixed and unique solution not merely in a general way, but in its particulars. The *precise way* that the "sages of old" worked out the various kinds of social constructions and norms is fixed and unique.

Ivanhoe makes his stance abundantly clear: Xunzi's position is that the way of the sages is complete, unchanging, and unique:

> [T]he rites that human beings follow, would seem to require regular adjustment and modification. Xunzi did not see things this way. He did not believe the world could change as much as we know it does. Though he believed that the rites went through a process of evolution, he believed that this process had reached a conclusion in the rites of the Three Dynasties. Xunzi did not provide an elaborate exposition of the process of the evolution of the *dao*, but he clearly believed that the sages had

brought the process to a successful conclusion and that the Confucian Way provided the unique solution which would be valid for all times. (1991, 318)

Ivanhoe quotes the following passage from Watson for support: "The Way is the proper standard for past and present. He who departs from the Way and makes arbitrary choices on the basis of his own judgments does not understand wherein fortune and misfortune lie" (1991, 318; W 153).[21] What does it mean to say, "The way is the proper standard for past and present"? One could take it to mean that there is a fixed way that is appropriate for all time. But this is not the only possible reading, nor the one that best fits a coherent interpretation of Xunzi. Notice that, while this English rendering may seem to suggest the idea of a "fixed" standard, the concept of fixity is not explicitly stated, nor is it to be found in the Chinese.[22] At any point, past or present, what serves as the proper standard is called by the name *dao*. It can serve as the proper standard because, given the tendencies of nature and the propensity of the circumstances (*shi* 勢), it leads in a productive direction, that is, toward harmony. Not to follow such a road would be a misfortune. The particulars of the path, however, are not fixed but context dependent. So, while Watson's translation is not incorrect, it is misleading. It seems to have led Ivanhoe into an interpretation that disregards the fact that Xunzi explicitly acknowledged that, for example, if sages were to arise again, in addition to reviving old names, they would create new ones.[23] This indicates that, even if Xunzi believed in a "unique solution," he apparently did not believe that it had been brought to completion.

Ivanhoe's premise of SFU leads him to go as far as to say that, for Xunzi, "The rites provide the only way out of the state of nature" (1991, 314). This cannot be Xunzi's view given his positive evaluation of the legalist policies of the overlords (*ba* 霸) as an inferior position to his own, but nonetheless a second best option which is better than nothing.[24] The problem with legalism, in Xunzi's eyes, is not that it fails to elevate a community from the state of nature,[25] but rather

---

21. Ivanhoe also cites two other passages in a footnote: "'When they (i.e. the rites) are properly established and brought to the peak of perfection, no one in the world can add to or detract from them" (W 94) and "Music consists of unchanging harmonies; rites are unalterable patterns" (adapted from W 117). See Ivanhoe 1991, 318n. I discuss these passages in sections 4.3.4 and 4.3.5.

22. 道者。古今之正權也。離道而內自擇。則不知禍福之所託。(86/22/74; K: 22.6b; W 153). This passage is discussed again in section 1.5.

23. "If true kings were to arise, they would certainly revitalize old names and create new ones." 若有王者起。必將有循於舊名。有作於新名。(83/22/11–12; K: 22.2a).

24. Xunzi offers a hierarchy of successful government: "A ruler who exalts ritual propriety and reveres virtuous people will be a true king. One who stresses law and loves the common people will be an overlord. One who is fond of profit and is deceitful will be in danger. And, one who engages in schemes and intrigue, and commits subversive and devious acts, will die." 君人者隆禮尊賢而王。重法愛民而霸。好利多詐而危。權謀傾覆幽險而亡。(58/16/4–5; K: 16.1) This passage reoccurs in K: 17.9, W 86, D 182; and (without the last sentence) in K: 27.1.

25. The overlord's legalist policies do have some merits. "Overlords are not like [true kings]. They open lands for cultivation, fill storehouses and granaries, and facilitate equipment usage. They carefully recruit and select scholar-officials of talent and skill, and then gradually lead them forward

that it fails to achieve much more than this. Legalism is capable of maintaining a degree of order and stability, and of accumulating and maintaining sufficient economic necessities with reasonably fair distribution. But it cannot deliver a high degree of harmony within a community or true contentment among its members. The state of Qin is an example.[26] Ivanhoe's claim illustrates a "slippery slope" phenomenon: while SFU does not necessarily entail that the rites are only way out of the state of nature, SFU sometimes slides into even more suspect interpretations.

Ivanhoe is not alone in advocating an SFU interpretation of Xunzi. For example, Munro writes:

> The *li* [rites] dictate that certain phenomena stand in definite relation to others, that the noble and base are distinguished from each other, and that some things should obey other things. There is a right way for one season to follow another and a wrong way, a right way for one natural body (mountain, river, planet, or element) to be related to another and a wrong way. There are antecedently fixed rules dictating which actions by all objects including man, are good or bad. (Munro 1969, 33)[27]

This is a "fixed uniqueness" position that at least seems to be of the strong variety.

In addition, in a review of *Virtue, Nature, and Moral Agency in the* Xunzi (edited by Ivanhoe and T. C. Kline), Aaron Stalnaker reaffirms a Strong Fixed Uniqueness position writing, "[T]he editors and contributors are right to develop an account of Xunzi as a moral universalist committed to the unique power and rightness of the Confucian Way *in all its specificity*" (Stalnaker 2002, 296; emphasis added). Beyond putting Stalnaker himself on record, this demonstrates that the scholars he refers to[28] (whatever their views might actually be) have at least given the impression that they support a SFU-type interpretation.

---

with praise and rewards, and correct them with severe punishments and penalties. In matters of life and death, and when the continuation or annihilation of lineages is at stake, they defend the weak and prohibit violence." 彼霸者不然。辟 [闢] 田野。實倉廩。便備用。案謹募選閱材伎 [技] 之士。然後漸慶賞以先之。嚴刑罰以糾之。存亡繼絕。衛弱禁暴。(27/9/39–40; K: 9.8; W 40).

26. "The state of Qin is in this category [of being extremely well ordered (*zhi zhi zhi* 治之至)]. Nevertheless it is in fear. Despite having numerous positive qualities concurrently and in the greatest possible degree, if one measures it by the success and fame of a true king, it is far inferior. Why is this? Because of the dearth of Confucians. Thus it is said, 'Pure, a true king; mixed, an overlord; otherwise one will be annihilated.'" 秦類之矣。雖然。則有諰矣。兼是數具者。而盡有之。然而縣之以王者之功名。則倜倜然其不及遠矣。是何也。則其殆無儒邪。故曰。粹而王。駁而霸。無一焉而亡。(61/16/67–69; K: 16.6; cf. K: 15.1d). *Xi* 諰 is interpreted here as *ju* 懼 (fear, dread), following Yang Liang.

27. This is based on a passage in book 19 (K: 19.2c; W 94; D 223–224), which is quoted in note 49 below. See also section 4.3.5.

28. Stalnaker cites the chapters by P. J. Ivanhoe, T. C. Kline, and David Nivison. He may also be thinking of Van Norden's contribution, though he does not explicitly cite it. See Hagen 2001a for my own review of the book in question.

1.2.2. Weak Fixed Uniqueness

Watson explicitly denies the "strong" part of SFU, but nevertheless holds a view of the way as fixed and singular. He writes:

> Xunzi maintained that, although political and social conditions invariably change, human nature and basic moral principles do not, and therefore the principles that were correct and brought order in the past will, if faithfully followed, do so again. He is thus calling not for a return to the precise ways of antiquity, but for a reconstruction of the moral greatness of antiquity in terms of the present. As he states in one of the sections not translated here, if you apply these *eternally valid moral principles* of the sages today, 'then Shun and Yu will appear again, and the reign of a true king will arise once more.' (Watson 1963, 6; emphasis added)[29]

The position that, rather than specific rules, roles, rites, categories, and so on being constant, it is some more general aspect which remains fixed, such as "basic moral principles," may be called "Weak Fixed Uniqueness" (WFU). The problem with this view, as found in Watson, is not that it is far off track—indeed, constructivism assumes that there are regularities in the world and that these should inform our constructs. Moreover, it is along these lines that "the connecting thread of the way" should be understood in the following passage: "If something did not change throughout the period of the hundred kings, this is enough to consider it a connecting thread of the way. One should respond to the ups and downs of history with this thread. If one applies constructive patterns to this thread there will not be disorder. But if one does not understand it, one will not know how to respond to changing circumstances."[30] However, it needs to be remembered that although certain moral principles may endure, and although they may find grounding in insights regarding human nature gleaned from long experience, they nevertheless may be legitimately formulated in more than one way. And, structures that realize them may both differ and evolve.

The real problem with WFU is that it tends toward overstatement, employing terms and expressions that are inappropriate in a description of the classical Chinese tradition—expressions like "eternally valid moral principles." It raises the question: Why has the interpretation slipped into such language?

Nivison also seems to have a WFU interpretation, but a more problematic

---

29. The text that he cites ("sec. 11," presumably 11.7c in Knoblock) discusses the problem of partiality in promoting officials. If a ruler simply sought out the truly able, "it would be like Yu and Shun had returned and the work of a true king had resumed." 如是則舜禹還至。王業還起。(41/11/84–85; K: 11.7c). The point, I take it, is that impartiality in making promotions is an enduring "basic moral principle" which will be effective in Xunzi's time just as it was in the times of Yu and Shun. However, to use the language of "eternally valid moral principles" is a stretch.

30. 百王之無變。足以為道貫。一廢一起。應之以貫。理貫不亂。不知貫。不知應變。(64/17/46–47; K: 17.11; W 87).

one than the one briefly stated by Watson. Rather than enduring "basic moral principles," Nivison believes that, for Xunzi, the *rules* that give moral principles form admit of only one correct formulation. He writes, "The set of rules that optimizes human satisfaction and minimizes conflict can be worked out essentially in only one way—the way the sages did it. It thus can be thought of as (we might say) an overflowing into the human social order of the necessity of the order of the universe as a whole" (Nivison 1996b, 48). The word "essentially" is enough for us to categorize this claim as the weak variety, though we must then take the phrase "the way the sages did it" as "roughly the way the sages did it" or else this would be an example of SFU. Also, note the connection being made between the order of the universe and the social order, with the fixity and "necessity" implied by the former carrying over into the later.

According to Nivison's interpretation, Xunzi does not believe that the human situation changes over time sufficiently to require modification of *dao*. He writes, "[I]f Xunzi thought that the 'Way' of the 'sages' was final and perfect, he must suppose that this human situation does not really change over historical time, and is not altered even by the events of history. It seems to me that Xunzi did tend to think this; but others in his day, such as the Legalists and the Daoists, would have none of it; and even Confucius seems to be ambivalent on the matter" (Nivison 1996a, 331). Just as Watson went from "basic moral principles" into "eternally valid" ones, Nivison here begins to sound like he is suggesting SFU, saying that Xunzi tended to believe that "the 'Way' of the 'sages' was *final* and *perfect*."

Although others have also suggested that Xunzi did not believe that conditions changed very much,[31] it is a much more plausible interpretation of Xunzi's understanding of history to say that, while he believed that nature (*tian* 天) and human nature (*xing* 性) had enduring regularities, he acknowledged the existence of significant social change. As Murase Hiroya puts it:

> Although, regardless of the period of human history, the given natural conditions for the most part don't change, if human circumstances vary greatly depending on the time period, this definitely depends wholly on the methods put into practice by people themselves, and especially on the question of how people interact toward nature, which continues its workings regardless of human [actions]. Thinking along these lines, Xunzi emphasized the responsibility of people themselves toward the order and disorder of society and the fortune and misfortune of people.[32]

---

31. See, for example, Ivanhoe 1991, 318–20. See also section 2.2 for a passage seeming to support this conclusion.

32. 所与の自然条件は人類史上いずれの時代もほとんど変りないのに、人間界の状態は時代によって大きく異っているとすれば、それはもっぱら人間自身の実践方法、とりわけ人間とは無関係の営みを続けている自然に対して人間がいかに対応するかということに決定的に依存している、というのである。こうして荀子は、社会の治乱や人間の吉凶に対する人間自身の責任を強調する。(Murase 1986, 23).

Were Xunzi to confront propositions such as: "the world could not change"[33] very much, or the "human situation . . . is not altered even by the events of history," he would in all likelihood respond with the same kind of hostility that he did to Mencius's thesis that human nature is good—and for substantially the same reasons. If our situation could not be changed, what need would there be for sages, or for their attunement of names and ritual propriety? What need would there be for Xunzi's own effort to articulate a way for society to achieve a stable harmony? That is, Xunzi had philosophical reasons to reject the view that the conditions of history are basically unchanging, even if direct historical evidence was lacking—which it was not. Xunzi was painfully aware that there were times of order and times of chaos. Further, he maintained, through the intelligent use of culturally constructed artifice we could transform ourselves morally, and establish a stable harmonious society. This would truly be a different "human situation" than the chaotic one that characterized the warring states period, in which Xunzi lived.

In any case, while it is sensible to speak of general ("weak") and enduring (more or less fixed, as far as we can see) principles, such principles would not necessarily have the privilege of being the only possible set of workable principles, nor would there be only one legitimate way in which they could be conceived or parsed.[34]

1.2.3. A Mixture of Methods

At this point I would like to draw attention to a complicating factor, the implications of which are often overlooked, namely, that Xunzi's *dao* is an amalgamation of various elements. It cannot, for example, simply be stated that *li* (ritual propriety) is the unique solution to humanities problems, because *li* must interact with other components of the system.

Consider Hansen's remark:

> How do we know that the Confucian *li* uniquely offers this positive outcome? It is hard, as I said, to find a direct argument, as opposed to these elaborate statements of faith. The direct argument he gives for *li* is his claim that *li* controls and channels desires. He must assume not only that *li* does this, but that it does it in a uniquely efficient way, the only way that preserves order and social harmony given human psychology and the background conditions. (1992, 312)

To the extent that this thesis is construed narrowly, or implies that *li* can operate alone as the solution, it is a flawed.

---

33. This statement was made in support of the claim that Xunzi held that the rites of the Zhou kings had reached perfection and would be "valid for all times." See section 1.2.1 for the extended quotation.

34. At the same time, however, Xunzi does see a *practical problem* in trying to have more than one set of self-coherent guiding principles concurrently. See section 1.3.1 below.

Xunzi did seem to believe that *li* (禮 ritual propriety) was necessary to facilitate social harmony in his time. However, this does not mean that he was taking a hard line on exactly what the content of *li* should be (i.e., *precisely* that of the later kings), or that it is unchanging (i.e., *always* that of the later kings). Rather, since what distinguishes *li* from *fa* (法) in the sense of "law" is the requirement of personalization, the content of *li*, by definition, should change as appropriate to meet changing needs. Xunzi was conservative, that is, he was reluctant to deviate from the proven successful ways and standards of the past. But, a conservative reluctance is still a good distance from the position that there is one and only one never-changing solution to the human predicament, and that this way has been found, articulated, and given form in singularly appropriate rules and standards. Nonetheless, even if the content of *li* is subject to change as appropriate, tempered by a conservative attitude, Xunzi clearly held *li* in high esteem.

However, one must remember—and this is the main point here—that Xunzi's system, while exalting *li*, does not rely on it exclusively. Laws and penalties are to some degree required, as is music, and appropriately attuned language. So, the system is not simple or pure; it is a mixture that is subject to change due to changing circumstances as well as refinements. His was a fluid conception of *dao* that stressed *li* as an important component, integrated with other aspects.

Extending these considerations to the idea of "basic moral principles," we can state a corollary to Xunzi's dictum that "A model cannot stand on its own, categories cannot apply themselves":[35] principles cannot stand on their own, nor can they organize themselves. Exemplary people are needed to interpret them, and coordinate them with circumstances. Further, since principles can compete, their relative weights must be assessed. This cannot be done in the abstract. A principle's weight in a particular case depends, in part, on the *degree* to which the principle is instantiated in that case. People must judge this. The accumulation of judgments based on principles applied to particular cases influences not only the understanding of those cases, it influences the understanding of the principles as well. That is, while principles may be thought of as enduring in some sense, specific conceptions must undergo ongoing reevaluation in attuning them to emerging contexts.

Thus, even weaker forms of "fixed uniqueness" interpretations, insofar as they imply a pure mechanism (e.g., ritual propriety alone) for instituting the way, or suggest that moral principles can be completely abstracted and held fixed and independent from an evolving social world, do not well describe Xunzi's position. Indeed, Xunzi's critique of his rivals is that they fixate on a single aspect of our condition, and fail to consider its relation to other aspects (see K: 21.4; W 125–26).

---

35. 故法不能獨立。類不能自行。(44/12/2; K: 12.1).

1.2.4. Variable Uniqueness

Perhaps we could salvage the uniqueness hypothesis by making it variable. Thus "Variable Uniqueness" (VU) would hold that there is just one best way to organize society (and articulate the relations in the natural world) while acknowledging that this way may change with the circumstances.[36] On this view, for any circumstance there must be exactly one best solution; a potential for two roughly equal solutions would be impossible. This seems an unlikely hypothesis. What would motivate the idea that Xunzi holds this meta-ethical position? It can't simply be that Xunzi held positions for which he argues aggressively, for taking a position on an issue does not commit one to a uniqueness theory. Positions are staked out in the context of known rivals. It may be thought that, given certain passages, some kind of uniqueness theory must hold. Indeed, one has to admit that there is a tension in Xunzi, that there are passages that at least seem to suggest there is only one way. In the following sections I will address some of the most relevant passages.

1.3. Dispelling Obsessions

1.3.1. No Two Ways?

In his recent book *Rituals of the Way*, Goldin maintains that, for Xunzi: "There is only one Way. The Sage Kings apprehended it, and their rituals embody it. There is no other Way, and no other constellation of rituals that conforms to the Way" (1999, 73). There is *prima facie* evidence for this claim that needs to be addressed. The opening paragraph of the "Dispelling Obsessions" chapter contains the following passage, which on Watson's translation reads: "There are not two Ways in the world; the sage is never of two minds."[37] Knoblock's and Homer Dubs's translations are similar.

　However, this passage should be understood with reference to other relevant passages. Consider the following passage from book 1 "Exhorting Learning": "One who [tries to] travel two roads [at the same time] will not reach one's destination. One who serves two lords will not please [them]. The eye cannot, when looking at two things, see them clearly. The ear cannot, when listening to two things, hear them well."[38] Xunzi is suggesting that practical problems arise when an individual—or a state—is not settled on a definite course: energies will not be aligned and attention will be divided. A similar problem is raised in book 14: "The ruler is the most exalted in the state. The father is the most exalted in the family. Exalting one [results in] order; exalting two [results in]

---

36. For more on this position, see section 2.2, "Uniqueness and Contingency."
37. 天下無二道。聖人無兩心。(78/21/1; K: 21.1; W 121).
38. 行衢道者不至。事兩君者不容。目不能兩視而明。耳不能兩聽而聰。(2/1/22; K: 1.6).

chaos. From ancient times to the present, there has never been a situation that was able to endure for very long with two exalted, each contending for respect."[39] Again Xunzi is indicating that, as a practical matter, having two *dao*s is not going to work very well. This point is also made in book 10, where Xunzi quotes a tradition that says, "When superiors are unified, so too are subordinates. When superiors are divided, so too are subordinates."[40]

Retranslating, and putting the passage in question into the context of the discussion in which it occurs, further makes the case:

> Generally, people suffer the misfortune of being deceived by one small corner and are in the dark about major ordering principles. When these are mastered, one may return to the classics. If one is in doubt about two [conflicting views] then there will be confusion. In the world there are not two holistic guiding discourses (*dao*), sages are not of two minds. Now, the feudal lords have different governments, the hundred schools have different theories, certainly some are right and some are wrong, some are well governed, some in chaos.[41]

Notice that Xunzi says that some of the feudal lords are governing well. It could be that only the rulers that follow the one right way achieve order, but the passage actually seems to suggest, on the contrary, that all the feudal lords govern differently and some of those various approaches are successful. This would be a less than straightforward way of making the claim that there is a single effective method of achieving order. The claim that is being made is that there is an inherent practical difficulty in achieving order, especially on a large scale, when there are competing doctrines about how to achieve it.

1.3.2. A State of Mind Allowing Access to Knowledge of Reality

Additional textual motivation for "uniqueness" interpretations can also be found in the "Dispelling Obsession" chapter. Schwartz addresses a theme in this chapter as follows:

> What the sage ultimately attains through his powers of reason is a comprehensive, impartial, "unbeclouded" view of reality. He totally understands that the human deliberative consciousness is a frail if precious possession. Not only can it be easily drowned in passion, it can easily become obsessed with some one lopsided aspect of reality which totally "beclouds" the grasp of the whole. "The sage knows that the great calamity in the mind's pursuit of true method is that the mind will become beclouded and obstructed." How does the sage maintain a transcendent overview?

---

39. 君者，國之隆也。父者，家之隆也。隆一而治。二而亂。自古及今。未有二隆爭重而能長久者。(53/14/22–23; K: 14.7).

40. 上一則下一矣。上二則下二矣。(35/10/84; K: 10.10).

41. 凡人之患。蔽於一曲而闇於大理。治則復經。兩疑則惑矣。天下無二道。聖人無兩心。今諸侯異政。百家異說。則必或是或非或治或亂。(78/21/1–2; K: 21.1).

How does man truly know the Way? The answer is "through emptiness, unity and quietude. The mind has never ceased to accumulate and yet it has what is called emptiness. It has never ceased to have different thoughts and yet it is pervaded with what is called unity. It has never ceased to be in motion and yet it has what is called quietude." . . . [I]t is also suggested that somehow "emptiness, unity, and quietude" are a necessary precondition of a truly "objective" grasp of reality. (Schwartz 1985, 314–15, quoting K: 21.5a, 21.5d; W 126, 127)

Hansen quotes the "empty, unified, and still" passage in support of the following conclusion: "[Han Feizi and Xunzi] both start with the authoritarian assumption of an absolute correct way. They assert what Zhuangzi denies, the possibility of achieving a frame of mind that gives unbiased access to it" (1992, 340). This leads Hansen finally to speculate thus:

I am most tempted to the hypothesis that Xunzi reverts to authoritarianism in the awareness that the analytical conventionalist argument does not get him home. His absolutist conclusion then uses the doctrine of a privileged preconventional vantage point. This brings him very close to Mencius, but since he looks *outward* with this special mindset, he claims to read the correct *dao* in nature. Here he uses the language of *empty*, *unified*, and *still*, the allegedly Daoist terms. But the doctrine is not pluralism; it is absolutism. (1992, 310)

His evaluation of Xunzi is an unflattering one:

The tradition expresses little doubt about the authenticity of the major segments of *The Xunzi*. There seems, however, to be at least two different thinkers writing there. One is a philosopher, aware of the philosophical issues motivating Zhuangzi's skepticism. The other is a dogmatic, toadying, propagandist for a draconian authoritarian social-political *dao*. He panders to rulers who are looking for ministers and a governing strategy. The central terms occur in both contexts. The philosopher sounds like a pragmatist faced with a form of relativism that he fully understands. The political dogmatist sounds as though he has no grasp of the philosophical problems of realism and relativism. (1992, 308)

Hansen, perhaps motivated by his desire to defend Daoism, fails to apply his well-articulated strategy of adopting the interpretation that makes the author more "reasonable" (see Hansen 1992, 10–11). Instead, he interprets Xunzi as philosophically schizophrenic.

But is a more reasonable interpretation possible? Or is a realist interpretation the only one that can adequately account for passages in "Dispelling Obsession" and the other scattered passages that seem also to support it? Below I will outline an alternative position. For now, let's just consider what I take to be the most critical passage. Knoblock's translation reads:

> Emptiness, unity, and stillness are called the Great Pure Understanding. Each of the myriad things has a form that is perceptible. Each being perceived can be assigned its proper place. Each having been assigned its proper place will not lose its proper position. . . . By penetrating into and inspecting the myriad things, he knows their *essential qualities*. By examining and testing order and disorder, he is fully conversant with their *inner laws*. (K: 21.4d–21.5e; emphasis added)

My reading of the passage is as follows:

> A state of receptivity, continuity, and equilibrium is called great clarity and insight. [For one with such clarity and insight,] of the myriad things, none having form lack perceptible features, none with perceptible features cannot be appraised, none that have been appraised will lose their station. . . . Keenly observing the myriad things, he appreciates distinctive features. He examines and compares [conditions leading to] order and disorder, and plumbs their depths.[42]

The difference between the two translations may at first sight seem stylistic, but the worldview behind the translations is fundamentally different. The import of the passage is that one who meets certain conditions is capable of a high degree of insight into relations relevant to achieving order, not that there is a univocal view of the universe, and all within it, to which a certain state of mind allows access.

1.3.3. Constructive Distinctions and False Dichotomies

Xunzi does not maintain that we simply make up a structure to describe what is itself unstructured. On the contrary, the world is not unstructured; it is over-structured. If we try to cut it at its joints, one cut restricts the next. Xunzi writes, "Whenever the myriad things are differentiated, each parsing will obscure (*bi* 蔽) others. This is the downfall common among ideologies."[43] For example,

> Mozi was blinded (*bi*) by utility and did not appreciate the significance (*zhi* 知) of cultural patterns. Master Song was obsessed with the satisfaction of desires and did not understand how to obtain this. Shen Dao was blinded by laws and did not appreciate the role of virtuous people. Shen Buhai was obsessed with technique and did not know knowledge. Huizi was blinded by language and did not understand

---

42. 虛壹而靜。謂之大清明。萬物莫形而不見。莫見而不論。莫論而失位。 . . . 疏觀萬物而知其情。參稽治亂而通其度。(80/21/41–42; K:21.4d–21.5e; W 128–129). I am tempted to read 莫論而失位 as "no one who arranges [the world] will lose the throne," but this neglects the parallelism with the two previous clauses.

43. 凡萬物異則莫不相為蔽。此心術之公患也。(78/21/7; K: 21.2; W 122). Cua, following Watson, translates the passage differently, but makes the point equally well. "[In general,] when one makes distinctions among myriad things, one's mind is liable to be obscured by these distinctions" (Cua 1985, 143). Knoblock gives an altogether different reading.

actualities. And, Zhuangzi was obsessed with *tian* and did not know the role of people.[44]

In the *Xunzi*, *bi* means being overly focused on one aspect of a situation such that one cannot accommodate competing ways of thought.[45] And, for this reason, one misses opportunities for forwarding the Confucian project of continually achieving harmony in an ever-changing environment. Criticizing competing schools of thought, Xunzi writes: "Each of these various attempts addresses merely one corner of the way. The *dao* embodies regularities while always changing. One corner is not sufficient to raise it up."[46] It is not that the way does not involve considerations of utility, curbing desires, legal measures, and so on. Rather, if one relies exclusively on distinctions drawn from focusing on just one of these, then one inevitably misses the opportunities available from considering things from other angles. As a holistic guiding discourse, *dao* indicates an effective and reliable way of governance that engenders social harmony. At any point in time this holistic discourse is called by the name *dao*. This, however, does not entail that its contents are unchanging. In fact, this passage asserts that they are always changing.

Bi leads one to take a distinction as a strict dichotomy not allowing consideration of other factors. A. S. Cua puts it this way: "All distinctions owe their origin to comparison and analogy of different kinds of things. They are made according to our current purposes, and thus are relative to a particular context of thought and discourse. Distinctions, while useful, are not dichotomies. In *bi*, a person attends exclusively to the significance of one item and disregards that of another" (1997, 206). *Ming* (clarity) being the opposite of *bi*, implies seeing various distinctions simultaneously and thus being in a position to begin to weigh them in relation to the particular circumstances and desired outcomes.

---

44. 墨子蔽於用而不知文。宋子蔽於欲而不知得。慎子蔽於法而不知賢。申子蔽於勢而不知知。惠子蔽於辭而不知實。莊子蔽於天而不知人。(79/21/21–22; K: 21.4; W 125).

45. In a lucid discussion of *bi*, Cua makes a very similar claim, writing: "Xunzi's point is that, depending on particular situations, yielding to or getting ahead of others, treating people equally or differently, and satisfying a few or many desires are valuable items for deliberation concerning a matter at hand. To seize upon one of these values and represent it as an all-or-nothing value in every problematic situation is to set up a misguided theory. . . . Since *bi* is contrary to reason (*li* 理), we may regard that state as one of irrational preoccupation with one side of a distinction at the expense of careful consideration of the other—an example of aspect obsession." (Cua 2003, 172–73; cf. Cua 1998, 227). Xunzi writes: "Seeing the desirable quality of something, one must sooner or latter consider its detestable (*e* 惡) qualities. Seeing the beneficial aspects of something, one must sooner or latter consider its harmful aspects. Weigh (*quan* 權) these aspects together, thoroughly gauge them, only then can one be confident whether the thing is desirable or detestable, whether to choose it or to reject it." 見其可欲也。則必前後慮其可惡也者。見其可利也。則必前後慮其可害也者。而兼權之。孰計之。然後定其欲惡取舍。(8/3/45–47; K: 3.13; Cua 1998, 260). The various aspects ought to be "weighed together" in order to form a truly considered judgment. For example, by focusing only on a short-term advantage, one may overlook reasons why a particular course of action could have long-run problems.

46. 此數具者。皆道之一隅也。夫道者。體常而盡變。一隅不足以舉之。(79/21/24–25; K: 21.4; W 126).

In order to do this one's mind should be empty, unified, and still. Xunzi writes, "Not using what is already stored up to disrupt with what will be received is called open-mindedness. . . . Not using one thing to disrupt another is called unity."[47] One must be able to maintain an open enough mind to evaluate various ways of dividing things up before one can competently articulate constructive divisions. This position may be seen as an extension of Confucius's view expressed in *Analects* 2.14, at least on Arthur Waley's reading of it: "A gentleman can see a question from all sides without bias. The small man is biased and can see a question from only one side" (1938, 91).[48]

1.3.4. Establishing Constructive Distinction

Ivanhoe's interpretation suggests that *dao* is some mystical entity (or principle) which stands independently of us, as a possible object of our understanding, and which, when understood and put into practice, makes the real world an ideal place. In a word, *dao* is treated as *transcendent*. He writes:

> [W]hereas Zhuangzi saw human distinctions as the source of all the world's ills, Xunzi saw them as the unique possibility for universal harmony and flourishing. If one could understand and master the *dao*, things would fall into place on a universal scale. The Way could protect one from all harm, offer one every benefit and bring peace, order, and prosperity to all the world. (1991, 317)[49]

I would argue, on the contrary, that Xunzi fully understood and appreciated the significance of Zhuangzi's insights into the conventionality of distinctions. In fact, Xunzi saw this conventionality as an opportunity to be proactive in shaping a harmonious cultural environment.[50] Xunzi's *dao* is not something out there waiting to be understood and *then* put into practice; the putting it into practice is integral to the understanding. Xunzi is explicit on this point: "One should study until one puts it [the way] into practice. To practice it is

---

47. 不以所已藏害所將受謂之虛。. . . 不以夫一害此一謂之壹。 (80/21/36–38; K: 21.5d; W 128).

48. 子曰：「君子周而不比，小人比而不周。」

49. Ivanhoe quotes the following passage from Watson in support of his position: "Through rites heaven and earth join in harmony, the sun and the moon shine, the four seasons proceed in order, the stars and constellations march, the rivers flow, and all things flourish; men's likes and dislikes are regulated and their joys and hates made appropriate. Those below are obedient, those above are enlightened; all things change but do not become disordered; only he who turns his back upon the rites will be destroyed. Are they not wonderful indeed!" (1991, 317; W 94). Note that there is nothing in this passage, even as translated here, which dictates a realist interpretation. See section 4.3.5 for more on this passage.

50. Virtually the same point is made by Tetsuo Najita regarding Laozi and Ogyū Sorai (a Japanese Confucian philosopher influenced by Xunzi). Najita writes, "[A]lthough Sorai firmly rejected Laozi's ideal of the natural community, he nonetheless retained in his overall theory Laozi's insight that Confucian ideas were artificial constructs and not extensions of the natural order. Whereas Laozi denounced them for this reason, Sorai endorsed them as creative constructions of the Sages" (1998, xvii–xviii).

to understand."[51] "Completely integrate one's learning, put it fully to use, and only then is one learned."[52]

It is difficult to construct a system of social arrangements that will produce order, harmony, and joy. Yet, sages have insight into how things hang together and a clearness of mind that enables them to weigh a variety of considerations without being obsessed with any single distinction. Over time they are able to differentiate strategies likely to be effective from ill-conceived ones. This does not imply that there is a unique solution. Another passage in "Dispelling Obsessions" explains: "If you guide [the mind] with constructive patterns,[53] support it with clarity, and let nothing destabilize it, this will suffice for it to establish right and wrong, and clear away doubts and suspicions."[54] Watson ends his translation of the same passage as follows: "it will be capable of *determining* right and wrong and resolving doubts" (W 131; emphasis added). It is instructive to note that the word "determining" here could be understood in the sense of ascertaining the truth of the matter, or in the sense of setting or establishing it. I suspect most readers of Watson's translation would assume the former was intended. But, the character being translated as "determining" (*ding* 定) really means something closer to the latter. Karlgren defines it as "settle, establish, fix" (GSR: 833z). Given certain conditions, the heart-mind is capable of establishing moral principles, which if followed will enable one to satisfy many desires over the long term.[55]

We also find passages, even in existing translations, which support the view that, far from being fixed for all time, the important distinctions must be reevaluated daily. For example: "[W]hen it comes to the duties to be observed between ruler and subject, the affection between father and son, and the differences in station between husband and wife—these you must work at day and night and never neglect" (W 85).[56] The meaning here is not that one should work hard at fulfilling fixed and rigid roles, but that the roles themselves must be fitted to one's personal circumstances, and this requires constant self-tailoring. One

---

51. 學至於行之而止矣。行之明也。(24/8/102–3; K: 8.11).

52. 全之盡之。然後學者也。(3/1/45–46; K: 1.13; W 22; H 252). Cf. "If categories of moral relations do not come through [in one's actions], or if one has not integrated consummate virtue and appropriateness (*ren yi*), one is not worthy of being called 'good at learning.' Learning is securing what one learns by integrating it." 倫類不通。仁義不一。不足謂善學。學也者。固學一之也。(3/1/44–45; K: 1.13; W 22).

53. See section 2.5 (near the end) for justification of the translation of *li* 理 as "constructive patterns."

54. 故導之以理。養之以清。物莫之傾。則足以定是非決嫌疑矣。(81/21/56–57).

55. Xunzi writes: "Is not long deliberation and taking into consideration what comes later excellent indeed!" 長慮顧後幾不甚善矣哉。(11/4/64–65; K: 4.11). Knoblock has "considering the long view of things and thinking of the consequences" for 長慮顧後, which amounts to the same thing. The context of the passage makes it clear that something of this nature is the intended meaning.

56. 傳曰。萬物之怪書不說。無用之辯。不急之察。棄而不治。若夫君臣之義。父子之親。夫婦之別。則日切瑳而不舍也。(64/17/37–38; K: 17.7; W 85). Watson's translation. See section 4.3.4 below, for my own translation.

must always be refining the important distinctions, as Edward J. Machle in a more literal translation of the same passage brings out, these are "patterns to be cut and polished daily" (1993, 117).

1.4. Confucian Constructivism

For Xunzi, when sages articulate moral categories, or devise ritualized rules of deference, they are not reporting on the true nature of things that an "un-beclouded" mind enables them to comprehend; rather they are developing constructs (i.e., something constructed by the mind[57]) that they believe will be constructive (i.e., useful, beneficial). For this reason, "constructivism" is a fitting label for this interpretation, playing on both senses of the word. The constructivist endeavors to construct constructive constructs, that is, devise productive artifice.[58]

Constructivism, as a philosophy of science, maintains that what counts as scientific knowledge depends on social conditions and the interests of individual scientists in addition to the constraints of the world that science seeks to describe. "For example, constructivists claim that the way we represent the structure of DNA is a result of many interrelated scientific practices and is not dictated by some ultimate underlying structure of reality"(Downes 1998, 624). This is not to say that constructivists deny a structured reality, they deny only that reality dictates a singular description. In Xunzi's language, "*Tian* can generate things but cannot articulate distinctions among them. Earth can support people but

---

57. Cua notes: "Xunzi does explicitly state that the sages are responsible for the existence of *li* through conscious or productive activity (*wei*)" (1985, 69). See section 1.6 for the passage in question, and sections 5.1 and 5.2 for more on the character *wei* 偽.

58. Broadly speaking, "Moral constructivism is a metaethical view about the nature of moral truth and moral facts (and properties), so called because the intuitive idea behind the view is that such truths and facts are human constructs rather than objects of discovery" (Timmons 1996, 106). There is, however, a form of constructivism that only partly resembles the theory I am ascribing to Xunzi. Onora O'Neill describes it as follows: "Unlike realists, constructivists deny that there are any distinctively moral facts or properties, whether natural or non-natural, which can be *discovered* or *intuited* and which provide the foundations of ethics" (O'Neill 1998, 631; emphasis hers). So far, so good. But, O'Neill continues her description, saying: "Unlike conventionalists or relativists, constructivists think that it is possible to justify universal ethical principles. . . . The distinctive feature of constructivism in ethics is the claim that universal ethical principles can be built out of quite minimal accounts of action and reason." She has in mind a more specific doctrine coined by John Rawls, "Kantian constructivism." Confucian constructivism, however, is hardly Kantian. While it does reason from what may be called minimal assumptions (e.g. that social harmony is desirable), it does not presume that there is one exclusive universally applicable system of morality. On Marcus Singer's account, "Constructivism maintains that moral ideas are human constructs and the task is not epistemological or metaphysical but practical and theoretical—[for Rawls] that of attaining reflective equilibrium between considered moral judgements and the principles that coordinate and explain them" (Singer 1995, 510). For Confucian constructivism the task is the practical realization of social harmony through an intelligent use of moral categories and norms. Ivanhoe uses the phrase "constructivist account" (2000, 239) as a contrasting position to his own. What he seems to have in mind here is the Kantian constructivism described above and should not be confused with the position I am taking.

cannot order them. The myriad things of the whole world, and all living people, await sages—and only then are they apportioned."[59] In other words, a constructivist denies that there are intrinsically appropriate descriptions of objects. As Xunzi says, "Name-concepts (*ming* 名) have no intrinsic appropriateness."[60]

For Xunzi *dao*ing is an art, or a craft. He writes, "The mind is the artisan and steward of the way,"[61] indicating that the mind is responsible both for giving the way shape and for overseeing its ongoing development. For example, naming for Xunzi is a practical matter. It is folly to try to have a different name for every individual thing, Xunzi tells us, just as it would be folly not to make any distinctions, calling everything by the same name. Things are named according to perceived similarities deemed sufficiently important and relevant to some task. When there is no longer any productive purpose in making finer distinctions we stop making them.[62] Further, as Cua has argued, "[G]eneric terms originate not from discovering 'essences' but from empirical comparison and analogy" (1985, 200 n4).

We can never reveal the one true description of reality, and to try to do so is not the Confucian project. It is not necessary to deny that we live in a world with preexisting interrelated aspects to hold that there is necessarily a creative and prescriptive element in any description of it. And, this allowance of creativity is not contrary to the Confucian and commonsense idea that there are more and less responsible ways to shape a version of our world. Xunzi recognized that names (and the categories and distinctions they signal) involve an element of conventionality. He took this as an opportunity to be proactive in shaping a harmonious cultural environment.

It is important, however, to stress the distinction between constructivism and mere conventionalism,[63] in which agreement is the sole standard of appropriateness. On the conventionalist view, the world is like a pie for which any

---

59. 天能生物不能辯物也。地能載人不能治人也。宇中萬物。生人之屬。待聖人然後分也。(73/19/78–79; K: 19.6; W 103). Cf. "The exemplary person is the beginning of ritual propriety and of a sense of appropriateness. . . . Thus, nature and the earth produce the exemplary person, and the exemplary person applies patterns (*li*) to earth and nature. . . . If there were no exemplary people, nature and the earth would not be patterned." 君子者禮義之始也。. . . 故天地生君子。君子理天地。. . . 無君子則天地不理。(28/9/64–66; K: 9.15; W 44–45).

60. 名無固宜。(83/22/25; K: 22.2g; W 144). For a justification of *ming* as "name-concepts," see section 3.2 and the glossary of key terms.

61. 心也者。道之工宰也。(82/22/40; K: 22.3f; W 147).

62. Xunzi writes, "After [we have perceived something] it is named accordingly, what is considered similar is given a similar name, what is considered different is given a different name. . . . Appreciating [the principle of] 'different names for different things' and thus, so as not to cause disorder, letting all different things have a different name, is as bad as letting all different things have the same name. . . . We press on dividing them up—where we make a distinction there is a distinguishing [term]—until we reach a point where there is no more [productive] distinctions to be made, and then we stop." 然後隨而命之。同則同之。異則異之。. . . 知異實者之異名也。故使異實者莫不異名也。不可亂也。猶使異實者莫不同名也。. . . 推而別之。別則有別。至於無別然後止。(83/22/21–25; K: 22.2f; W 143–44; Graham 1989, 265).

63. For a critique of the conventionalist side of Hansen's interpretation of Xunzi, see Van Norden 1993.

slice can be considered equally well made. There is no pattern or structure that favors one way of slicing over another. Thus our cutting imposes a structure on what was itself unstructured.

The constructivist, on the other hand, groups things together on the basis of their perceived qualities and human interests. While these groupings have no privileged status, they have their basis in both natural patterns and propensities, as well as the interests of those doing the grouping. Categories are not considered purely natural kinds.[64] Nevertheless, this does not imply that any grouping is as good as any other. Categories are not univocal, but neither are they arbitrary. They answer to some purpose or use. Xunzi writes, "The myriad things share the same world but have different forms. They lack an intrinsically appropriate articulation, but have a use for people. This refers to the art of discriminating regular patterns (*shu*)."[65]

An important aspect of constructivism is that it allows for creative pluralism rather than implying that there is a unique solution to the ways in which the world may be legitimately divided. For a realist, distinctions are supposed to "truly" reflect the physical or moral world, and two mutually contradictory distinctions cannot both be "true." But, it is possible for two systems to be roughly equally good with respect to satisfying some common purpose while at the same time being composed of different, mutually contradictory, distinctions. If in an Aristotelian virtue system disposition x is a virtue, while in a Confucian system it is a vice, the realist must say that at least one of them is wrong. They cannot both have described x truly, as a virtue and a vice. For the realist, a claim about x is a claim about how the world really is, and thus can be (at least theoretically) judged independently from any other distinction. But for the constructivist, one component of a system cannot be judged independently of its role in the whole system, since what is at issue are consequences that depend on the interaction of everything in the system. So, since it is possible that both systems could be roughly equally good at satisfying similar purposes, it is possible that x is a virtue in one system and a vice in another, given the different dynamics of those systems—just as monkshood is both a medicine and a poison. Clearly, though,

---

64. Consider the status of marsupial mice. Would a taxonomy that grouped them with ordinary mice rather than with their genetically closer relative the kangaroo be less "true," or even just plain wrong? Xunzi would not think "truth" is an appropriate standard of assessment. I hasten to concede that it may indeed be useful, given the purposes of biology, to group kangaroos together with marsupial mice. But, this is a very different claim than that of the strong realist.

65. 萬物同宇而異體。無宜而有用為人。數也。(31/10/1). Knoblock translates *shu* 數 as "the natural order of things," whereas Dubs renders it "an art." Knoblock's translation reads: "The myriad things share the same world, but their embodied form is different. Although they have no intrinsic appropriateness, yet they may be of use to humanity: this is due to the natural order of things" (K: 10.1). Cf. Dubs's translation, "All things are present together in the world, but have different forms. Of themselves they are not appropriate; but they are used by men—this is an art" (D 151). As I read it, they each capture one element of its meaning. That is, *shu* 數 simultaneously carries the meanings of "regular patterns" as well as "art." The idea is that the process of skillfully utilizing the regular patterns of the various aspects of our surrounding conditions is an art.

these considerations would hardly suggest that every distinction is as good as every other. On the contrary, the standard is efficacy toward the realization of some worthwhile goal.

The constructivist project involves an element of creativity in the process of moving toward the goals of community cohesion, political stability, and harmonious intercourse. These values are in turn justified by their important role in the satisfaction of people's desires. If everyone tried to satisfy one's own individual desires whimsically, one would end up frustrated. Xunzi writes:

> Departing from the way and choosing from the inside [i.e., according to one's original desires] is like exchanging two for one. How can there be a gain? The [fulfillment of] one's desires accumulated over a hundred years would be exchanged for the dubious [gratification] of a single instance. Anyone who does this does not understand the calculations involved.[66]

Dao is the name for a path forged with an eye to the deep and broad satisfaction of human needs and wants. Such a path is not easily found, and following our immediate inclinations tends to lead us astray. Xunzi believed that by appreciating the accumulated wisdom and experience of the sage kings, and the lessons of their successes, we have confidence that we are "on the right track" as we continue the endeavor to make our way.

1.5. Morality as Moral: A Problem for Nivison

Now that both realist and constructivist views have been introduced, we are in a position to confront a meta-ethical "problem." Nivison identifies Xunzi's problem as "how to secure the Confucian tradition of moral rules and values against a variety of voices . . . and how to do this in a nonarbitrary way" (1996b, 52). He addresses this problem by reflecting on the position of the Qing Dynasty Confucian thinker Zhang Xuecheng.

The main point of his discussion is that the sages come up with their moral system *piecemeal* (and this, as Nivison points out, can reasonably be traced back to Xunzi's idea of *ji wei* 積偽, the accumulation of constructive activity). This addresses the question of why a person cannot simply make up their own way and claim that it is on par with the way of the sages. "The mistake in the question is that I shouldn't be comparing myself with some person or persons in the past, but with a (perhaps still continuing) *historical process*" (1996b, 53; emphasis in original). Nivison, however, is not entirely satisfied, and he hesitates to attribute Zhang's position to Xunzi, calling it a "decent revision" (54). Moreover, he finds the position somewhat problematic on its own. He writes:

---

66. 離道而內自擇。是猶以兩易一也。奚得。其累百年之欲。易一時之嫌。然且為之不明其數也。(86/22/77–78; K: 22.6c; W 154).

"There is a price to be paid for a view like this: (1) The positive moral order is a historical product, perhaps still unfolding, not final. (2) A present-day person or ruler in the right 'position' can keep on creating, if a need exists and it is that person's function to meet it" (53–54).[67] Why does Nivison tally these on the negative side of the ledger? For a constructivist these are not costs.

Elsewhere, after explaining that Xunzi gives consequentialist reasons to follow *dao* and what amount to aesthetic reasons to love it, Nivison wonders whether this gives an account of "morality as *moral.*" He writes, "Morality is an illusion, really, in this point of view" (1996b, 274). What exactly is taken to be an illusion on this view? *Dao*, embodied as it is in the norms of ritual propriety, is not illusory. Only morality as conceived in moral realist terms is illusory. Here is the issue for Nivison: "one may still ask whether utility plus cosmic beauty account for morality as *moral*—whether, e.g., they can show me why I am doing something morally *wrong* if I fail to observe mourning for my parents" (274; emphasis in original). Confucians have ample resources for critique of such a person. On the other hand, I would readily concede to Nivison that on this view there is no claim regarding actions mapping to any other realm where what *really is wrong* is kept track of. But for whom is this a problem? From the constructivist perspective, what Nivison considers problems are nonissues.

Henry Rosemont has said, "Confucian philosophers never considered the philosophical question of the meaning of life, but rather focused their energies on constructing a value system in which everyone could find meaning *in* life" (1971, 213). Similarly, we could say, Confucians were not concerned with the question of whether some activity *really* was moral, but rather were concerned about constructing a world imbued with moral meaning. Making a related point, Takeuchi Yoshio writes, "Morality [for Xunzi] is not conduct based on our natural constitution, it is something artificial which rectifies and ornaments our nature, that is, it is *wei* 偽 (artifice)."[68] Morality is not something given. It can be found neither in our nature nor the nature of the world. It is something devised, in full consideration of the constraints of our condition, both to improve ourselves and the state of our circumstances, making our journey through the world meaningful.

Perhaps Nivison worries that on the view that he outlined the ancient sages would lose their authority. While sages could not be viewed as absolute authorities from this viewpoint, innovation in keeping with the spirit of the tradition need not diminish the importance of the sages. Indeed, it makes the appearance of new sages all the more important—and it is new sages that Xunzi's educational philosophy is designed to produce.

---

67. It should be noted that the process of constructing a moral order is more complicated than implied in Nivison's statement. As an example, see section 3.4, "Naming: The Ruler's Prerogative?"

68. 道徳は天性に本づく行でなく、性を矯飾する人為的のもの即ち偽である。(Takeuchi, p. 105). *Wei* 偽 is discussed in sections 5.1 and 5.2.

There is always a role for sages to revive the old and make it relevant to the contemporary. In this way evolving standards are both "projections" of tradition and to some degree novel. As Abe Yoshio explains it, "Since the authority of the later kings is something that one should recognize as a projection of the former kings, one can acknowledge that for Xunzi the new *li* established by the later kings have the same dignity as the *li* of the former kings."[69]

Nishi Junzō goes further, claiming: "For Xunzi there is no given order or morality. All of that people personally choose and establish."[70] This claim is problematic as it stands and needs to be qualified. While morality is a social product (in which the sages have a key role), there are constraints—both natural and historical—that restrict individual choice in its construction. Xunzi recognized moral construction as a continuous and complex negotiation between various levels of society (the masses, the ruler, and the elite).[71]

Xunzi likewise appreciated the importance of balancing the enduring lessons of history and the evolving needs of the present. He writes, "*Dao* is the proper balance (*quan* 權) of past and present.[72] Those who depart from *dao* and make choices from personal inclinations do not appreciate that on which fortune and misfortune depend."[73] Interpreting this passage Feng Youlan writes: "Thus, when people make choices, they must put the prudence and wisdom of their minds to work, and weigh the various aspects of advantages and disadvantage in a balance, in order not to be 'confused regarding weal and woe.' In this way, '*dao* is the proper balance of ancient and present.' This is the *dao* of the following passage: '*Dao* is not the *dao* of *tian*, nor the *dao* of earth. It is the way people conduct themselves.'"[74] *Dao* is the balance: the way made by thoughtful, prudent people.

The root metaphor behind the character *quan* 權 is the sliding weight of a steelyard, and in the context of this passage it means "balance" or "weigh against

---

69. いずれにせよ、荀子はこの後王の権威は先王の投影として承認すべきだというのだから、後王によって制定される新礼は、先王の礼と同等の尊厳を有するものと認められる。(Abe 1964, 61).

70. 荀子にとっては、所与の秩序・道徳はなく、すべては人が自ら択び自ら定めるものである。(Nishi 1969, 44).

71. See, for example, section 3.4 for a discussion of the dynamics involved in attuning names.

72. I have chosen to translate this in a way that maintains an ambiguity in the text. Considering the larger context, the meaning is probably that *dao* is the proper balance both of the past and of the present. This is generally how it is taken, and my discussion assumes this reading as well. However, it could also mean *dao* involves finding the proper balance between the past, on the one hand, and the present, on the other. In other words, as is suggested at the end of my discussion of the passage, it could mean the balance between tradition and current needs. Cf. Knoblock's translation: "The Way, from antiquity to the present, has been the right balance" (K: 22.6b).

73. 道者。古今之正權也。離道而內自擇。則不知禍福之所託。(86/22/74; K: 22.6b; W 153).

74. 故人在去取之際，必以心慮知，權衡各方面之利害，而不致「惑於禍福」。「道者，古今之正權」也。此道即所謂「道者，非天之道，非地之道，人之所以道也」。(Feng 1961, 361; cf. Fung 1952, 290, for Derk Bodde's translation; cf. also Kakimura and Azuma 1995, 428). The passage cited is: *Xunzi* 20/8/23–24; K: 8.3.

each other" (see Graham 1978, 184). It may be considered the ongoing balancing of conditions relevant to maintaining harmony in the midst of changing circumstances.[75] And though the primary meaning is balance, it may be thought to continue to suggest the other aspects of its meaning. It represents a kind of power, an authoritative influence. It implies the nimble adjustment to change, adaptability, flexibility. When used as an adverb it has the sense of "tentatively." And as a verb, in addition to "to weigh" or "to assess," it means, "to handle a task provisionally." Thus the meaning of the passage seems to be that *dao*ing has always been a matter of finding the proper balance for one's time and circumstance. Acting in accordance with these considerations is contrasted with following one's own shortsighted desires and feeling. *Dao* is a path forged, and still being forged, by the exemplars of tradition. It is a product of the always-accumulating wisdom of a tradition in an endeavor to achieve and maintain social and human values. Following such a path leads to fortunate circumstances, whereas following our immediate inclinations leads to misfortune.

Also, when considering the import of this passage, we would do well to remember that Xunzi also wrote, "Those who are good at articulating the ancient necessarily need to show that it is applicable in the present."[76] Indeed, one may read the passage in question to state, "*Dao* is the proper balance of tradition and the current situation." In fact, this interpretation is supported by a passage in the "Dispelling Obsessions" chapter which describes *dao* as the balancing of various dichotomized categories including the past and present:

> Sages know the peril of ideology of the mind, and see the misfortunes of obsessing on one thing and being blind to others. Thus [they neither obsess on nor are blind to] . . . [among other things] the ancient or the present. They simultaneously set out the myriad phenomena and impartially hang them in a balance. For this reason, the multifarious distinctions do not obstruct each other and thereby throw their arrangement into chaos. What do we call this balance? "*Dao*."[77]

The idea of balancing tradition with present needs and conditions could be considered a corollary to one of Xunzi's principles of clear mindedness that I noted earlier: "Not using what is already stored up to disrupt what will be received is called open-mindedness."[78] For Xunzi, to see only the traditional

---

75. It is in fact the same character used by Mencius when he approves of using one's *discretion* regarding the ordinary norms of *li* in extraordinary cases, such as saving someone from drowning.

76. A fuller and more literal translation puts the statement into context: "Those who are good at articulating the ancient must have a tally to the present. Those who are good at articulating *tian* must have verification of its relation to people. Generally speaking, theoreticians value coherent distinctions and conformity to experience." 故善言古者必有節於今。善言天者必有徵於人。凡論者貴其有辨合有符驗。 (88/23/44-45; K: 23.3b; W 163).

77. 聖人知心術之患。見蔽塞之禍。故 . . . 無古無今。兼陳萬物而中縣衡焉。是故眾異不得相蔽以亂其倫也。何謂衡。曰。道。 (79/21/28-30; K: 21.5a-b; W 126-27; H 274).

78. 不以所已藏害所將受謂之虛。 (80/21/36-37; K: 21.5d; W 128). See section 1.3.3.

would be a form of *bi* (obsession). As David Hall and Roger Ames contend, "Both pragmatists and Confucians would consider the question of how one might balance the demands of novelty with the claims of tradition to be one of the most significant social questions" (1999, 156).

1.6. A Case in Point

Citing a passage that likens the art of instituting social norms with pottery, Ivanhoe suggests that through the effort of the sages cultural patterns are brought to "perfection." He writes, "The sages brought these cultural patterns to a state of perfection through a long and arduous process of trial and error, just as a potter learns to fashion bowls and develops the art of pottery" (1991, 313–14). He offers the following translation adapted from Watson in support of this position:

> [A]ll rituals and social norms are produced by the conscious activity (*wei* 偽) of the sages; essentially they are not products of man's nature. A potter molds clay and makes a vessel, but the vessel is the product of the conscious activity of the potter, not essentially a product of his human nature. A carpenter carves a piece of wood and makes a utensil, but the utensil is a product of the conscious activity of the carpenter, not essentially a product of his human nature. The sage gathers together his thoughts and ideas, experiments with various forms of conscious activity, and so produces rituals and social norms and sets forth laws and regulations. (Ivanhoe 1991, 314; cf. K: 23.2a; W 160)

There is nothing in this passage that suggests that the product is perfect, or that it is a unique solution. On the contrary, this passage supports a constructivist interpretation. Just as not all forms will make equally good bowls, not all social norms will be equally constructive. But also, just as there may be more than one form that makes a good bowl, so too there may be more than one set of social constructs that are conducive to harmony. Further, just because someone has made a good bowl, which may serve as a model for the next generation of bowl makers, that fact does not rule out the possibility of refinement, or that changing circumstances may call for alterations. In fact, human aesthetic sensibilities require that bowls be different. What makes a potter authoritative is sustained quality in difference, not replication.

*   *   *

As mentioned earlier, this chapter is intended to characterize some general features common among many interpretations of Xunzi (although those interpretations may differ substantially in other ways). And, I have promised to look beneath those surface features in chapter 2. Thus, in the following chapter, I explore the concepts of *li* 理 and *lei* 類 (patterns and categories), and their relation to *tian* 天 (nature and its propensities). This takes us to the most fundamental aspects of Xunzi's thought, but we will find a correlative interdependence rather than a foundation. Understanding this relation between *li* and *lei* as mutually entailing will then facilitate our understanding of *zhengming* 正名, or, in more general terms, why naming works the way it does in Xunzi's thought (discussed in chapter 3). Even ritual propriety, the topic of chapter 4, exhibits an analogous nature, that is, social patterns simultaneously shape, and are shaped by, the conduct of exemplary people.

Li and *Lei*: Constructive Patterning of Categories

In the previous chapter, I argued that many scholars view Xunzi as maintaining that the *dao* 道 of the ancient sages was the uniquely effective way to achieve a harmonious society. In strong versions of this interpretation, Xunzi is thought to regard the way of the sage-kings as perfect in every detail. The first half of this chapter discusses how certain interpretations of the concepts of *li* 理 and *lei* 類, patterns and categories, tend to support this type of theory. In the second half, I question the viability of these interpretations and offer a constructivist alternative, which views categories as human constructs designed to be constructive. On this view, there is not one true way to understand the world and our roles and responsibilities in it. Rather, constructivism allows conceptual room for pluralism, as well as for progress without teleology. While some ways of organizing social constructs are more conducive to forming a harmonious society than others, conceptually ordering our world is an ongoing process that has no final or perfect articulation.

2.1. The Patterns of "Heaven"

One explanation underlying the purported uniqueness of the way is that *li* 理 (pattern)[1] refers to a kind of rational structure or "reason." This is the view we see expressed, for example, in John Knoblock's characterization of *li* in the introduction to his translation of the *Xunzi*: "wherever a distinctive pattern provided the order of a thing, there was *li*. It was the principle of order that provided the pattern, regulated the thing, and made it recognizable as that thing and function as that thing functions. It is the reason and rationality common to the minds of all men" (1988, 80). He goes on to say that, "The *li* is the rational basis of all order. It is natural order, and it is reason."

This interpretation is also suggested in his translation of *lei* 類. Since *li* is reason, *lei*, which is taken as the unique set of categories truly based on it, are thought of as "proper logical" categories, as in the following: "When knowledgeable, he [the gentleman] understands the interconnections between

---

1. I will use the word "pattern" as a gloss for *li* 理. Later, I will suggest the phrase "constructive patterns" to signal that *li* are patterns picked out for their positive effect. A. S. Cua has expressed valid worries about the use of "pattern" as a translation for *li*. See Cua 1997, 201. Nevertheless, rendering *li* as "pattern" is judged to best serve our purposes here. See also the glossary of key terms.

phenomena and can assign them to their proper logical category" (K: 3.6). There is, however, nothing in the text that corresponds with either "proper" or "logical."[2] The passage merely says, "The intelligent (*Zhi* 知)[3] categorize with clarity of mind and penetrating insight."[4]

A. C. Graham expresses a similar view to that of Knoblock. Referring to Xunzi's philosophy, he says: "Morality has the pattern (*li*) by which it is knowable by thought; man has, presumably in his nature, the equipment by which, although his desires run the other way, it is possible for him to know it" (1989, 249). Although Graham avoids the word "reason," the view expressed seems to be that morality has a rational pattern and we have the capacity, reason, to know it in the abstract.

Another formulation of a similar idea is that the world is "naturally ordered" and we are equipped with mental faculties that can discern this order. This view is expressed by Robert Eno: "*Zhengming* ['Rectification of Names'] constructs a model of the proper function of language on the basis of the claim that the role of 'names' (generally, substance words) is to distinguish differences in 'realities' (*shi*). The world is pictured as a field of objects that are naturally ordered into sets on the basis of sameness (*tong*) and difference (*yi*). Man is innately equipped to distinguish these two primal qualities" (1990, 146, cf. Puett below). On this view, since sameness and difference are the "primal qualities" of things, and since we are given mental faculties that can discern sameness and difference, we can thus divide things up in accord with their true nature. Only things that are truly the same will be grouped together. This way we generate a set of real categories.[5] As Donald Munro puts it, "In the *Xunzi* the universe is presented as an ordered entity, each object having definite relationships to others. But the pattern cannot be grasped unless a person develops his mind" (1969, 157).

A different view, with similar implications, is that knowledge of the true nature of things is attained through mystical experience. For example, Chad Hansen attributes to Xunzi the position that "a *mystical*, unbiased, apprehension of the correct *dao* is possible to Confucians" (1992, 313, cf. 342; emphasis added). Adding detail to the *mystical knowledge* interpretation, Henri Maspero's account reads as follows:

---

2. Phrases like "proper categories" are ubiquitous in translations of the *Xunzi*. Often there is nothing corresponding to "proper" in the text. The resulting "translation" seems to indicate something along the lines of a realist position. But the only justification I can see for the addition of the key word suggesting that position is the prior assumption of it.

3. See the glossary of key terms.

4. The extended passage reads: "The *junzi* is the opposite of the small man. The broad-minded *junzi*, [respecting] the way things hang together, leads the way. The small minded, fearful of doing what is appropriate, are tied in knots. The intelligent categorize with clarity of mind and penetrating insight. The simple minded follow the model with uprightness and honesty." 君子小人之反也。君子大心則 [敬] 天而道。小心則畏義而節。知則明通而類。愚則端慤而法。(7/3/16–17; K: 3.6).

5. Strictly speaking, it would only be the sage, being free from obsession, who properly exercises his cognitive faculties.

Xunzi has borrowed from the mystical school certain of its techniques, and seeks to attain truth not by reasoning (by that one risks "by being wrong on a single point, being in the dark with relation to the Great Doctrine," the sole truth, as happened to Mozi, Songzi, and so many others), but by a meditation pushed very far, to the point where the spirit, freed from all surface phenomena, grasps the very nature of things directly and becomes capable of knowing them and naming them without mistake. (1978, 351–52)

On this view, though we go about arriving at the truth differently (through meditation rather than reason), in the end we know the real set of categories. However, this seems to involve a deeper conception of reality than simply nature. Paul Goldin's account at times also suggests that the true nature of things, for Xunzi, is not nature itself, but some deeper level of reality. He writes, "Xunzi enjoins us rather to inquire into the ontic presence that lies behind everything we see in the world—and then to bring ourselves into harmony with that force" (1999, 104).

Tian 天, interpreted as "Heaven," is sometimes thought to be some more "ultimate" level of reality that is taken as akin to reason. Consider Benjamin Schwartz's statement: "[T]he 'objective' order of society embodied in *li* [ritual propriety[6]] and law is also on some level embedded in the order of Heaven and . . . in fashioning the human order the sages do not freely invent but actually make manifest a universal pattern somehow[7] already rooted in the ultimate nature of things" (1985, 316). Schwartz fleshes out "Heaven" in terms of "the ultimate nature of things," but that does not answer for us whether this ultimate nature is to be read from the world of things or whether the world of things is somehow already in accordance with some more primary order. Schwartz's view of Xunzi's position toward logic seems to suggest a rationalist reading. "[Xunzi's] attitude toward 'logic' is that the sages in their cogitations had not only developed whatever logic was required for their needs but had already embedded it in a language which provided a complete and comprehensive map of reality" (314). The logical nature of "the order of Heaven," having been reasoned out through the "cogitations" of the sages, was used to create a perfect language which truly captured the unique set of real logical categories. Or so this interpretation seems to have it.

Let's now consider in more detail Michael Puett's reasons for his claims, which I outlined in the opening pages of chapter 1, that the sages were not involved in true creation at all, but rather in bringing about a preordained result.

---

6. While "*li*" in this passage refers to 禮 (ritual propriety), the "order of Heaven" described here seems to apply to both *li* 理, patterns generally (paradigmatically those found in nature), and *li* 禮, patterns of social behavior. See section 2.3 for a discussion of the relation between *li* 理 and *li* 禮.

7. The use of the word "somehow" here suggests that Schwartz himself found this relation mysterious.

Remember his interpretation of "Heaven" and its relation to the normative order: "the sages' acts of creation involve not arbitrary inventions but the bringing to humanity of a normative order rooted, ultimately, in Heaven" (2001, 72).[8] Puett's conception of the normative order being rooted in "Heaven" seems to include two components of Heaven, (1) "Heavenly faculties," which we use to perceive the world, and (2) Heaven as the object of knowledge. These two are linked, it seems, such that "correct" use of the Heavenly faculties allows us (or at least the sages) to discern the "proper," Heavenly privileged, categories. Puett sees this relation as teleological. Correctly utilized faculties, given by Heaven, enable one to know It. "Heaven thus gives man the faculties which, if used properly, will guide his actions. In order to further highlight the implicit teleology here, Xunzi refers to the final stage of this process of cultivation as 'knowing Heaven'" (68). What we will know when we know Heaven is predetermined by Heaven, mediated by our Heavenly faculties.

As for ritual and morality, these were "generated from the Heaven-given mind" (Puett 2001, 70). Puett argues that the usage of the word *sheng* 生 (generate) rather than *zuo* 作 (create) indicates that sages were not innovating when they "gave birth" to ritual and morality (see Puett 2001, p. 72). He recognizes that he has to account for the passage that says: "If true kings were to arise, they would certainly revitalize old names and create (*zuo*) new ones."[9] He explains: "Xunzi agrees [with the Mohists] that sages must now arise and innovate (*zuo*), but he strongly limits the ways in which sages can do so: innovation must be based in the correct use of the faculties given by Heaven, thus allowing the sage to discern accurately similarities and distinctions in the natural world"[10] (72).

This description does not give much room for innovation, except where innovation means innovating a system that could only have been innovated correctly in one way—but that would be discovery, not innovation. Rather than abandon the conclusion that the sage does not innovate, and move his analysis in a constructivist direction, Puett sticks to a teleological view. It may seem he would have to abandon his thesis of a strict distinction between *sheng* and *zuo*, and say that neither *sheng* nor *zuo* involves true innovation. Instead, however, he suggests that only names *qua* labels are innovated, while the categories that underlie them are determined.[11] Names may vary, but the patterns of Heaven

---

8. Cf. Goldin 1999, 54: "[Xunzi] postulates instead a set of Sage Kings, who *knew the Way of Heaven*, and established a code of ritual for future generations to follow." Emphasis added.

9. 若有王者起，必將有循於舊名，有作於新名。(83/22/11–12; K: 22.2a; W 141). See Puett 2001, 71, for his discussion of this passage.

10. It seems here that one aspect of "Heaven" is thought to be the natural world properly categorized.

11. Puett is not alone in this interpretation. Graham writes: "the divisions marked by naming are subjective for Zhuangzi but objective for Xunzi. . . . although naming is conventional, the divisions they mark are inescapably there" (1991, 285). Similarly, Van Norden takes Xunzi as endorsing the following: "the distinctions among things in the world picked out by the (arbitrarily chosen) words of Chinese are themselves objective" (2000, 132 n61). See section 3.2.

admit only one formulation.[12] "Names are created by a sage only after he has correctly differentiated reality by properly using the faculties with which he was born. Thus, Xunzi . . . has limited the arbitrariness of such conscious activity by defining it normatively as the process of correctly using one's Heaven-given faculties" (Puett 2001, 71–72). In the process of "knowing Heaven," sages are said to have "correctly differentiated reality," and to be able to "discern accurately similarities and distinctions in the natural world" (68, 71, 72). On this basis, the sage is thought to have "generated" rites, duties, laws, and standards, where the word "generated" (from *sheng* 生, to give birth to) is not thought to involve innovation on the part of the sage. "Xunzi consistently contends that the rites, duties, laws, and standards instituted by the sages were generated (*sheng*), not created (*zuo*)" (70).

Intriguing though it is, we have to reject the thesis that the use of *sheng*, as opposed to *zuo*, implies that what is "generated" does not involve any innovation. Xunzi writes,

> The potter makes a vessel using a clay mold. If this is so, then the vessel is generated (*sheng* 生) from the conscious activity of the potter, not original human nature. The carpenter carves wood to make a vessel. If this is so, then the vessel is generated by the conscious activity of carpenter, not original human nature. The sage accumulates thoughts and deliberation, and practices conscious activity thereby generating ritual propriety combined with a sense of appropriateness, and gives rise to laws and standards. If this is so, then likewise ritual propriety combined with a sense of appropriateness and laws and standards are generated by the conscious activity of the sages, not original human nature.[13]

Any given vessels, as products of potters and carpenters, are not generated the one and only possible way they could have been. So too with the roles and standards "generated"[14] by the sages. Puett tries to get around this by submitting that Xunzi's use of artisans as a metaphor for sages suggests not innovation but merely technical expertise in "generating" *liyi*. This suggestion is clever, but not

---

12. Puett does occasionally use language that suggests his position may allow some wiggle room in defining concepts, but he makes it clear that, if any, it is very little.

13. 故陶人埏埴而為器。然則器生於工人之偽。非故生於人之性也。故工人斲木而成器。然則器生於工人之偽。非故生於人之性也。聖人積思慮習偽故以生禮義而起法度。然則禮義法度者是生於聖人之偽。非故生於人之性也。(87/23/23–25; K:23.2a; W 160). See section 1.6, which includes Ivanhoe's adaptation of Watson's translation, for more on this passage. Puett does quote this passage himself, and he admits: "If Xunzi claims that ritual and morality are not based on nature but are rather an artificial construct of the sages, and if Xunzi portrays such a sagely construction as comparable to the construction of artisans, then he would certainly appear to be moving toward the notion of sagely creation advocated by the Mohists" (2001, 66). However, Puett sticks with his distinction, maintaining that artisans in their "activity of everyday craft" are meant to be seen as engaging in "carefully trained activity" which merely "generates" implements uncreatively (66, 67).

14. Note too that elsewhere *li* is described as being "fashioned" (*zhi* 制). See section 4.1, and the footnote near the end of section 3.3.

entirely compelling. *Liyi* is *wei* 偽 (artifice/the product of conscious activity), generally understood from its components as "man-made" (人為).[15] This would be a surprising choice as a technical term for someone who wanted to say that the role of people is limited to bringing out a teleologically determined result, a "normative order rooted, ultimately, in Heaven" (72).

2.2. Uniqueness and Contingency

The views expressed in the preceding section seem to suggest that a complete articulation of the way of the sage kings would hold universally and for all time, circumstances not withstanding. Ivanhoe, Munro, and most recently, Goldin have explicitly expressed this view. Ivanhoe states that rites are "unalterable patterns" (1991, 321) and that "the Confucian Way provided the unique solution which would be valid for all times" (318). Munro writes: "There are antecedently fixed rules dictating which actions by all objects including man, are good or bad" (1969, 33). Goldin makes a similarly strong claim: "The Way is not merely the intermingling of *yin* and *yang*, but the eternal and unchanging Way that governs all the processes of the cosmos" (1999, 103–4).[16]

Schwartz goes as far as to suggest that *li* (ritual propriety) is a kind of "natural law." Consider the following extended quotation:

> It [the cosmic dimension of *li*] is a dimension which seems to run against any view that interprets Xunzi's notion that "Man makes culture" to mean that culture is an arbitrary "conventional" (in the Greek sense of *nomos*) invention. . . . Here the word *li* is elevated to the status of a principle of order governing both the cosmos and the human order. The western idea of convention and contrivance suggests that what has been made might have easily been made in some other fashion. . . . To Xunzi, however, the good order of society which he describes is the universal order of civilization. Hence, when we speak of the sages as "making it" or "forming it," we find that what they actually do is *make manifest* the overall pattern appropriate to the end of harmonizing the centrifugal tendencies found in the individual human organism. It may not be innate in the individual but it seems to be latently present in the objective cosmic order. The *li* is in essence a kind of "natural law" in the stoic and medieval sense. Like natural law, it is not self-enacting. Yet it would appear that what the ancient sages did in bringing the order of society into existence was not invent an arbitrary system of *li* but "discover" it by a process of arduous reflection. Again, one need not imagine here a Platonic realm of eternal forms and yet in some sense *li* are part of the larger cosmic pattern and as such are much more than simply utilitarian devices. They are certainly not arbitrary conventions. (1985, 301–2; emphasis in original)

---

15. See section 5.2 for more on this.
16. As can be seen in a quotation in section 1.2.2, Burton Watson also uses "eternal" language, namely, "eternally valid moral principles" (1963, 6).

Although we can agree that the *li* are not arbitrary, much of this characterization sounds excessively deterministic. While he tells us not to imagine Platonic forms, Schwartz nevertheless writes that "*li* is elevated to the status of a principle of order governing both the cosmos and the human order," that it is "latently present in the objective cosmic order," and that it is a kind of "natural law." Below I will offer an alternative understanding of *li* as continually changing and contingent on our situations and interests, and which does not imply that there is a single correct and universally valid articulation of *li*.

But, for the moment, consider that "uniqueness" could be tied to contingency such that problems always have some single uniquely effective solution, with specifics dependent on circumstances. The constructivist would balk on accepting even this much as necessarily the case. Whether or not there is a single best solution to a problem, even given a specific set of circumstances, depends on those circumstances. That is, there may in some cases be a clear and uniquely favorable alternative, but the constructivist can see no reason to declare in advance that in each case this would be so.

Hansen's conception of the sage as pathfinder seems to imply this "contingent uniqueness" interpretation. "Heaven sets the natural regularities that make some *dao*s promote stable, harmonious satisfactory human life more effectively than others. The configuration of the forest dictates a path as much as does the intended destination. Given a social goal, the natural structure (the forest) determines the optimal *dao*. But it does so via the creative work of the pathfinder" (1992, 312).[17] This sounds like a constructivist metaphor except for the use of the singular "the optimal *dao*." Why would we assume that there is always only one best way to get through a forest? Hansen seems not to appreciate the constructivist implications of his own metaphor.[18] Complex practical problems generally allow for a variety of solutions, each with both merits and demerits relative to competing solutions. That is, solutions typically involve tradeoffs.

Frequently, however, when sentiments of contingency to circumstances are expressed with regard to Xunzi, they are coupled with claims such as those mentioned in chapter 1 (sections 1.2.1 and 1.2.2). For example, Ivanhoe claims, "[Xunzi] did not believe the world could change as much as we know it does"[19] (1991, 318). Nivison also at times seems to suggest something like

---

17. Cf. "The creative sage-kings have blazed the uniquely efficient path to that goal [the survival of the human species] in the natural context" (Hansen 1992, 312). And, "Objective or absolute justification of 'realist' traditionalism are available by making maximizing survival and effectiveness the test of *the correct* system of names (*dao*)" (Hansen 1983, 182).

18. Xunzi uses a similar metaphor when he likens the rites to markers to assist in crossing a river (96/27/10–11; K: 27.12 and 64/17/48–49; K: 17.11; W 87). Such markers signal a way across, marking known dangers and relatively safe alternatives. But there may be more than one way to cross a river. The rites, being taken from successful points of the tradition, mark a known way, not necessarily the only way. See section 4.4.

19. It is this consideration that led Ivanhoe to his above-mentioned conclusion that "the Confucian Way provided the unique solution which would be valid for all times" (Ivanhoe 1991, 318). An extended quotation can be found in section 1.2.2.

this. For example, he writes: "if Xunzi thought that the 'Way' of the 'sages' was final and perfect, he must suppose that this human situation does not really change over historical time, and is not altered even by the events of history. It seems to me that Xunzi did tend to think this" (1996a, 331). Thus whether the justification is absolutist or conditional, since conditions are thought not to change significantly, the conclusion tends to be that the way and its categories are uniquely correct and do not change.

The claim that Xunzi thought that circumstances do not significantly change is generally simply stated without reference to supporting passages. Presumably, the following passage is seen as making the point plain enough:

> Fools say, "The ancient and present are different circumstances, so the ways which bring order and chaos will differ." And the masses are deluded by this. . . . Why are sages not deceived? I say it is because sages use themselves as the measure. Thus they use their understanding of people to measure people, their understanding of circumstances to measure circumstances, and their classifications to measure classifications. They use their theories to measure achievement, and their way to view the whole. They take measure of the continuities between the ancient and the present. Their categories do not become contrary; over a very long stretch of time their patternings remain similar.[20]

Graham[21] interprets Xunzi's answer to the question raised in this passage as follows: "Why is the sage not deceived? Because he can think out the ideal form of government himself" (1989, 257). Graham's interpretation seems to be the result of two points. They are, as he translates them: (1) "Past and present are one; if kinds are not violated, however long it continues the patterns are the same;" and (2) "The sage is one who measures by himself."[22] Taking these ideas together, the sage is thought to be able to reason out a solution that will forever apply.

The passage does support the notion that human and natural propensities are enduring and that some basic moral principles are likely to endure as well. Xunzi points out that the masses are confused by claims that lessons from the past are inapplicable. The sage considers the past success or failure of theories to be important. But Xunzi also, elsewhere, states, "Those who are good at articulating the ancient necessarily need to show that it is applicable in the

---

20. 夫妄人曰。古今異情。其以治亂者異道。而眾人惑焉。. . . 聖人何以不欺。曰。聖人者。以己度者也。故以人度人。以情度情。以類度類。以說度功。以道觀盡。古今一度也。類不悖久同理。(14/5/33–36; K: 5.5; D 74; Graham 1989, 257).

21. Graham's analysis of Xunzi's philosophy in his *Disputers of the Tao* seems supportive of a constructivist reading up to the point where he says: "However, no one [including Xunzi] had yet questioned that in discovering his wisest course man also discovers what Heaven has decreed for him" (Graham 1989, 247).

22. See Graham 1989, 257, for more of his translation.

present."[23] Graham's interpretation that the sage can "think out the ideal form of government" is not entailed by the first passage, and is not compatible with the second. Xunzi believes that there are more and less effective ways of dealing with persistent features of the human condition, but he does not posit an abstract ideal to be reasoned out.

Further, as Edward J. Machle notes: "Xun speaks of 'responding to changing conditions' 15 other times [in addition to two discussed by Machle], and it is *yi* (moral common sense, the *aisthesis* of the *phronimos*) that guides the application of unchanging *li* [ritual propriety] in a changing world. This fact alone should turn the edge of the charge of rigid authoritarianism that some have aimed at Xun Qing" (1993, 130). Machle himself, however, clings to a conception of "unchanging *li*," though he accepts that the application of it changes in response to a changing world. But can *li* really be separated from the application of it? The standard for *li* is in the exemplary person's application.[24]

2.3. Relation of *Li* 理 and *Li* 禮

Li 禮 (ritual propriety) is thought to be based on *li* 理 (patterns) which are in turn considered the real design of nature. In Ivanhoe's words, "The Confucian rituals . . . provide a way to realize an orderly design inherent in the world" (2000, 240). Eno best describes this presumed relation. "In describing a world sliced into pieces and roles, and a human mind that learns truth by distinguishing classes, the *Xunzi* designs rationalizing theories that make its ritual ethics appear to be an analogue of Nature. By providing *li* with this structural affinity to Nature, it becomes possible to claim that ritual is an extension of Nature's organizing principles" (1990, 147). Later he adds:

> The notion of study as the delineation of the bounds of knowledge relates to our earlier discussion of the *Xunzi*'s taxonomic portrait of the world. As we noted there, when the *Xunzi* slices the world into pieces and principles, it does so not only for objective entities but for life conceived as situations and roles. This analogous structure between natural and ethical worlds allows the *Xunzi* to make an implicit but clear claim to the effect that ritual *li* embody *intrinsic principles of ethical existence* fundamentally equivalent to principles of natural existence, or "*li*" [理]. Ritual *li* are, in essence, the extension of natural principles into the human sphere.[25] (1990, 152; emphasis mine)

---

23. A fuller quotation puts the statement into context: "Those who are good at articulating the ancient necessarily need to show that it is applicable in the present. Those who are good at articulating *tian* necessarily need to show its relevance to people. Theories are valued for coherent distinctions and conforming to experience." 故善言古者必有節於今。善言天者必有徵於人。凡論者貴其有辨合有符驗。 (88/23/44–45; K: 23.3b; W 163).

24. See chapter 4, especially sections 4.2 and 4.7.

25. Contrast this with the interpretations of Chen Daqi and Jiang Shangxian given in section 1.1.

If one can learn the "truth" regarding the classes (*lei* 類) of things in the world, and the rational structure (*li* 理) that underlies them, and if a particular set of articulated ritual roles and norms (*li* 禮) are considered "an analogue of Nature," then one might conclude that the Confucian Way could be known and justified with more than good degree of confidence. Bryan W. Van Norden goes as far as to claim that Xunzi "held what might be described as an 'intellectualist' position: Confucianism can be justified with almost mathematical certainty" (1996, 3).

Eno states that there is a "continuity between natural principles and ritual forms" (1990, 163). Fair enough. There is analogy that holds between them. *Li* 理 are the patterns we understand in the world around us generally, and *li* 禮 are the patterns we understand specifically in our social world. Without patterns the world would be chaotic, incomprehensible.[26] But must this continuity between *li* 理 and *li* 禮 involve "natural principles" which are absolute and whose absoluteness carries over to ritual forms, as Eno's description seems to suggest?

2.4. Dissenting Views:
Li and *Lei* as Mutually Influencing

The notion that the activity of naming in the Chinese tradition broadly involves bringing about order, rather then merely discerning a preexisting order, has been discussed by David Hall and Roger Ames: "Not only are names used to name the order, they are also used for effecting order in what is to be named. The *Guanzi* describes this function of names: 'Names (*ming* 名) are the means whereby the sages organize the myriad phenomena'" (1987, 274). This claim is made in the context of a discussion of Confucius, and is not explicitly applied to Xunzi.

Similarly, in his book on Xunzi's moral epistemology, Cua offers an interpretation of the relation between *li* 理 and *lei* 類 as mutually influencing.

> Both observation and purpose of discourse may thus be regarded as providing the *li* or rationales for assigning things to different classes (*lei*). *Li*, in this way is a rationale of classification. Alternatively put, *li* is implicit in the notion of *lei*. On the other hand, to give a *li* of *x* is not simply to give a rationale, say, for the existence of *x* as a particular object, event, or state of affairs; it is also to presuppose that *x* belongs to a certain *lei* or class. Consequently, the *li* of *x* has to be understood in terms of the *lei* to which *x* belongs. . . . [J]ust as every *lei* has *li* as a basis, every *li* involves *lei* as

---

26. Cf. "In Chinese Confucianism, to be 'reasonable' (*heli* 合理) is to think and act in accordance with the order of things as mediated through tradition. *Li* 理 understood here as 'pattern' or 'coherence' is inclusive of the more narrowly defined *li* 禮 as ritual. It entails being aware of those constitutive relationships that condition each thing and which, through patterns of correlation, make the world meaningful and intelligible" (Hall and Ames 1999, 157).

a precondition;[27] that it is through *lei* that *li* is manifest, and it is through *li* that we attain *lei* (i.e., rest satisfied with our classification). (1985, 54)[28]

Later, in *Anticipating China*, Hall and Ames, citing Cua and making the same point, give a reformulation of their original claim as it applies to Xunzi. "On the one hand, *li*, which involves the mapping out of patterns, can only operate on the basis of assumed classifications (*lei*); at the same time, it is the mapping operation of *li*, including and excluding on the basis of perceived similarities and differences, that establishes classifications (*lei*) in the first place." They go on to make explicit their position that for Xunzi the distinctions that demarcate a world are not necessary ones: "One appropriates an always-interpreted world through language acquisition and enculturation, and then continues the historical process of world-making. Distinctions, as ad hoc conventions, are always contingent and performative. Thus, as a distinctly historicist thinker, Xunzi makes no appeal to transcendent principles or necessary distinctions" (1995, 208). Unfortunately, little textual evidence from the *Xunzi* has yet been given in support of these interpretations.[29]

2.5. The Constructivist View

It may be helpful to begin a reconstruction of the concept of *li* 理 by considering its nonphilosophic meaning. Knoblock explains that, "As a verb, it means to cut along the veins of a piece of jade or to lay out fields according to the requirements of land forms" (1988, 80).[30] To *li* a field or a piece of jade involves an element of creativity. The creation is not *ex nihilo* but rather complementary

---

27. Cua gives credit to Wei Zhengtong for this idea. Wei writes, "Every *lei* (category) has its *li* (rationale) for becoming a category. That is, *li* is the grounds for the category. Thus, *li* are seen through *lei*, and *lei* are completed through *li*. Any single thing initiates a category, and *li* is what is contained therein." 每一類有其成類之理，理即成類之根據。故理由類而見，類由理而成。凡 單舉類者，理即涵其中。(Wei 1974,19). Cua also cites Chen Daqi 1954, 73.

28. Cua cites a study that supports the view that classification and perceived similarity do in fact influence one another. The study concludes: "changes in grouping (produced by the replacement or addition of objects) lead to corresponding changes in the similarity of the objects. These results shed light on the dynamic interplay between similarity and classification. It is generally assumed that classifications are determined by similarities among the objects. The preceding discussion supports the converse hypothesis: that the similarity of objects is modified by the manner in which they are classified. Thus, similarity has two faces: causal and derivative. It serves as a basis for the classification of objects, but it is also influenced by the adopted classification" (Tversky 1977, 344).

29. Cua's claim, however, is part of a lengthy and complex argument. See Cua 1985, especially "Phases of Argumentation," 39–87. Also, note that the following passage expresses the dependency of patterns on categories, the often-overlooked side of the relationship between the two. "[The consummate social person (*ren ren* 仁人)] appropriates ritual propriety combined with a sense of appropriateness as a tapestry of cultural patterns (*wen* 文), and appropriates ethical relations and categories as constructive patterns (*li* 理)." 禮義以為文。倫類以為理。(51/13/42; K: 13.7).

30. Cf. "*[L]i*, often translated 'reason' or 'principle'; originally probably [meant] 'to mark out fields,' but later 'to carve jade according to its veins'—not following the veins could ruin the jade" (Machle 1993, 128). See glossary of key terms for more on the original meaning of *li* 理.

to what is given, necessarily emphasizing some features and suppressing others. There are veins in jade, and they influence the way the jeweler will shape it. But, would two experts at carving jade cut the same piece of jade in exactly the same way? Their respective incisions would be best thought of as interpretations, which bring certain features to light at the expense of others.[31] Articulating the *li* relative to a given topic highlights and brings into focus particular aspects of it, and orders the subject matter accordingly. It should also be kept in mind that *li* is an activity[32] as much as it is a pre-existing structure. *Li* involves the *highlighting* of patterns. *Li* is *li*-ing, that is, patterning, highlighting particular aspects of a subject matter for some purpose. One does not cut a piece of jade to *reveal* the way *it is*, but to bring forth a beautiful way it can be.

Wing-tsit Chan makes the following observations:

> An examination of ancient Confucian Classics reveals several surprising facts. One is that the word [*li*] does not occur in most of these Classics. It is not found in the *Analects*, the *Spring and Autumn Annals*, the *Yi li* (Book of Ceremonial), the text of the *Book of Changes*, or the *Great Learning*. Secondly, where the word does occur, it does not mean principle but means to put in order (*zhi*) or to distinguish. The earliest occurrence of the word is probably in the *Book of Odes*, where it occurs only once, in the sentence *wo jiang wo li*, which may be rendered to read, "We define our boundary and form (*li*) small divisions." Professor Demiéville thinks that *li* here means pattern. The implication is unmistakable, but the word is definitely used as a verb. (1964, 123)

Chan further notes that, in the *Book of Rites*, "The term *li* appears nineteen times, chiefly as a verb, meaning to order" (1964, 124). And, in the *Zhuangzi*, "The ideas of *li* as pattern and putting to order are prevalent" (125). In reference to the *Xunzi*, Chan writes:

> Aside from the many uses of the word in the sense of putting to order the meaning of *li* as order and pattern (*wen li*) is also very prominent. Likewise, the meaning of moral principle (*yi li* or *dao li*) is outstanding. What is more significant is that Xunzi not only talked about the principle of the world (*tian xia zhi li*) but also "the great principle" (*da li*). Furthermore *li* is considered universal, permanent, and unchangeable, thus making principle absolute. (1964, 126)

Although it may be tempting to read *da li* in the singular, which seems to motivate a universalistic reading, it is more likely that its meaning in the *Xunzi* is something closer to "great (or broad) principles and patterns" as opposed

---

31. Note that not everybody is equally qualified to cut jade.
32. The *li* of a finished piece of calligraphy is still temporal and dynamic, always suggesting movement.

to particular ones. Chan himself comes close to noticing this. Immediately after attributing a kind of universalism to Xunzi, he remarks: "At the same time, Xunzi mentioned the principle of silkworms, the specific principle of a specific thing" (1964, 126). Reading *da li* as "broad patterns and principles" as opposed to "particular patterns and principles" would better fit with Xunzi's discussion of broad and particular name-concepts (*ming* 名) in the *Zhengming* chapter immediately preceding his claim that "name-concepts have no intrinsic appropriateness."[33]

Forming categories (*lei*) is a process of extending an exemplary case on the basis of these highlighted patterns. Knoblock's own translation of a brief passage makes the point. "[Sage ministers] draw inferences from the categories by analogical extension and connect things with comparable cases in order to handle those cases for which there is no paradigm in the model."[34] Rather than everything nicely fitting into a "proper logical category" (as he often translates *lei*), categories either accommodate or exclude instances based on analogical reasoning, grounded in perceived patterns, in comparison to more paradigmatic cases. If a sage, having a developed sense of appropriateness, takes an instance as relevantly similar to paradigmatic cases, then it is counted as an instance of that category. A fuller account of this process is given as follows:

> They model the later[35] kings, unite ritual propriety (*li*) and appropriateness (*yi*), as well as unify and regulate measures. They use the shallow to grasp and keep hold of the broad. They use the ancient to grasp and maintain the present. They use particulars (*yi* 一) to grasp and manage the myriad. If they are of the category of authoritative persons with a sense of appropriateness,[36] although they may live among birds and beasts, they make distinctions easily as if black from white. They rely on observations and are suspicious of changing to what has never been heard of and never been seen. They start with one corner and respond to it by promoting unified categories. There is nothing about which they are confused or ashamed. Extending the model, they systematize it, like enigmatically fitting together a tally. These are the Great Confucians.[37]

Since every circumstance, just like each piece of jade, is unique, and since categories are always grounded in particular instances, they require a degree of

---

33. 名無固宜。(83/22/25; K: 22.2g; W 144). See section 3.2 for more on this passage, and for a justification of the translation of *ming* as name-concepts.

34. 推類接譽以待無方。(49/13/5; K: 13.1).

35. The text actually says "former kings" here, but since he is describing the best category of Confucians, and since he makes it clear elsewhere that it is the later king that should be followed, I take it that the "later kings" is what is intended. I am following Knoblock in this regard.

36. Note that this is what makes the Great Confucians qualified to author names.

37. 法先王。統禮義。一制度。以淺持博。以古持今。以一持萬。茍仁義之類也。雖在鳥獸之中若別白黑。倚物怪變。所未嘗聞也。所未嘗見也。卒然起一方。則舉統類而應之。無僟[作]。張法而度之。則晻然若合符節。是大儒者也。(24/8/97–100; K: 8.10).

reinterpretation in every application. As Xunzi succinctly puts it: "A model cannot stand on its own, categories cannot apply themselves."[38] Deciding how a rule applies in a given situation requires an interpretation of the situation, the rule, and the relation between the two. Similarly, in order for categories to function constructively they need to be applied by competent and sensitive interpreters. Those who both appreciate the function and importance of constructively formulated categories, and have cultivated their character to the point of developing the virtue of public spiritedness, qualify as Great Confucians capable of authoring categories. Xunzi writes: "Their purposes have comfortably settled on the public good; their conduct has comfortably settled into self-cultivation. And, they thoroughly appreciate the significance of the guiding principle of categories. Such a person may be called a 'Great Confucian.'"[39]

Realizing that categories, which rely on the process of patterning for their rationale, have a conventional aspect, Xunzi saw that they might be designed to facilitate social harmony and personal fulfillment. They could be crafted as tools to serve constructive purposes. As with any tool, they are assessed by how well they perform their function. Thus, the legitimacy of a distinction lies in its workability rather than a special status it might have resulting from its rational structure or correspondence with some deeper level of reality. Consider Xunzi's criticism of Master Song's doctrines. "[Master Song] made alterations to them [the concepts of honor and disgrace] with a single morning's deliberation. His theory will certainly not work in practice. This is analogous to using mud balls to dam up a large river or sea. It is like using the Jiao pygmies to support Mount Tai. In no time they will stumble and fall and it will break into pieces."[40] The problem is not that Master Song's way of marking out the categories of honor and disgrace fails to correspond to how things really are, but that it is not serviceable. His case exemplifies the folly of arbitrarily and carelessly crafting distinctions.

When constructive categories (which includes norms defined by *li* 禮) are successfully instituted, social harmony (or what may be called the "flourishing of human connectedness") can be realized.[41] This is called "hitting the mark." Xunzi makes it clear in the following passage that this "hitting the mark" does not have to do with a correspondence with *tian*; rather, the standard is set by people, specifically those who lead society in a constructive direction and are thereby worthy of being examples to others: "The way of the ancient kings

---

38. 故法不能獨立。類不能自行。(44/12/2; K: 12.1).

39. 志安公。行安脩。知通統類。如是則可謂大儒矣。(25/8/122; K: 8.12).

40. 慮一朝而改之。說必不行矣。譬之是猶以摶涂塞江海也。以焦僥而戴太山也。蹎跌碎折不待頃矣。(69–70/18/112–13; K: 18.9).

41. To say that social harmony can be realized is not to posit a fixed ideal waiting for a corresponding achievement in practice. Success in realizing a harmonious situation is always a matter of degree, leaving room for improvement. And, just as the world is always in flux, constructive responses to changing circumstances will always be needed. Further, there is no presumption that there is only one constructive way to respond to a given situation.

was the flourishing (*long* 隆) of human connectedness (*ren* 仁).[42] This is hitting the mark in putting it [a way, a doctrine] into practice. How would I describe 'hitting the mark'? I say it consists in ritual propriety combined with a sense of appropriateness. 'The way' is not the way of *tian* 天, neither is it the way of the earth. It is that by which the people are led; it is the path of the exemplary person."[43] This passage problematizes the claim that Xunzi's *dao* is one in which social patterns are extensions of the ultimately real patterns of *tian*, whether *tian* is considered natural, metaphysical, or rational. Why is it that people rather than *tian* serve as the standard for patterns? It is because prior to the patterning of the sage, *tian* is unpatterned.[44] "*Tian* can generate things but cannot articulate distinctions among them. Earth can support people but cannot order them. The myriad things of the whole world, and all living people, await sages—and only then are they apportioned."[45]

Reminiscent of the *Analects* 15.29, "People are able to broaden the way, it is not the way which broadens people,"[46] Xunzi states that:

Nature (*tian* 天) and the earth are the beginning of life. Ritual propriety and a sense of appropriateness (*li yi* 禮義) are the beginning of good government (*zhi* 治). The exemplary person (*junzi* 君子) is the beginning of ritual propriety and of a sense of appropriateness. Acting on them, stringing them together, increasingly emphasizing them, and bringing about fondness for them, is the beginning of the exemplary person. Thus, nature and the earth produce the exemplary person, and the exemplary person applies patterns (*li* 理) to earth and nature. . . . If there were no exemplary people, nature and the earth would not be patterned.[47]

---

42. Knoblock renders *long* 隆 "exalting," which is consistent with commentaries implying something "lofty" or "eminent," or the making of it so. This is reasonable, and I too use "exalting" for *long* in other passages. In addition to "high" or "lofty," *long* has the sense of "abundance" or "flourishing." Stressing the idea of flourishing in combination with the conception of *ren* as "human connectedness" expresses what it might look like when a king has "hit the mark" in putting the way into practice. However, acceptance of this reading of the passage is not critically important to my argument. In the end, there is little difference, since exalting something should result in its flourishing, that would be the point of exalting it. Similarly, if we took a more conventional translation of *ren*, say "human heartedness," or even "benevolence," the result of elevating it should be the deepening of social bonds, in keeping with the Confucian project of fostering social harmony.

43. 先王之道。仁之隆也。比中而行之。曷謂中。曰。禮義是也。道者非天之道。非地之道。人之所以道也。君子之所道也。(20/8/23–24; K: 8.3). Cf. A. C. Graham's translation: "The Way is not the Way of Heaven, nor the Way of Earth, it is what man uses to make his way, what the gentleman adopts as the Way" (1989, 242–43).

44. This is not to say that *tian* is unstructured. See sections 1.4.3 and 1.5. Cf. *Laozi* 1: "Lacking names, the beginning of the world. Having names, the mother of the myriad things." 無名天地之始。有名萬物之母。 Naming is what brings the myriad things into existence *as the myriad things*.

45. 天能生物不能辯物也。地能載人不能治人也。宇中萬物。生人之屬。待聖人然後分也。(73/19/78–79; K: 19.6; W 103).

46. 子曰：人能弘道，非道弘人。

47. 天地者生之始也。禮義者治之始也。君子者禮義之始也。為之貫之。積重之。致好

Here we have a statement of the virtuous cycle connecting the development of exemplary persons with the development of *liyi* 禮義, ritual propriety combined with a sense of appropriateness. People striving to be exemplary, the *shi* 士,[48] acting in accordance with ritual propriety, following the model of their teachers, thus develop an intellectual appreciation for *li* as well as a habit of acting in accordance with them. They also develop a kind of "practical wisdom" regarding how to apply *li* to novel circumstances:[49] this is *yi*. As times change and as the cultural tradition develops greater understanding, *li* may be modified,[50] but this is not something outside the *liyi* scope just described. Modification of *li* is a special case of using one's developed sense of appropriateness in the application of *li*.

It is only after one has gone through this process of developing *yi*, that one is exemplary, that is, worthy of being an example.[51] The *junzi*'s continual interpretation of *li* through action is the "beginning of *liyi*" all over again for the next generation of *shi* and posterity as well, filtered through each successive generation. In this way, the *junzi* is the beginning of *liyi*; and, acting in accordance with one's developed sense of what *li* call for in each situation, as well as the attendant growing fondness for these cultural patterns, is the beginning of becoming a *junzi* oneself. It is only the *junzi* who is capable of "applying the patterns to earth and nature," and to moral categories as well. And this is what the *junzi* is in effect doing when interpreting and applying and thus redefining *li* 禮, the most important set of patterns (*li* 理). Since patterns are applied by the *junzi* with an eye to good government, I will often translate *li* 理 as "constructive patterns" signaling that these are patterns picked out for their positive effect, not for their representing exclusive ontological truth. For example:

> Generally, in conducting affairs, what contributes to good government should be
> established. If it does not contribute to constructive patterns then abandon it. This is
> called "hitting the mark" in conducting affairs. Generally, in realizing theories, those
> that contribute to constructive patterns should be acted on. Those that do not should
> be given up. This is called "hitting the mark" with theories. In conducting affairs,
> missing the mark is called treacherous affairs. In realizing theories, missing the mark

---

之者。君子之始也。故天地生君子。君子理天地。 . . . 無君子則天地不理。 (28/9/64–66; K: 9.15; W 44–45).

48. See Ames and Rosemont 1998, 62.

49. Cf. *Mencius* 4A.17, and *Analects*: 9.3.

50. See section 4.3.4 below.

51. Cf. "[The *junzi*'s] social relations are characterized by categories which follow from a sense of appropriateness (*yi*)." 其交遊也。緣義而有類。 (45/12/27; K: 12.3). This is what is meant by *zhengming*. The *junzi*'s behavior is attuned with a set of "names" which indicate categories that are constructed from a developed sense of appropriateness grounded in the successful elements of one's tradition. The concept of *zhengming* will be further addressed in the next chapter. Note that Xunzi provides a description of the most important relational categories earlier in the same section (i.e., K: 12.3).

is called a treacherous way. Treacherous affairs and treacherous ways are abandoned in a well-governed age, but followed and acquiesced to in a chaotic one.[52]

What is our guide for making constructive distinctions? It is *yi*, our developed sense of appropriateness. Speaking of social divisions, Xunzi asks and then answers himself: "How are we able to put social divisions into practice? I say it is *yi*. If *yi* is used in forming divisions then there will be harmony."[53] Harmony is realized by setting up categories through the use of our developed sense of what will be conducive to it. That is, given our accumulated understanding of how things hang together, we make social division (and the same holds true for categories in general) with a mind to making the most out of our circumstances. "If a sincere mind applies a sense of appropriateness then constructive patterns will result."[54]

A problem with the characterization of the *junzi*'s "knowing Heaven" as knowing the ultimate patterns of reality is that for the *junzi* knowledge is always practical. Xunzi goes as far as to say that "The sage is somewhat exceptional for not seeking to know *tian*."[55] *Tian*, in this case, stands for propensities of nature which are outside people's power to influence. This statement does not imply that the sage does not have a sophisticated appreciation for these propensities, but knowing the workings of nature are not what Xunzi's *junzi* seek. They have practical ends in view. Chen Daqi put it this way, "Xunzi thought that what need not and should not be sought is knowledge concerning the metaphysics of the myriad things in nature. He though we do need to and ought to seek

---

52. 凡事行有益於理者立之。無益於理者廢之。夫是之謂中事。凡知說有益於理者為之。無益於理者舍之。夫是之謂中說。事行失中謂之姦事。知說失中。謂之姦道。姦事姦道。治世之所棄。而亂世之所從服也。(21/8/31–34; K: 8.4). The *Concordance to the Hsün Tzu* (1966), from which I quote the Chinese text for the *Xunzi*, notes that the first occurrence of *li* 理 is written *zhi* 治 in another edition. (D. C. Lau's *A Concordance to the Xunzi* [1996], simply has *zhi* instead of *li*, apparently judging *li* to have been the result of a corruption. The meaning of the characters *zhi* and *li* overlap in that both imply a sense of orderliness. The use of *zhi* in the first instance indicates the sense of "order" intended throughout the passage, that is, the sense of "good government." The parallelism helps infuse this sense of order in each occurrence of *li* that is repeated, since *li* occupies in the second clause the place of *zhi* in the first. This both enriches and clarifies the passage. The reason this is important is that *zhi* being replaced by *li* results in translations like Knoblock's "paths of action and undertakings that hold benefit for what *accords with order* should be established" (K: 8.4, emphasis added). This may be mistaken as a statement of some kind of correspondence with an independent principle of order, when the passage simply advocates establishing sound governmental practices.

53. 分何以能行。曰義。故義以分則和。(29/9/71; K: 9.16a; Goldin 1999, 75).

54. 誠心行義則理 (7/3/27–28; K: 3.9).

55. 唯聖人為不求知天。(62/17/10; K: 17.2b; W 80). Cf. "Regarding the myriad things of *tian* and the earth, [*junzi*] do not devote themselves to explaining how these things are as they are, but rather are devoted to the skill of utilizing their resources." 其於天地萬物也。不務說其所以然。而致善用其材。(45/12/25; K: 12.3). Sages and *junzi* do have an appreciation for how things hang together, but they do not concentrate on studies of things which are beyond human influence and which have no bearing on how one should live. They do not seek to understand, for example, why the seasons are the way they are. Rather, appreciating certain regularities about them, they want to make sure crops are planted at appropriate times.

knowledge concerning the science[56] of the myriad things in nature."[57] One might better say: we should seek knowledge of how to work with nature's regularities in a productive way, but not to know her inner secrets. Xunzi himself asks rhetorically:

> Which is better, emphasizing *tian* and pondering it,
>   or systematizing things and livestock?
> Which is better, following *tian* and singing its praises,
>   or curbing its forces and utilizing them? . . .
> Which is better, contemplating things as if they were given,
>   or patterning them so as not to miss their potential?
> Which is more important, the source from which things are produced,
>   or that by which they are completed?
> Thus, if one neglects people and ponders *tian*,
>   one will miss the actual situation regarding the myriad things.[58]

Tian has its propensities, but it is up to people to conceptually as well as practically organize them. The organization is done with a mind to getting the most out of it in terms of social harmony. It is an ongoing process, and while there may be progress, in the sense of improvements over past accomplishments, it is not teleologically approaching a singular or perfect arrangement. The conceptual organization of the world is formalized in language, particularly in name-concepts (*ming* 名). This is the subject of the next chapter.

---

56. Xunzi has been accused of being antiscientific, and contributing to China's supposedly antiscientific attitude. To speak of Xunzi's attitude toward science is, of course, anachronistic. Nevertheless, if we are to do so, the distinction may be better drawn by saying that he would have been for practical science and engineering, but would have been opposed to theoretical science that borders on metaphysical speculation. And, for the record, let's remember that China was technologically ahead of the rest of the world before the modern scientific and industrial revolutions.

57. 荀子所認為不必求且不應求的，是有關天地萬物的形而上學上的知識，荀子所認為必須求且應當求的，是有關天地萬物的科學上的知識。 (Chen Daqi 1954, 25).

58. 大天而思之。孰與物畜而制之。從天而頌之。孰與制天命而用之。. . . 思物而物之。孰與理物而勿失之也。願於物之所以生。孰與有物之所以成。故錯人而思天。則失萬物之情。 (64/17/44–46; K: 17.10; W 86; Graham 1989, 240).

Zhengming: Naming as a Constructive Project

3

Building on the understanding of *li* 理 and *lei* 類 as patterns and categories that are mutually influencing, in this chapter I present an interpretation of *zhengming* 正名 (attuning names) that does not assume a realist view of language. In the process, I challenge the view of several interpreters of Xunzi regarding the status of names (*ming* 名), maintaining that Xunzi's view is consistent with the activity we see not only in his own efforts to influence language, but in those of Confucius as well. Based on a reconsideration of translations and interpretations of key passages, I argue that names are regarded neither as mere labels nor as indicating a privileged taxonomy of the myriad phenomena. Rather, Xunzi conceives them as constructs designed to facilitate social goals. In addition, I will suggest an alternative to overly simplistic understandings of how appropriate names are fashioned and of who is responsible for their form.

3.1. The Constructive Use of *Zhengming* in the *Analects*

The phrase *zhengming* 正名, often translated "the rectification of names," occurs in only one passage in the *Analects*:

> Zilu inquired, "If the lord of Wei were to entrust you with the governance of his state, what would you do first?"
>
> The Master answered, "Wouldn't it necessarily be the attunement of names (*zhengming*)?"
>
> Zilu replied, "That is what you would do? You sure go roundabout. Why this attunement?"
>
> The Master responded, "You are a bumpkin. With respect to that which he is ignorant, the exemplary person (*junzi* 君子) defers. . . . There is nothing lax in the exemplary person's attitude toward language, period!"[1]

A number of scholars, going back at least to Arthur Waley, have regarded this passage as an interpolation (see Waley 1938, 22). Nevertheless, although

---

1. 子路曰：衛君待子而為政，子將奚先？子曰：必也正名乎！子路曰：有是哉？子之迂也！奚其正？子曰：野哉，由也！君子於其所不知，蓋闕如也。. . . 君子於其言，無所苟而已矣。*Analects* 13.3.

it is possible to challenge the authenticity of this passage, and to question whether Confucius himself explicitly articulated the idea of attuning names, the importance of the process of *zhengming* in the Confucian tradition can hardly be questioned. As Chad Hansen puts it, "the rectification of names can be regarded as a genuine Confucian teaching *in the sense that* without it, the ethical system of Confucius would be considerably less coherent" (1983, 181n; emphasis in original).

Examples generally considered to illustrate the *zhengming* process often appear to infuse new meanings into existing terms. And, it is widely accepted that Confucius, though claiming to be a mere transmitter and not an innovator (*Analects* 7.1), did precisely this. For example, Confucius's usage of the term *ren* 仁 apparently struck his followers as so unusual that they asked him repeatedly for clarification of its meaning. Roger Ames and Henry Rosemont Jr. make the same point: "The fact that Confucius is asked so often what he means by the expression *ren* would suggest that he is reinventing this term for his own purposes, and that those in conversation with him are not comfortable in their understanding of it" (1998, 50). In addition, prior to Confucius's time *junzi* merely indicated a political category, and *li* 禮 was limited to formal ritual matters. Confucius imbued these terms with moral content. Similarly, as Huang Chun-chieh puts it, "The word translated as meaning 'duke' is *gong*. Confucius changed the meaning of this word from 'rulership' to 'public,' that is, people at large" (1993, 62).

Confucius could be accused of what C. L. Stevenson termed "persuasive definition." "A 'persuasive' definition is one which gives a new conceptual meaning to a familiar word without substantially changing its emotive meaning, and which is used with the conscious or unconscious purpose of changing, by this means, the direction of people's interests [or attitudes]" (1963, 32).[2] Though often suspect, persuasive definition can be legitimate. If the emotive quality attached to the new meaning can be adequately defended, then it may be deemed appropriate. For example, the word *junzi*, when used to mean "prince," would have emotively connoted "honorable." When Confucius redefined this term to mean "people of high moral character," the "honorable" connotation followed. Since the case can be made that it is really such a virtuous person—and not the mere prince by birth—who is deserving of honor, the move is appropriate. Describing Xunzi's view, Watanabe Takashi writes, "Making names is trying

---

2. As an example, a libertarian may characterize government-subsidized medical care as "stealing." The idea is that since the money to pay for medical treatment must come from somewhere, the subsidy must be "taken" from the people to whom it really belongs. The implication is that we should not approve of this since we all know (or feel) that "stealing" is wrong. Persuasive definitions are, of course, open to critique. In this case, one could answer that if governmental funding of medical care is "stealing," then so too is most everything else that governments do (to which the libertarian—but not necessarily those whom they wish to persuade—might all too eagerly agree), and that, further, "what belongs to whom?" and "who has a claim to what?" are not always easy questions to answer.

to precisely define concepts and to make an appropriate language. . . . Things should be given appropriate names according to their value."[3] *Zhengming* requires that the evaluative force of words be appropriately directed.

Much of the *Analects* is devoted to this process of recharacterizing and giving new meanings to evolving concepts so that they would be responsive to the needs of the times. For example, the *Analects* records many statements like the following: "*Junzi* make appropriateness their basic character, put it into practice by observing ritual propriety, expresses it with modesty, and complete it by living up to their words. Such are *junzi* indeed!"[4] Here Confucius is neither describing the way *junzi* happen to be, nor postulating an external source of authority. He is rather *stipulating* a reconceived category (*lei* 類). As Paul Goldin describes Confucius's reevaluation of the category of *junzi*: "The only *junzi* worthy of the name, in other words, were people who lived up to the highest moral standards, regardless of whether they were noble or base by birth" (1999, vii).

Zhengming, like most of classical Chinese doctrines, is fundamentally ethical in nature. Rectifying names is not so much a task of getting them right in an epistemological sense as designing them to be effective for social and ethical purposes. It is because *zhengming* was such a critical component of Confucius's project that he reacted so strongly when Zilu failed to see its importance even when told explicitly.

As we explore the notion of *zhengming* in the *Xunzi*, we will do well to keep in mind that *zhengming* is the process that Confucius is constantly engaged in throughout the *Analects* as he answers questions about various ethical concepts. It is not a process of explaining what is already there in language, or of what exists prior (logically or temporally) to our mental activities. *Zhengming* is an effort to go beyond how a term is used or what it means, and to stipulate how it *should be* used and what it *should* mean. While this stipulation involves a creative element, we will see that it is one that operates within boundaries and answers to standards.

3.2. Names Have No Intrinsic Appropriateness

For understanding Xunzi's conception of naming, perhaps the most critical passage is a controversial one from the *Zhengming* chapter. Burton Watson's translation reads: "Names have no intrinsic appropriateness. One agrees to use a certain name and issues an order to that effect. . . . Names have no intrinsic reality [*shi* 實]. One agrees to use a certain name and issues an order that it should be applied to a certain reality" (W 144).

---

3. 制名とは概念を正確に規定し適正な言語化を試みることである。...それぞれの価値にふさわしい呼称が与えられるべきだとした。(Watanabe 1973, 807).
4. 子曰：「君子義以為質，禮以行之，孫以出之，信以成之。君子哉！」*Analects* 15.18.

Bryan Van Norden argues that the first claim concerns the question of which sounds constitute words, and the second claim addresses which of these words are made to correspond to each type of thing. He writes, "First, it [weak conventionalism] claims that it is a matter of convention which combinations of phonemes are words and which are not. Second, weak conventionalism asserts that the connection between a particular symbol and the thing that it is a symbol for is arbitrary and contingent. This seems to be all that Xunzi is asserting in this passage" (1993, 376). This interpretation seems to regard *ming* 名 as a mere symbol, a label, if you will. Thus, Van Norden takes the first claim to involve the formation of labels, and the second claim to involve attaching these labels to (presumably already given) categories.

Benjamin Schwartz expresses a similar view: "[Xunzi's] view that it [language] is a human creation leads him to adopt the view that there is no 'inherent' relation between the sounds of words and their meanings. . . . As for the names of categories of institutions, ranks, laws, and *li*, the lucid minds of the sage-kings made it possible for them to assign all these categories of experience to their proper classes, categories, and relations, and once they had done so they conventionally assigned certain meanings to certain sounds" (1985, 312). Schwartz implies that there are "proper" classes, categories, and relations regarding institutions, ranks, laws, and *li*, that are somehow real (they seem to be mapping to "categories of experience" that only the lucid minds of sage-kings perceive) and the only contingent aspect of naming is the assigning of sounds.

The very idea of *zhengming*, however, militates against a narrow understanding of *ming* as label. Although consistency in the sounds and written forms of words is important for communication, *zhengming* is not primarily concerned with using sanctioned labels. As a primarily ethical doctrine, *zhengming* has two sides: the name (*ming*) and the actual situation (*shi* 實); stipulating appropriate categories, and living up to the standards set by them.[5] Xunzi includes the following in a short list of measures to foster customs conducive to peace and prosperity: "equalize words and conduct, and unite guiding principles with categories."[6] Although the word *zhengming* is not used here, this can be taken

---

5. Hu Shih also notes these two sides to *zhengming*: "The object is, first, to make the names stand for what they ought to stand for, and then to so reorganize the social and political relations and institutions as to make them what their names indicate they should be. The rectification of names thus consists in making the real relationships and duties and institutions conform as far as possible to their *ideal* meanings which, however obscured and neglected they may now have become, can still be re-discovered and re-established by proper study and, literally 'judicious' use of names" (Hu 1963, 26; emphasis in original). Hu sometimes sounds as though he leans toward a realist interpretation. For example, it is not entirely clear how strong a sense of "*ideal* meanings" he has in mind here. The idea of *rediscovering* these ideal meanings seems to suggest that there is something fixed which is to be rediscovered. On the other hand, his rendering of *zhengming* as a "judicious use of names," links naming with the exercise of judgment. See also Hu's remark quoted in the final footnote of this chapter.

6. 齊言行。壹統類。 (16/6/14; K: 6).

as a succinct description of it. Conduct must match words, and the categories that the words call forth should be attuned to a guiding discourse. When categories, and the terms which represent them, prescribe appropriate principles of conduct, behavior is accordingly guided. And, at the same time, acting in accordance with these categories further reinforces them. When categories are fitting, then living up to them is *zhengming*.[7] When they are not, then to *zhengming* is to reconstruct them in a constructive way. In other words, attuning names involves making the actual situation congruent with a constructive ethical vocabulary. Thus, one must both attune behavior and the ethical concepts that give behavior its guidance.

We should keep in mind here that the *Guanzi* also suggests that, rather than serving as a mere symbol for preexisting and unproblematic classifications, the idea of imposing order on the world is central to the meaning and usage of *ming*. "Naming (*ming*) is the means by which sages arrange the myriad phenomena."[8] Also, the *shiming*, a Han dynasty dictionary, defines *ming* as follows: "Naming is clarifying. Applying names to actualities enables clear demarcations."[9]

In addition, *ming* is ubiquitously translated in the Japanese literature on Xunzi as *gainen* 概念 (concept).[10] The introductory remarks preceding Murase Hiroya's Japanese translation of parts of the *Zhengming* chapter are particularly revealing. First he says that *ming* can mean either a "term" (J: *meiji* 名辞) or "concept" (J: *gainen*). He writes, "For the word *ming* 名, as mentioned before, there are both cases in which it indicates a 'term', that is, a symbol, as well as cases where it indicates the meaning of the symbol, that is, a 'concept.'"[11] However, he states that in the case of *zhengming, ming* refers to the former (Murase 1986, 147). But consider his translation of the "intrinsic appropriateness" passage

---

7. Cf. "[W]hen a son does not live up to his obligations, the 'name' (*ming*) of being a son requires ethical correction. Ideally, correction of misconduct will be accompanied by a transformation of the person's character. In this sense, rectifying names (*zhengming*) is a procedure for rectifying misconduct. This Confucian view finds a partial affinity with that of Arthur Murphy: 'The term "brother," in the statement of a ground of obligation, is not a practically noncommittal term. To be a brother is not just to be a male sibling—it is a privilege, a burden and, whether we like it or not, a commitment'" (Cua 1997, 204). See K: 12.3 for Xunzi's definitions of family members, which states, for example, that to behave as an older brother is to be kind, loving, and friendly, while to behave as younger brother is to be respectful and conscientious. 請問為人兄。曰。慈愛 而見友。請問為人弟。曰。敬詘而不苟。 (45/12/19; K: 12.3).

8. 聖人之所以紀萬物也。 *Guanzi*, "Xinshu."

9. 名，明也，名實使分明也。 *Shiming*, "Shiyanyu."

10. For example, Kaizuka Shigeki writes, "[For Xunzi,] knowledge comes about by making names, that is to say 'concepts' (*gainen* 概念), and by seeking a coincidence with actualities having objective existence. This is assured by what we should call the subject's inherent phenomena-recognition ability. But the concepts were based on a social viewpoint established by a kind of social agreement." 客観的な存在にあたる実にたいして名すなわち概念を製してその一致を求めるこ とによって知識が成立する。それは主観の先天的ともいうべき事物認識能力によって保証さ れるのであるが、その概念は人間が一種の社会的な約束によって定められるという社会的な立 場で基礎づけたのであった。 (Kaizuka 1961, 173). Cf. Kakimura and Azuma 1995, 446; Kaji 1971, 44; and Watanabe 1973, 807 (see section 3.1). See also *ming* in the glossary of key terms.

11. なお、「名」という語には、前述の通り、「名称」＝シンボルを指す場合と、 シンボルの「意味」すなわち「概念」を指す場合とがある。 (Murase 1986, 148).

(rendered into English): "It is not the case that names (i.e., symbols) carry meanings which are valid by nature; they are established by nothing more than the mutual agreement of people."[12] Despite his explicit indication that he takes *ming* to merely mean "symbol" in this case, Murase nevertheless interprets the passage to say that what is established by agreement is not the symbol *itself* but rather the *meaning it will carry*.

We find similar assessments in the Chinese scholarship as well. For example, Xunzi quotes the saying "the sage does not love himself" (though he loves people and is himself a person) as an example of "using *ming* to disorder *ming*."[13] The problem, as Lao Siguang observes, involves a "discrepancy in the scope of the concept" (概念之範圍差異), that is, an equivocation between the *ming* (name-concept) *ren* 人 as "other people" and *ren* as "people, including oneself" (see Lao 1968, 274).

In a similar vein, Lin Lizhen writes:

> It seems from his selected examples [of fallacies], Xunzi's notion of names evidently already surpassed the range of ordinary so-called "terms," it is also not absolutely identical with what we call "concept" (C: *gainian*) in logic. What he calls *ming*, besides including "term" or "concept," really already simultaneously includes "judgment" and "disputation" [lit. speech which differentiates]. . . . On Xunzi's view, the product of disputation is something unavoidable based on what is pressing in the current situation.[14]

On Chenyang Li's understanding, *ming* includes "not only names in the sense the English word usually means but also descriptions" (1999, 64). He says that Xunzi "did not speculate about what kinds of things there are in themselves apart from human awareness. It is clear that, for him, naming and classification are the same process; it is we who do the classification on the basis of our experience of things" (69). And his interpretation stresses "the active role of the knower in the process of knowing" (69). He writes, "In knowing, the mind/heart is not passively dependent on what the senses register. It processes what the senses register and produces judgment on what things are and how to name them" (70). Further, Xunzi's "taxonomy," Li says, "does not distinguish natural kinds and artificial kinds, both being 'things.' We divided 'things' further and further into lesser general categories depending on our needs" (85).[15]

---

12. 名称（名＝シンボル）はもともとそれによって通用する意味を担っているわけではなく、人びと相互の約束によってかく定められたにすぎない。(Murase 1986, 166).

13. This applies also to the saying, "killing a robber is not killing a person" (see 84/22/30; K: 22.3a; W 145).

14. 由所舉的例子看來，荀子觀念中的名，顯然已經超越了平常所云「名稱」的範圍，亦不與邏輯上所說的「概念」完全一致。其所謂名，除了包含名稱或概念外，實已兼括「判斷」及「辨說」。...在荀子看，辨說的產生，乃是基於時勢所迫，不得已而有的現象。(Lin 1978, 65).

15. Li at one point writes, "Xunzi developed a realist theory of names" (1999, 68). It is unclear

This last point refers to a passage[16] that occurs immediately prior to the "intrinsic appropriateness" passage and discusses broad and specific *ming*. The broadest *ming* (*da gong ming* 大共名) is "thing" (*wu* 物), and the narrowest *ming* is one for which no more useful distinctions (*bie* 別) can be made. What is broad or narrow is not the label but the meaning indicated by it.

The idea that *ming* means something like "concept" supports John Makeham's translation and interpretation of the passage in question. His translation reads: "A name has no intrinsic appropriateness; rather, the appropriateness of a particular name is demarcated by being ordained. . . . A name has no intrinsically appropriate object [*shi*]; rather, its appropriate object is demarcated by being ordained" (1994, 63).[17] On Makeham's view, not only are the names *qua* labels conventional, but what is picked out by a name is also a matter of convention.[18] Makeham writes, "[T]he ruler determines what object a name demarcates. By ordaining a particular denomination the ruler establishes boundaries which serve to demarcate one object from another. Only then is a name made a matter of convention" (59).

In the final section I will consider the degree to which naming can be considered simply the prerogative of the ruler. Be that as it may, on Makeham's interpretation there seems to be no necessity to demarcate an object in correspondence with any univocal standard. The demarcation of an object, to which a name refers, has no "intrinsic appropriateness" (*gu yi* 固宜); the boundaries are demarcated by being "ordained" (*ming* 命). In other words, the sage has a hand in defining the boundary conditions, which are not thought to be inherently preexisting.

This stands in contrast to Goldin's treatment of the passage in his recent book on Xunzi. Completely ignoring the second claim, he offers an excerpt of the passage that includes the first claim only. He immediately concludes: "Thus, while the names themselves are arbitrary, there can be no discussion over

---

in what sense he means this. Given the other things he says, he could not mean the strong realist position that I have been arguing against.

16. 83/22/21–25; K: 22.2f; W 143–44; Graham 1989, 265.

17. Cf. Graham's translation of the key phrases, "Names have no inherent appropriateness, we name by convention. . . . No object belongs inherently to a name, we name by convention" (1989, 266). Wing-tsit Chan's translation seems ambiguous on this point. He translates, "Names have no correctness of their own. The correctness is given by convention. When the convention is established and the custom is formed, they are called correct names. If they are contrary to convention, they are called incorrect names. Names have no corresponding actualities by themselves. The actualities ascribed to them are given by convention. When the convention is established and the custom is formed, they are called names of such-and-such actualities. But some names are felicitous in themselves. When a name is direct, easy to understand, and self-consistent, it is called a felicitous name" (1963, 126). Hansen's translation of this passage leans in the constructivist direction. However, his interpretation is more radical, suggesting that there are no standards for the appropriateness of distinctions other than mere convention. See Hansen 1983, 79–81. For my own translation of this passage, see section 3.4 below.

18. The convention is not arbitrary; things are grouped together that are judged to be relevantly similar, perhaps simply to each other, or to a paradigmatic case.

what gets named" (1999, 96; emphasis in original). In other words, "[W]hile the actual names of objects may be a trivial matter, the objects themselves are not open to interpretation" (99). Even the venerable A. C. Graham, at times, expressed what seems to be a similar position: "[T]he divisions marked by naming are subjective for Zhuangzi but objective for Xunzi. . . . For Xunzi on the contrary, although naming is conventional, the divisions they mark are inescapably there" (1991, 285). Whatever Graham may have intended here, at least we can say that statements of this nature might lead one in the direction of an interpretation like that of Goldin.

Hansen takes the passage in question, and others in the *Zhengming* chapter, to indicate a conventionalist strain in Xunzi's thinking. But Hansen thinks that Xunzi articulates two contradictory views and, in the final analysis, he considers Xunzi to be an "absolutist."[19] Interestingly, those who find fault with Hansen's interpretation tend to fault the conventionalist side rather than the absolutist side of his interpretation.[20]

Robert Eno is not convinced that the "intrinsic appropriateness" passage contradicts a realist interpretation of Xunzi. He writes:

> Interpretation of the *Xunzi*'s theory of language has focused on the phrases, "Names have no intrinsic appropriateness," and "Names have no intrinsic reality," to argue that the *Xunzi* takes a conventionalist approach to language.[21] However, when viewed as a whole, the *Xunzi*'s theory of language is realist. Although individual words are initially chosen arbitrarily, their consistent use and syntactic relations in language create a perfect correspondence[22] between the elements and structure of language and the objects of the world and their relations. It is this characteristic of language that allows the text explicitly to limit its conventionalism: "Names can be intrinsically good: those that are straightforward and simple, without contradiction (*fu*) are called good names."[23] Implicitly, names *may* "contradict"[24] reality. (1990, 272 n65)

19. "But the other Xunzi—the political absolutist—also comes through even in philosophical sections. This theorist is an uncritical absolutist. He asserts the possibility of direct access to the correct *dao*" (Hansen 1992, 309). Cf. Hansen 1992, 310; see section 1.3.2.

20. For Van Norden's critique of the conventionalist side of Hansen's interpretation of Xunzi, see Van Norden 1993.

21. Here Eno cites Hansen 1983, 81.

22. There is a kind of correspondence that makes sense when talking about a theory of truth, and could function in the early Chinese tradition as well. But it is not Eno's "perfect correspondence between the elements and structure of language and the objects of the world and their relations." Rather, statements about states of affairs can correspond to those states of affairs, not as they are absolutely, but as they are given an interpreting scheme. While categories themselves do not map to something ultimately real, statements can correspond with what is the case, where both the statement and what is the case are interpreted through the same scheme. This is roughly the kind of correspondence theory of truth that John Searle defends. See Searle 1995, 199–226. The kind of correspondence Eno appeals to is no longer tenable, and attributing that view to the *Xunzi* makes it less interesting, and is unwarranted.

23. 名有固善。徑易而不拂。謂之善名。 (84/22/27; K: 22.2g; W 144). I read this passage as follows: "There are names which are intrinsically apt. Names which are easy and straightforward, and do not conflict, are called 'apt' names."

24. Cf. Knoblock's translation of another passage: "Things of the same class do not become

Eno's rebuttal focuses on the lines immediately following the "intrinsic appropriateness" passages. In particular he seems to stress that names can be "intrinsically good" and that good names (*shanming* 善名) are "without contradiction (*fu* 拂[25])." And, he seems to assume that this refers to the possibility of names contradicting *reality,* rather than each other.

Shanming, felicitous names, are those that are "straightforward and simple" and don't conflict with each other. Felicitous names involve such things as labels signaling relationships between categories. Consider Confucius's definition of *zheng* 政 (to govern) in terms of *zheng* 正 (proper): "Governing (*zheng* 政) is making proper (*zheng* 正)."[26] The word *zheng* (proper) is ultimately conventional as a label. Considered independently, one could say the same of *zheng* (to govern). However, considered together this is an example of felicitous naming, since the same pronunciation, as well as one character deriving from the other, signals an analogy between the two meanings. The meanings are also influenced by the relationship. Concepts are often defined in classical Chinese in precisely this way. The definition of naming mentioned near the beginning of this section, "Naming (*ming* 名) is clarifying (*ming* 明)," is a fitting example. Both the label and the conceptual aspect of names can relate in felicitous ways without implying realism.

Eno also claims, "The notion of making distinctions (*bian*), which is no more than a 'true' perception of natural divisions in the constitution of the world, is inextricably linked to the idea of creating proper order" (1990, 146). He offers two passages from Xunzi in support of this claim. I will take them up in turn and then consider their implications.

The first passage is: "Making fair equity (*pingjun*) universal, with all ordered according to their distinctions (*zhibian*): in this the hundred kings were alike; this is the great role (*fen*) of ritual and law (*lifa*)" (1990, 146–47).[27] I read this passage somewhat differently: "Everything in the world is distinguished and

---

contradictory even though a long time has elapsed because they share an identical principle of order." 類不悖雖久同理。 (14/5/36; K: 5.5). My translation reads: "Categories are not unreasonable, although a long time may pass, they will exhibit similar constructive patterns." Here *bei* (contrary, absurd) is used rather than *fu* (go against). Constructive categories and the relations they highlight are thought to be enduring. Cf. Criticizing the doctrines and policies of the prime minister of Qi, Xunzi says, "They are as absurd (*bei*) and preposterous as decreasing what one has in insufficient quantities while emphasizing what one has in surplus, and in this way seeking the success and fame of Kings Tang and Wu. Ruling in this manner is like lying down to lick the sky, or rescuing a hanging man by pulling on his feet. Such doctrines will certainly not work in practice. The more one acts on them the farther away from one's goal one becomes." 損己之所不足。以重己之所有餘。若是其悖繆也。而求有湯武之功名可乎。辟之是猶伏而咶天。救經而引其足也。説必不行矣。愈務而愈遠。 (60/16/44–45; K: 16.4). Similarly, Xunzi make an analogy between the "great stupidity" of forsaking *liyi* 禮義 and "desiring longevity and slitting one's throat" 是猶欲壽而殁 [刎] 頸也。 (60/16/47–48; K: 16.4). In each case, there is a practical contradiction. Well-conceived categories do not lead people to such absurdities, even after a long time.

25. Yang Liang interprets *fu* as *weifu* 違拂, meaning to go against (see Wang 1988, 420).
26. *Analects* 12.17 政者，正也。 See also Hu 1963, 24.
27. Eno's translation. It should be noted that Xunzi is quoting here. While it is not clear exactly where the quotation ends, the fact that it is repeated in K: 11.9a up to and including the part translated here suggests that this is likely all part of the quotation.

adjusted, everything is ordered and differentiated. This is what was similar among the hundred kings, and is the great role of ritual propriety and law."[28] On either reading, this passage does not state that the way the hundred kings differentiated things and brought order to the world was "identical," as one would think "natural divisions" would be, and as Eno often translates the word *tong* 同.[29] First, *tong* 同 does not mean "identical," but rather "similar."[30] If two things are relatively similar they may be loosely called "the same" or "alike" when the respect and degree of similarity is understood, without implying that the items are identical. Further, in this passage, it is not distinctions themselves that are claimed to be the same, but rather *the fact that* things were regulated and disciplined into order in the reign of each king. And, when we look at the larger context of the passage, what it really amounts to is the importance of division of labor and delegation. The sage kings were all good at making sure things and affairs, and the responsibilities for them, were divided up so as to enable effective management. This was a critique of Mozi, who is characterized, unfairly,[31] as suggesting that a king should rely merely on his own personal efforts.

The second passage Eno offers is: "Duties (*fen*) divided without disorder above; talents without exhaustion below: this is the ultimate of order according to distinctions" (1990, 147).[32] Here Xunzi is concerned with not over burdening people. Thus he advocates allocating responsibilities according to individual abilities, that is, what each person can manage.

Eno's point, that *bian*, "making distinctions," is linked to the idea of creating order, is well taken. However, his idea that *bian* "is no more than a 'true' perception of natural divisions in the constitution of the world" is suspect. When we consider the two passages he offers, this claim does not follow. The

---

28. 天下莫不平均。莫不治辨。是百王之所同也。而禮法之大分也。(40/11/62–63; K: 11.5b). Karlgren says that the seal form of *ban* 釆, also read *bian*, is similar to that of *ping* 平 and that this *bian* 釆 is cognate to *bian* 辨 "distinguish," which occurs in the second clause (see GSR: 195a). *Ping* can be a loanword for *ban* with a sense similar to *bian*. Reading *pingjun* as "distinguished and adjusted" makes more sense along side *zhi bian*, "ordered and differentiated" than something like Eno's "fair equity." Knoblock has "unbalanced and unadjusted" for *bu ping bian* which is not bad as a "middle way."

29. Note Eno's use of "identical" as a translation of *tong*: "Things which are of identical type and essence are perceived by the *tian*-like faculties [i.e., sense organs] identically." (1990, 272 n64, brackets in original, quoting *Xunzi* 83/22/16; K: 22.2c). More frequently he uses "sameness," but in keeping with his realist understanding of the text, he seems to have in mind a sense of sameness which implies strict identity. See Eno 1990, 145–46.

30. Cf. *Mencius* 6A: "As a rule, the same category (*tong lei* 同類) selects out the mutually similar." 故凡同類者，舉相似也。 *Ju* 舉 has the senses of choose, elect, and promote. It implies that there was an element of choice and indeterminacy, as well as advocacy, which underscores the prescriptive element of *lei*. It is not that a *lei* is articulated to express the singularly correct groupings of identicals, but rather its purpose is to promote particular groupings based on selected elements of perceived similarities.

31. See *Mozi*, book 11, "Obeying one's Superior," for his description of how governmental responsibilities should be divided up.

32. Eno's translation. 分不亂於上。能不窮於下。治辨之極也。 (22/8/55; K: 8.6).

first passage stresses the importance of having attuned names (*zhengming*) by suggesting that each of the Hundred Kings did this well, but does not imply that they necessarily did it the same. In fact, common sense together with scant historical records would suggest the contrary. The second passage identifies two criteria for judging success in creating order via a set of distinctions. Such criteria are the kind a pragmatist might use to adjudicate between competing claims. A realist, one would think, would be more interested in somehow loftier concerns than the practical matter of achieving orderly government by assigning duties according to the particulars of each individual's skills and abilities.

3.3. Attuning Names

To see why *zhengming* is best understood in a constructivist manner, it is helpful to keep in mind the mutually entailing relationship between *li* 理 and *lei* 類, which was discussed in the previous chapter, for it is intimately bound up with the *zhengming* process. Whenever one engages in *zhengming* one is marking a *lei* (category) of some kind or another (it could be a moral category as well as a physical one) and of some scope (it could be a relatively "general name," *gongming* 共名, or a more "specific name," *bieming* 別名). Just how the category should be delimited depends on the *li* (patterns) of the matter in question. However, these patterns are not foundational; they in turn depend on previously conceived categories. As Cua succinctly put it, "[J]ust as every *lei* has *li* as a basis, every *li* involves *lei* as a precondition" (1985, 54; see section 2.4).

Some interpreters of Xunzi's thought, however, take names (*ming*) and categories (*lei*) to represent privileged groupings, their special authority being assured by virtue of their correspondence with the deep structure of the universe. Names and categories are grounded in *li* taken as "principles of natural existence," or in "the Way" as the "plan and pattern" of reality.

Eno provides the clearest description of this position, and thus, though mentioned in the previous chapter (section 2.3), it bears repeating. He writes:

> [W]hen the *Xunzi* slices the world into pieces and principles, it does so not only for objective entities but for life conceived as situations and roles. This analogous structure between natural and ethical worlds allows the *Xunzi* to make an implicit but clear claim to the effect that ritual *li* embody *intrinsic principles of ethical existence* fundamentally equivalent to principles of natural existence, or "*li*" [理]. (1990, 152; emphasis mine)

Eno further maintains:

> *Zhengming* constructs a model of the proper function of language on the basis of the claim that the role of "names" (generally, substance words) is to distinguish differences in "realities" (*shi*). The world is pictured as a field of objects that are naturally

ordered into sets on the basis of sameness (*tong*) and difference (*yi*). Man is innately equipped to distinguish these two primal qualities. (1990, 146)

Eno attributes to Xunzi a worldview in which "realities"—thought of as substances or natural objects, as well as social and ethical phenomena such as rituals and roles—are somehow "naturally ordered," and that people are equipped to recognize that order and then represent it in language.

Schwartz articulates a similar view. He writes:

> Both [the Mohists and Xunzi] are convinced that a *truly correct language* which provides a clear and unambiguous picture of both the natural and human world is a product of conscious human activity. What divides them fundamentally is Xunzi's belief that such a language has already been created by both the people and the sage-kings of old. . . . Yet clearly Xunzi is quite prepared to draw on their [i.e. Mohist] categories to provide us with a more precise defense of what he considers to be the *true language* of the sage-kings. . . . Xunzi believed not only that the sages had clearly established the fundamental logical categories and classes [i.e. *lei*] but that they had also solved the problem of applying them to reality so that what they had bequeathed was a *complete map of social reality*. (1985, 312–13; emphasis added)

Goldin likewise expresses a similar view. He writes: "In the term *dao* 道, or Way, Xunzi postulates a single and universal ontology. The Way is the way of the universe, and the 'plan and pattern' [*jing li* 經理] of reality, and theories are 'heterodox' if they do not conform to it. The exalted rectification—or rectification of names—is a tool that the philosopher can use to distinguish lewd[33] antinomies from truths compatible with the Way" (1999, 98).

Goldin offers the following translation of a key passage as support for this position:

> Names are that by which different objects are designated. Propositions connect the names of different objects in order to sort ideas into one. Disputations and explications do not differentiate [between] reality and name in order to illustrate the Way of movement and quietude [this statement is inherently ambiguous in the Chinese original as well]. Designating and naming are the application of disputations and explications. Disputations and explications are the mind's image of the Way. The mind is the craftsman and manager of the Way. The Way is the plan and pattern of order. . . . Using the correct Way to distinguish lewd [doctrines] is like leading [i.e. stretching] rope to determine the crooked and straight. For this reason, heterodox explications cannot [cause] chaos, and the Hundred Schools have no place to hide.[34]

---

33. It is unclear exactly what Goldin has in mind here. The word "lewd" does have an archaic sense roughly equivalent to "vulgar" in the sense of "common." However, Goldin also uses "lewd" as a translation of the character *jian* 姦 (composed of three women) meaning wicked and deceitful, and which—in anther context—could mean "adultery."

34. Goldin's translation of *Xunzi* 84/22/38–43. (1999, 98, brackets and ellipsis in original. Cf.

This is a rich passage, and deserves explication. Retranslating, I will break it up and consider it part by part. But first, to broaden the context of the passage, I will begin with the immediately preceding passage, which reads:

> When things and events (*shi* 實) are not understood (*yu* 喻), assign a name (*ming* 命). When this naming is not understood, specify (*qi* 期).[35] When specifications are not understood, explain (*shuo* 説). When explanations are not understood, make incisive distinctions (*bian* 辨). Thus, specifying, naming, making distinctions, and explaining are important language patterns (*wen* 文) of practical use (*yong* 用), and they are the beginning of the kingly enterprise. Making actual things or events understood when the name is heard is the practical use of names. Accumulating and completing cultural patterns is the beauty of names. Achieving both practical use and beauty is called "knowing names" (*zhi ming* 知名).[36]

This is plainly a discussion of increasing levels of clarification involved in the process of communication. Now, let us begin the part quoted by Goldin. My translation reads:

> Name-concepts (*ming* 名) are that by which different[37] actualities (*shi* 實) are specified (*qi* 期). A phrase unites the names of different actualities thereby to state a single meaning. Distinctions and explanations, by not "differing" [i.e. varying] names and tokens, illustrate the *dao* of movement and stillness.[38]

It should be kept in mind that this part of the chapter deals with Xunzi's response to the paradoxes of the sophists. The meaning of the last sentence of the quotation, which is often translated such that it sounds like a non sequitur, can be understood by looking at it in that light. The import of the sentence is that by being consistent in the use of names with respect to the things to which names refer, one can discourse about the way while avoiding paradoxes.

K: 22.3f; W 147–48). Puett's account is similar to Goldin's. See Puett 2001, 72, for his translation and analysis of this passage. For the Chinese text, see the notes below.

35. See the glossary of key terms for justification of my interpretation of *qi* as "specify."

36. 實不喻然後命。命不喻然後期。期不喻然後説。説不喻然後辨。故期命辨説也者。用之大文也。而王業之始也。名聞而實喻。名之用也。累而成文。名之麗也。用麗俱得。謂之知名。 (84/22/36–38; K: 22.3f; W 146–47; H 281–82; D 290; Mei 1951, 59–60; Duyvendak 1924, 241; Wang 1988, 422–23).

37. I read *lei* 累 as *yi* 異 here, as most translators do. The visual similarity combined with the fact that the phrase *yi shi* 異實 occurs in each of the next two statements support this alteration. (However, *lei* also occurs just shortly before this passage, where it means "accumulate.") Duyvendak suggests, further, that the alternative (the unamended text) does not make much sense. He renders it, "Names serve to define joined realities" (1924, 241). Or, putting it in my own words, "Names are that by which specifications bind (*lei*) together actual objects." To a constructivist way of thinking, this makes pretty good sense. I believe it is a viable alternative.

38. 名也者。所以期累實也。辭也者。兼異實之名以論一意也。辨説也者。不異實名以喻動靜之道也。 (84/22/38–40; K:22.3f; W 147).

Specifying (*qi*) and naming (*ming* 命) are the practical uses of distinctions and explanations. Distinctions and explanations are how the mind represents *dao*.[39]

Rather than being "eternal and unchanging" yet "ultimately ineffable,"[40] as Goldin understands Xunzi's *dao*, it is rather because *dao* is always in flux that it resists a final articulation.[41] Nevertheless, as this passage indicates, Xunzi did not regard *dao* as something mysterious and beyond expression. On the contrary, he regarded it as something that we can discuss, making distinctions and offering explanations, as we do when we lay down stipulations and give reasons for choosing to characterize things the way we do. Not only can the way be discussed, it is at root "discourse" (*dao*).

The mind is the craftsman and manager of *dao*.[42]

Here we have the relation between *dao* and the mind stated plainly. It is not a picture of a passive mind reflecting an independent and prior *dao*. Rather, the mind crafts the way. And once crafted, *dao* does not become fixed or static. The mind must continue to manage the way.

Dao is regulating and patterning (*jing li*) order (i.e., good government).[43]

Dao is active, it is verbal, it is something one does. In reference to this passage Eric Hutton explains, "*Jing* [經] originally referred to the neat arrangement of vertical threads that make up the warp of a loom, and by extension, it came to mean 'order,' where this could be either the 'ordering structure' of an object, or the *act* of arranging something" (2002, 366; emphasis mine). He continues, "[T]he occurrence of the word 'craftsman' (*gong* [工]) in the sentence prior to this one in the text suggests that Xunzi is thinking in terms of an analogy with crafts, which also gives one reason to take *jing* in its original sense" (380 n50).

The passage continues:

[When] one's mind is in accord with *dao*, explanations accord with the mind, and phrases accord with explanations. There is precise naming (*zhengming*) and specify-

39. 期命也者。辨説之用也。辨説也者。心之象道也。 (84/22/40; K: 22.3f; W 147).
40. "The Way is not merely the intermingling of *yin* and *yang*, but the eternal and unchanging Way that governs all the processes of the cosmos. Xunzi avoids lengthy characterizations of the Way because it is ultimately ineffable" (Goldin 1999, 103–4).
41. "Each of these various attempts addresses merely one corner of the way. The *dao* embodies regularities while always changing. Addressing one corner is not sufficient to raise it up." 此數具者。皆道之一隅也。夫道者。體常而盡變。一隅不足以舉之。 (79/21/24–25; K: 21.4; W 126).
42. 心也者。道之工宰也。 (82/22/40; K: 22.3f; W 147). I keep close to Goldin's translation here to highlight that even his translation, in this instance, suggests a constructivist interpretation.
43. 道也者。治之經理也。 (84/22/40–41; K: 22.3f; W 147).

ing, "stuff" is clear and understood, distinctions differentiate without going to far [i.e., splitting hairs] and categories are extended [by analogy][44] without including contraries. Listening accords with refined patterns (*wen* 文), and distinctions are made with exhaustive reasoning.[45]

It is somewhat ironic that Goldin omits this part of the passage, for it is here that, at first blush, it seems as if his conception of *dao* as a "single and universal ontology" finds its best support. What does it mean for one's mind to be in accord with *dao*? It may seem from this part of the passage that *dao* comes first, and then the mind is either in accord with it or not. But, how can that mesh with the mind being the craftsman and manager of *dao*, which is stated just two sentences earlier? A change of perspective has taken place. When Xunzi first speaks of the mind as the craftsman and manager of *dao*, he is speaking of defining a discourse that conduces to orderly, patterned government. But then he wants to make a claim about the condition for communicating with clarity. He tells us that when we are thinking and speaking according to constructively designed patterns of discourse (*dao*), we can be clear and understood without lapsing into fallacy and paradox. This does not contradict his claim that *dao* is ultimately a human construct. While the image of the "craftsman and manager of the *dao*" suggests the idea that language and the categories it marks are socially constructed, Xunzi makes the qualification here that, given a linguistic convention X, it is sensible to talk about whether some "actual thing or event" (*shi*) legitimately counts as an X, that is, whether it qualifies according to the conventions that set the boundaries of the category marked by X.

Continuing with the translation of the passage:

Taking a precise course and distinguishing it from what is perverse and deceptive (*jian* 姦), is like stretching a cord to oppose crooked and straight. For this reason improper (*xie* 邪)[46] explanations are not able to cause disorder, and the hundred schools have nowhere to flee.[47]

---

44. Cf. Knoblock's translation of the following passage: "They draw inferences from the categories by analogical extension and connect things with comparable cases in order to handle those cases for which there is no paradigm in the model." 推類接譽 [與] 以待無方。(49–50/13/5–6; K: 13.1). Cf. also a similar passage: "If there is a law (*fa*) carry it out. If there is not, proceed (*ju*) by analogical extension (*lei*)." 其有法者以法行。無法者以類舉。(26/9/13; K: 9.2; W 35). *Ju* has the senses of "to choose" or "to promote," the passage thus suggests contingency.

45. 心合於道。說合於心。辭合於說。正名而期。質請而喻。辨異而不過。推類而不悖。聽則合文。辨則盡故。(8/22/41–42; K: 22.3f; W 147–48). This section Goldin chose to omit in his excerpt.

46. Sometimes glossed as "evil," *xie* 邪 is the opposite of *zheng* 正, and means "crooked, awry, askew" or "heretical, irregular," and by extension "improper, illegitimate" and even "wicked or depraved." Perhaps most tellingly, in Chinese medicine it indicates unhealthy influences that cause disease—just as ill-conceived distinctions can lead to moral and social degradation.

47. 以正道而辨姦。猶引繩以持曲直。是故邪說不能亂。百家無所竄。(84/22/42–43; K: 22.3f; W 148).

When a constructive way has been clearly articulated, and the terms of discourse are set, that is, when it is clear what is the way and what is not, sophists will not be able to confuse people with their word games.

This whole passage was supposed to support the following claim: "One way or the other, the consequence is inescapable: within Xunzi's system, once names are chosen, they demand strict compliance. For names represent *reality*, and their abuse results in a faulty characterization of the world" (Goldin 1999, 97; emphasis in original).

Indeed, the image of stretching a cord signals some standard against which names are measured.[48] The mind, being like a carpenter, develops tools appropriate for its trade. The carpenter uses a chalk line or a carpenter's square to manage the sides and corners of his product, keeping them in line with his intentions. The sagely mind constructs distinctions which when adhered to forward the project of achieving a stable harmonious society, and thwart the efforts of those who would use language to confuse others and disrupt social cohesion. But those standards are practical conventions, which do not correspond to some singular independent and preexistent truth.

Consider Xunzi's response to Master Song's assertion that "Being humiliated is not disgraceful" (見侮不辱). Xunzi employs a distinction (honor or disgrace that is merely circumstantial as opposed to that which is moral) to clear up the confusion caused by Master Song's assertion, but before that he lays out the theoretical groundwork:

> Ordinarily, discussions must first establish ample standards of correctness (*zheng* 正) and only then is one able to assent [to a conclusion]. If there are no such standards, then "what is" and "what is not" are not distinguished, and arguments and controversies will not be resolved. Thus it is said: "The great and lofty of the world, the boundaries of 'this' and 'not this' (and value distinctions), what gives rise to

---

48. Although the metaphor of a carpenter square might lead one to imagine some transcendent form (i.e., the Right Angle) which sets a standard independent of human intentions, Xunzi's use of a variety of other metaphors militates against the idea that he was thinking about it in anything like this manner. For example, he uses images of sharpening metal, cutting, and polishing, as well as the carving of utensils and the molding of pots, none of which suggest a corresponding singular and fixed standard (see sections 4.4, 5.2, and 5.3). Similarly, his metaphor of the rites as markers that enable people avoid deep spots while fording rivers does not suggest that there is only one route across (see latter part of section 4.4). Further, the metaphor of a straightening board, while suggesting the idea of shaping something to meet a certain form, does not suggest that there is a privileged shape for the frame itself. Consider: the straightening board metaphor is twice paired with the metaphor of sharpening metal (K: 1.1, W 15 & K: 23.1, W 157), and once followed by the metaphors of carving utensils and molding bowls (K: 23. 3c, W 164). The message is that there must be strenuous effort applied in producing a good product. As for the point of the carpenter's square metaphor, it is that by maintaining clear standards we can avoid being taken in by fallacious arguments. The metaphor simply is not addressed to the question of whether or not these standards themselves have a conventional element. Also, see section 1.5 for how the metaphor of a balance (*quan* 權) implies indeterminacy.

differentiating duties and naming forms, this is kingly government."[49] Therefore, ordinarily, when discussions turn to specifying (*qi* 期), assigning names (*ming* 命),[50] and saying "this is" and "this is not" (including making value distinctions), people should take the sage kings as their teachers.[51]

There are two levels of standards employed by Xunzi. One is the standard an established distinction sets. It is when Xunzi is discussing this level that he sounds the most authoritarian. Perhaps, as Lee Yearley has suggested, Xunzi intended these kinds of remarks to have a particular effect on less sophisticated audiences (see Yearley 1980, 469). As for the merits of distinctions themselves, they answer to the standard of efficacy in achieving a level of order and stability in a community in which the common people as well as the elite can find contentment in a generally happy and fulfilling social life.[52] Although Xunzi rails against those like Master Song[53] who all too often make alterations in important distinctions without due care, the fact that there is a standard of efficacy at work does not imply that the distinctions based on this standard represent one true "reality."

Xunzi does not assume that there can be a singularly correct articulation of reality. Asserting a pragmatic justification for the classification of things, Xunzi writes: "Among the myriad things, different concrete things have similar appearances. There is no intrinsic appropriateness, but there is a use for people. This refers to the art of discriminating regular patterns (*shu* 數)."[54] The world

---

49. Here it is clear that Xunzi is concerned about the boundaries of concepts, of what is to count as "this" and what as "not this." Specification is a part of this process in a continuum from naming to explaining (*shuo*), and finally to making incisive distinctions (*bian*).

50. Morohashi defines *qiming* 期命 as 約束して定めること, that is, "something which is fixed by agreement." *Sadameru* 定める means "to establish, stipulate, decide, determine, set (a date)." This combination also occurs in the passage preceding the passage cited by Goldin, quoted above.

51. 凡議必將立隆正然後可也。無隆正則是非不分。而辨訟不決。故所聞曰。天下之大隆。是非之封界。分職名象之所起。王制是也。故凡言議期命是非以聖王為師。 (69/18/102–4; K: 18.9). Notice that Xunzi does not suggest that the sage kings are absolute authorities in this matter, but only that we can and should learn from them.

52. See book 9, "Kingly Regulations," for Xunzi's descriptions the relationship of mutual support between the people and the good and wise ruler. There Xunzi writes, "A ruler is good at grouping. If the grouping and the guiding discourse (*dao*) are mutually coherent (*dang*), then the myriad things all receive what is suitable to them. [For example,] the six domestic animals all will get to grow to maturity, and members of all classes will get to live out their full life span." 君者善群也。群道當則萬物皆得其宜。六畜皆得其長。群生皆得其命。 (29/9/75–76; K: 9.16a; W 46).

53. "[Master Song] made alterations to them [the concepts of honor and disgrace] with a single morning's deliberation. His theory will certainly not work in practice. This is analogous to using mud balls to dam up a large river or sea. It is like using the Jiao pygmies to support Mount Tai. In no time they will stumble and fall and it will break into pieces." 慮一朝而改之。說必不行矣。譬之是猶以塼涂塞江海也。以焦僥而戴太山也。躓跌碎折不待頃矣。 (69–70/18/112–13; K: 18.9). Cf. "Their reflections are not deep; their choices are not circumspect; their determination of what to accept and what to reject is flippant and careless. This is why they are in danger." 其慮之不深。其擇之不謹。其定取舍楛僈。是其所以危也。 (10/4/32; K: 4.7).

54. 萬物同宇而異體。無宜而有用為人。數也。 (31/10/1; K: 10.1). With Knoblock, I also

has regularities that may be patterned, categorized, and named based on the potential usefulness for human purposes. This process is an art.

Describing the process of categorizing and naming, Xunzi writes:

> After [we have perceived something] it is named accordingly, what is considered similar is given a similar name, what is considered different is given a different name. . . . Appreciating [the principle of] "different names for different things" and thus, so as not to cause disorder, letting all different things have a different name, is as bad as letting all different things have the same name. . . . We press on dividing them up, where we make a distinction there is a distinguishing [term] until we reach a point where there are no more [productive] distinctions to be made and then we stop.[55]

Xunzi says we depend on our senses to make distinctions. And he does indicate, as Okamoto Tetsuharu notes, "Under similar conditions, the senses operate similarly, and so bring about similar results."[56] Nevertheless, distinctions are not simply determined by the senses. Kodama Rokurō describes it this way: "According to Xunzi, in the heart-mind there is a faculty of knowing, and in the five senses—the ears, eyes, nose, mouth, and shape—there is a faculty of sensation. The phenomena of the external world are 'caught' by the five senses, and this signal is sent to the heart-mind. The judgment of what that signal means occurs in the heart-mind."[57]

What does Kodama mean by "a faculty of knowing"? He uses the combination 徵知, lifted from the *Xunzi*, which can be understood by its components

supply the word "intrinsic," reading, 無宜 as 無固宜. I also agree with Knoblock that *shu* here suggests something like "natural order of things" in the sense of "regular patterns" (*shu* 數 = *guilü* 規律). But I believe it may at the same time be suggesting the process is an "art." (See GSR: 123r.) Cf. Dubs's translation: "All things are present together in the world, but have different forms. Of themselves they are not appropriate; but they are used by men—this is an art" (D 151). The import of the passage is that the process of skillfully utilizing the "regular patterns" of the various aspects of our surrounding conditions is an "art."

55. 然後隨而命之。同則同之。異則異之。. . . 知異實者之異名也。故使異實者莫不異名也。不可亂也，猶使異實者莫不同名也。. . . 推而別之。別則有別。至於無別然後止。(83/22/21–25; K: 22.2f; W 143–44; Graham 1989, 265).

56. 同じような状況のもとでは、天官は同じように作動し同じような作動結果をもたらす。(Okamoto 1986, 74–75). Note that Okamoto interprets the Chinese word *tong* 同 as *onajiyō* 同じよう (similar) rather than simply *onaji* 同じ (the same). The relevant passage reads: "What do we rely on to determine the similar from the different? I say, we rely on the senses. Generally speaking, when people experiences things of similar category and similar quality, their senses regard the thing similarly." 何緣而以同異。曰。緣天官。凡同類同情者。其天官之意物也。同。(83/22/15–16; K: 22.2c; W 142).

57. 心に徴知（知る）の機能があり、耳目鼻口形の五官には感覚という機能がある。外界の事象は五官によってキャッチされ、その信号が心に送られる。心ではその信号が何を意味するかを判断する、と荀子は考察している。(Kodama 1992, 394). Cf. "According to the *Zhengming* chapter, names are necessary in order to differentiate actual similarities and differences. And the basis on which these are established is taken to be perceptions of the senses and the cognition of the mind." 「正名篇」によれば、名は現実の異同を弁ずるために必要で、これを制定する根拠は五官の知覚と心の認識によるとする。(Abe 1964, 62).

as knowing the sign, indication, or symptom. Thus it does not seem to suggest any special knowledge beyond the phenomenal experience. That is, it does not seem to suggest that through the senses we are able to understand the ideal or essential nature of things, or anything in that vein. To describe how this faculty gets its data, Kodama uses the word *kyatchi* (キャッチ) from the English "to catch," which can mean "to get information on or about something," and has usages including the way a camera "catches" the action in a photo. But what is "caught" by the senses is the phenomena, not principles underlying the phenomena. The phenomena is caught as image, sound, smell, taste, and shape, and the heart-mind must then makes judgments or decisions (J: *handan* 判断) regarding its meaning or significance (J: *imi* 意味)—and this is an interpretive process which depends in part on the purposes at hand.

Also, not all concepts and categories are equally dependent on immediate sense experience. And it is the more abstract categories, such as *junzi*, that are most important to Xunzi. In this type of case it is particularly clear that the process of categorization cannot be done automatically by the senses. Consider Okamoto's remarks regarding Xunzi's view of names of social phenomena:

> What kind of conduct will be taken as what degree of high merit, and what kind of prize will the person who does this action receive? While holding the various ceremonies, what kind of expression is materially fitting? There must be mutual agreement among people regarding these matters (sometimes, as a matter of fact, this mutual agreement might be a one-sided coercion). It is after this mutual agreement on the object, that the mutual agreement regarding the name has meaning. If there is no mutual agreement on the object, the object doesn't exist.[58]

In other words, at least for some objects, not only are the boundaries of the object dependent on mutual agreement, such agreement is a prerequisite for the object to exist at all. Watson's translation of the following passage assumes a different view: "[T]he wise man is careful to set up the proper distinctions and to regulate names so that they will apply correctly to the realities they designate. In this way he makes clear the distinction between eminent and humble and discriminates properly between things that are the same and those that are different" (W 142). This translation seems to imply that some things really are the same, and they thus represent the objective kinds that proper names are supposed to identify. I read the passage as follows: "Therefore the wise make distinctions and fashion (*zhi* 制) names, using them to identify objects. In this

---

58. どんな行為がどの程度に高い勲功とされ、その行為者はどんな褒賞を受けるのか。さまざまな儀礼をとり行うにあたって、物的にどのような表現が適当か。こういうことについて、人びとの合意がなければならない（時として、事実上は、合意は一方的な強制であるかもしれない）。実についてのこの合意の後に、名についての合意が意味を有するのである。実についての合意がなければ、実が存在しないのである。(Okamoto 1986, 66).

way noble and base are made clear, and things that are similar are distinguished from those which are different."[59]

The key difference between the two translations is that the former takes there to be a single ultimate pattern and the latter allows for a number of patterns. On the latter reading a choice is made. The sage, considering the purposes relevant to the distinction, and focusing on the patterns relevant to those purposes, chooses to group things that are similar with respect to the selected patterns. As Cua points out: "[C]lassification in general depends on similarities adjudged to be important for the purpose at hand. . . . This point appears quite clear in Xunzi's remark that 'just as there are no laws (*fa*) that can stand by themselves [without men who carry them out], there are no classes (*lei*) that can by themselves be applied'" (1985, 46; brackets in original). One looks for patterns in the matter at hand such that picking out those patterns in particular ways is useful for influencing people to behave in a way that conduces to social harmony. As Yearley explains it, "Xunzi's emphasis on the importance of ideas obsessing people arises from his view that language forms attitude, action, and emotion. He thinks that our ideas control our perceptions and actions. Objects in the world draw us because of our ideas about the world or our perspective on it; even our 'spontaneous' desires are reinforced or diminished by the ideas we hold" (1980, 470). Xunzi is keenly aware of the perlocutionary force of language.

3.4. Naming: The Ruler's Prerogative?

If, on Xunzi's view, the distinctions and categories delineated by naming are human constructs, rather than "natural divisions," who is responsible for assuring the adequacy of the naming process (*zhengming*)? One interpretation is that Xunzi takes it to be the prerogative of sage kings to set the terms of discourse, for their clear-mindedness and lack of bias uniquely equips them to make sagacious judgments. Makeham puts it this way: "The kingly prerogative to decide how objects should be tailored and the resulting distinctions fixed as names, meant that for Xun Qing [Xunzi], consensus regarding a term's usage came after the king had decided what should be named and how" (1994, 59).

This is not to say that kings decide arbitrarily when they set terms. They have social aims, and must determine whether their distinctions will further those ends given the propensities of their circumstances. A ruler cannot command that his distinctions will be productive. Some distinctions will serve better than others. Thus, a king must be careful how he decides.

But the naming process, for Xunzi, is more complicated than simply a top down imposition, where naming conventions are the dictates of a wise king

---

59. 故知為之分別制名以指實。上以明貴賤。下以辨同異。 (83/22/14; K: 22.2b; W 142). The underlying metaphor of the character *zhi* 制 is "to cut out cloths," thus "to fashion" (*zhi* 製) (see GSR: 335a–b). Its meanings include: make, institute, stipulate, establish, regulate, and govern.

alone.[60] After all, Xunzi himself was no king, yet he strove to affect the moral agenda through the *zhengming* process. The same is true of Confucius, as we saw earlier. The simple assertion that naming is the king's prerogative is inadequate. Even if Xunzi considered himself a sage, in terms of the objective hierarchical social structure he was still just a scholar, albeit a wise one, who wished to have an influence.

Recall a passage quoted earlier: "The wise make distinctions and set terms, using them to identify actual objects."[61] This may be interpreted as discussing the "wise among rulers," still indicating that it is the ruler's prerogative. However, in a Confucian system, while an authoritative king clearly sets the moral tone, his main function was to promote the worthy, filling the ranks of government with people who possess the moral and intellectual qualities that make them competent to participate in achieving, maintaining and enhancing harmonious social conditions. Rosemont goes as far as to say, "Xunzi's ruler has one major political function to serve, namely, the appointment of the officials who will otherwise manage the state's affairs" (2000, 22).[62] Thus, in determining conventions the ruler would likely seek recommendations from those most capable, in this case, "the wise." While it is the ruler's *responsibility* to see to it that names are attuned, the wise ruler is first and foremost one who surrounds himself with wise advisors. Xunzi quotes a traditional saying, "Recognizing the worthy is called enlightenment."[63] It turns out to be the role of the exemplary person, more than anybody else, to influence terminology positively. "Exemplary people apply patterns (*li* 理) to earth and nature. . . . If there were no exemplary people, nature and the earth would not be patterned."[64]

---

60. Analogous claims are made about the kingly imposition of ritual. For example, Masayuki Sato writes, "[W]hether *Li* was conducted in the central government or local governments, *Li* as a political method was expected to emanate from rulers and be relayed to his subordinates" (2003, 418). Like the top-down account of naming, this account of the formation of *li* is also an oversimplification. See the next chapter for more on *li*, ritual propriety.

61. 故知者為之分別制名以指實。 (83/22/14; K: 22.2b; W 142).

62. In other words, "Xunzi's monarch was to reign more than to rule" (Rosemont 2000, 22). At least it can be said that the ruler had a fairly limited number of important things to do. Xunzi writes: "With care, he recruits, selects, and reviews scholar officials of talent. He encourages them with awards and praise, and curbs them with the prospect of severe punishment. He chooses those scholar officials who know how to take care of business, and employs them to carry out the affairs of state. By this means ample stocks will accumulate, sufficient for both useful things and adornments." 安謹募。選閱材伎之士。然後漸賞慶以先之。嚴刑罰以防之。擇士之知事者使相率貫也。是以厭然畜積修飾。而物用之足也。 (30–31/9/114–16; K: 9.19b; W 53; D 147–48). Note: This is not a description of a True King, but of a second best type, an overlord (霸 *ba*). Here we see Xunzi's concession to the legalists that they are capable of a certain degree of, and certain kinds of, success in governance.

63. 知賢之謂明。 (79/21/20; K: 21.3; W 125).

64. 君子理天地。 . . . 無君子則天地不理。 (28/9/65–66; K: 9.15; W 44–45). Cf. "The *junzi* is the opposite of the small man. The broad-minded *junzi*, [respecting] the way things hang together, leads the way. The small minded, fearful of doing what is appropriate, are tied in knots. The intelligent categorize with clarity of mind and penetrating insight. The simple minded follow the model with uprightness and honesty." 君子小人之反也。君子大心則 [敬] 天而道。小心則畏義而節。知則明通而類。愚則端愨而法。 (7/3/16–17; K: 3.6). Cf. also, "The way is not the way

Also, consider the role of remonstration 諫 (*jian*), an important and enduring signature of the Confucian governmental structure.[65] The ruler is not an infallible authority. "Tradition has it: 'One should follow the way, not follow one's lord.'"[66] As further evidence that Xunzi did not take the ruler's judgment to be the final word, consider his advice to generals: "There are three instances in which [a general] is not subject to the commands of his lord. Though he may be put to death, he cannot be made to take a position that is untenable. Though he may be put to death, he cannot be made to attack where he will not win. Though he may be put to death, he cannot be made to deceive the common people."[67] The exemplary person may be considered to be in an analogous position. When there is a severe conflict between the ruler's orders and what would be appropriate, the exemplary person follows the way, not his lord.

In fact, those who have made themselves authoritative through study and moral training have duty to engage the ruler on moral matters. As David Hall and Roger Ames point out, "Scholars, teachers, and intellectuals within their respective societies, as well as members of the world community, may then [when culturally informed] take up the duty of remonstrance" (1999, 155). Xunzi writes: "When a ruler is involved in schemes and affairs which go too far, and one fears they will endanger the state, high officials and senior advisors are able to approach and speak to the ruler. Approving when one's advice is used and leaving when it is not is called 'remonstrance.'"[68] Xunzi recognizes rulers do

---

of *tian* 天, neither is it the way of the earth. It is that by which the people are lead; it is the path of the exemplary person." 道者非天之道。非地之道。人之所以道也。君子之所道也。(20/8/24; K: 8.3). And also cf. "The exemplary person is certain to make discriminations. Everyone likes to talk about what they find to be felicitous (*shan*), but the exemplary person does this extremely well." 君子必辯。凡人莫不好言其所善。而君子為甚焉。 (14/5/53; K: 5.9 & K: 5.6). There seems to be layers of meaning here. Everybody is "fond of talking about what they are good at" (好言其所善), and the exemplary person is very good at making distinctions. But also the exemplary person is fond of and exceptional at talking about what it means to be *shan* 善, to be morally adept.

65. Cf. "A principle characteristic of Confucianism as a political vision is its stress upon the duty of 'remonstrance (*jian* 諫).' the mutual obligations of rulers and ministers require that the latter are expected to behave not only as functionaries mediating decrees of the rulers, but as responsible advisors, as well" (Hall and Ames 1999, 154). See K: 29.2–3.

66. 傳曰。從道不從君。 (50/13/19; K: 13.2).

67. 所以不受命於主有三。可殺而不可使處不完。可殺而不可使擊不勝。可殺而不可使欺百姓。 (55/15/51–52; K: 15.1e; W 66).

68. 君有過謀過事。將危國家。殞社稷之懼也。大臣父兄有能進言於君。用則可。不用則去。謂之諫。 (50/13/12–13; K: 13.2). In reference to this passage Knoblock quotes the *Liji*: "It is a matter of ritual for men who are ministers not to make a display of remonstrance. One should remonstrate up to three times, and if one's advice is not taken, then one should flee" (Knoblock 1990, 325 n11; *Liji*, "*Quli*," Knoblock's translation). Cf. "King Wen took note of the fate of Zhou of Yin, and thus took control of his heart-mind and governed it cautiously, this way he was able to employ Lü Wang for a long time and not lose the way in his personal conduct." 文王監於殷紂。故主其心而慎治之。是以能長用呂望而身不失道。 (79/21/12–13; K: 21.2; W 123). Watson interprets *yong* 用 (to use, employ) as "to benefit from the good advise," which seems to be apt in this context. A similar account is given of Cheng Tang employing Jie of Xia. Jie and Zhou Xin, on the other hand, are said to have failed to recognize the merits Guan Longfeng and Qi, the prince of Wei, respectively. See K: 21.2.

not reason in a vacuum. They are, and ought to be, influenced by those around them.

However, Xunzi is also concerned that a constructive agenda may be undermined if external opposition arises and publicly contradicts the "party line." The traditional form of critique in the Chinese tradition was not confrontational. Rather, disagreements with the ruler were raised in accordance with rules of propriety. Xunzi lays plain the criteria for a constructive discussion as follows:

> Do not answer those whose questions are crude and insubstantial. Do not question those whose answers are crude and insubstantial. Do not listen to those whose explanations are crude and insubstantial. Do not engage in discriminating discourse with those of contentious spirit. If they have arrived where they are via the *dao*, only then engage them. If they have not, avoid them. Thus, if they respect ritual propriety only then can one speak meaningfully with them about the direction of the way. If their disposition is considerate only then can one speak meaningfully with them about the patterns of the way. If their demeanor is deferential only then can one speak meaningfully with them about transmitting the way.[69]

It is not that there is only one moral path and that the ruler has access to it, but that in order to preserve the value of solidarity, there are limits to the ways in which articulation of competing moral conceptions may be expressed. Observance of deferential ritual formalities is indicative of cultural attainment, qualifying one for having a contributing voice in the discussion of the way.

Turning to a different but related issue, it has been suggested that Xunzi's philosophy may be criticized for serving only the interest of the elite. Hansen sarcastically remarks, "[Xunzi] simply assumes the authority and interests of the ruling class. He all-too-frequently starts his arguments from the *obviously* correct and cultivated sensibility of the *junzi* (superior man)" (1992, 312; emphasis in original).[70] While it is possible for Xunzi's views to be appropriated by an unworthy elite for self-serving purposes, there are a couple problems with Hansen's charge. First, it seems to equate the authority of the ruling class with that of the *junzi*. Second, it lumps together the very different considerations of *authority* of a group on the one hand, and the *interests* of that group on the other. Insofar as the claim is that Xunzi attributes a large degree of authority to the *junzi*, this is quite accurate. But we must keep in mind that a *junzi* is not merely a person of high station, but one worthy of such responsibility. Xunzi

---

69. 問楛者。勿告也。告楛者。勿問也。說楛者。勿聽也。有爭氣者。勿與辯也。故必由其道。至然後接之。非其道則避之。故禮恭而後可與言道之方。辭順而後可與言道之理。色從而後可與言道之致。(3/1/39–42; K: 1.12; W 21). Cf. K: 14.1.

70. Cf. "The absolutist Xunzi takes the authority of the *junzi* (gentleman) and the political leader for granted. Their choices are the unquestioned standard of *shi* (this:right) and *fei* (not this: wrong)" (Hansen 1992, 309).

does not merely "assume" that *junzi* are authoritative. Rather, having developed
the sensibilities that qualify one to be authoritative is a good part of what it *means*
to be a *junzi*.[71] *Zhengming* would require that those in authority be authoritative.
By suggesting that the *junzi* acts out of a narrow self-interest, Hansen implies
that Xunzi is using *"junzi"* in an arbitrary and even immoral way.

The Confucian *junzi*, being interested in what is appropriate rather than
what is profitable, is not (at least in theory) self-interested. And, whether the
ruling class is authoritative depends on whether or not the king surrounds himself with morally cultivated people and aspires to such cultivation himself. By
placing authority in the hands of the cultivated, Xunzi does not privilege their
interests, but rather offers a scheme which is designed to be in the best interest
of everybody. The ruler's care for the people is thought to have a stabilizing
effect, keeping the ruler happily in power. It follows that it is in the long-term
best interest of the ruler to take care of the people, and this aspect plays a part
in Xunzi's pitching his program to rulers.[72] But the beauty of the system is that
it is balanced, and is designed to be mutually beneficial.

In theory, positions of influence are open to people of any class, since the
junzi is thought to rise through the ranks by virtue of both moral and scholarly
achievement. As mentioned in the introduction, Xunzi writes: "Although one
may be a descendent of commoners, if one accumulates culture and learning,
is upright in personal conduct, and is able to devotedly apply oneself to the
observance of ritual propriety with a sense of appropriateness, such a person
should be brought up to the status of chief minister or high official."[73] Thus,
people achieve a status where influence on the moral agenda is possible by first
cultivating themselves. Through this process they become qualified to exercise
their growing influence with competence and compassion.

And, finally, even the common people play a role in the naming process, as
can be seen from a passage we encountered earlier (this time offering my own
translation):

> Names do not have intrinsic appropriateness. They are arranged by decree. Ar-
> rangements that are settled upon to the point of becoming customary are called
> appropriate. If something differs from the arrangement then it is called inappropriate.
> Names do not have intrinsic actual objects. By arranging the objects, we thereby

---

71. Cf. "[T]he Confucian idea of 'authority' entails indispensable moral and aesthetic content"
(Hall and Ames 1999, 158).

72. "If a ruler of the people desires ease and stability, there is nothing like fair policies and
loving the people. If he desires glory, there is nothing like exalting ritual propriety, and respecting
scholar officials. If he desires achievements and fame, there is nothing like esteeming the virtuous,
and employing the able in government. These are the crucial points of a ruler. If these three points
are properly dealt with, then all remaining matters will be properly dealt with." 故君人者。欲安
則莫若平政愛民矣。欲榮則莫若隆禮敬士矣。欲立功名則莫若尚賢使能矣。是君者之大節也。
三節者當。則其餘莫不當矣。(26/9/22–23; K: 9.4; W 37; D 125).

73. 雖庶人之子孫也。積文學。正身行。能屬於禮義。則歸之卿相士大夫。(9/26/3;
K:9.1; W 33).

name them. If the arrangement has become fixed and has succeeded in becoming customary, the term may be called the object's name.[74]

While those in high station have a particular responsibility regarding the generation and maintenance of effective terminology, if a term or corresponding distinction does not resonate with the common people[75] and thus fails to become customary it is found to be "inappropriate." A doctrine that involved harsh punishments for those who did not follow the king's imposed terms would be a legalist one, not a Confucian one. The Confucian would rather seek to persuade by convention and authoritative example.[76] The appropriateness of an attempt at persuasion is judged ultimately by whether it resonates with the people.

Also consider that the *Zhengming* chapter begins with a description of how the latter kings employed ready-made names,[77] following the Yin, the Zhou, and names fixed by ritual usage. This implies that names are both cumulative and change over time.[78] And, importantly, Xunzi writes here that for common names the latter kings followed established customs. In each case there was a legitimating authority that served to stabilize a widely shared terminology. For common names this legitimating standard was popular usage—what had taken root and become customary.[79]

The view that naming is the sole prerogative of sage-kings is unsatisfactory, as is the view that Xunzi's philosophy serves only the interest of the ruling class. Rather, the process of *zhengming* is better thought of as a complex negotiation

---

74. 名無固宜。約之以命。約定俗成謂之宜。異於約則謂之不宜。名無固實。約之以命實。約定俗成。謂之實名。 (83–84/22/25–27; K: 22.2g; W 144). Cf. Watson's and John Makeham's translations of this passage quoted earlier (section 3.2). Also note that the *shi* 實 of 約之以命實 is thought by some commentators to be an accidental addition. See Wang 1988, 420.

75. The character *su* 俗 explicitly refers to the lower of the common people.

76. "The exemplary measure themselves with a stretched cord. In their contacts with others they use a bow-frame. Because they measure themselves with a stretched cord, they may be taken as a model worthy of emulation everywhere. By using a bow-frame in their contact with others, they are thus able to be magnanimous and tolerant." 故君子之度己則以繩。接人則用枻。度己以繩。故足以為天下法則矣。接人用枻。故能寬容。 (14/5/47–48; K: 5.7).

77. This refers to "the ready-made names of the latter kings." 後王之成名 (82/22/1; K: 22.1; W 139). *Cheng ming* 成名 may also suggest that the skillful adoption of names is how the latter kings achieved (*cheng*) their fame (*ming*).

78. Note the similarity here with Confucius's discussion of the evolution of the rites in *Analects* 2.23: "The Yin dynasty was based on the rituals of the Xia, what was added and subtracted can be known. The Zhou dynasty is based on the rituals of the Yin, what was added and subtracted can be known. If there is a dynasty which inherits Zhou culture, although a hundred ages may pass, it can be known." 殷因於夏禮，所損益，可知也；周因於殷禮，所損益，可知也。其或繼周者，雖百世，可知也。

79. Cf. Hu Shih's interpretation of Xunzi's naming process: "Being an extreme humanist and always demanding historical evidence, Xunzi dismissed the mysterious origin of names and substituted for it a theory which derives the names from sense experience and mental activity. But he retained the view that names were first 'instituted' by acts of governmental power, although he did not deny that the later governments had the same power to institute new names and to *ratify* and rectify the *names that had arisen form time to time without governmental sanction*" (Hu 1963, 159; emphasis added).

between the ruler, the moral and intellectual elite, and the people. The goal is a morally efficacious language, though there is no assumption that the categories agreed upon represent a preexisting natural and moral taxonomy, or map precisely to a specific ontology. Thus, as this negotiation continues, names, and the concepts they indicate, are susceptible to constructive change. As we will see in the next chapter, an analogous account can be given for Xunzi's conception of *li* (ritual propriety 禮).

The Nature of
Ritual Propriety

4

In the preceding chapters I focused on the mutual relation between patterns and categories, and the manner in which morally efficacious concepts, as the product of intelligent patterning, are stabilized in language. I have thus far only briefly discussed the relation between *li* 理 as pattern and *li* 禮 as ritual propriety (section 2.3). In this chapter, I will focus on the concept of *li* 禮 (ritual propriety), showing that it can be understood as contingent and evolving, but not arbitrary—as it is tied to both tradition and contextual appropriateness. That is, I will offer a characterization of Confucian *li* as a rich and layered concept, as both grounded in tradition and yet open to change. At the same time, while elaborating on various aspects of *li*, I will challenge the view that, for Xunzi, the rituals of the sage kings were uniquely valid.

Li are pragmatic devices that give concrete form to vague ideals, and encourage and facilitate the development of virtues, that is, admirable character traits. They have some naturalistic basis in that they are justified in terms of their efficacy in creating and maintaining social conditions conducive to human flourishing, and in this human nature cannot be ignored. Nevertheless, they are neither determinate nor exclusive, for they are dependent not only on nature but also on the contingencies of their historical development. Further, they are context dependent, and fundamentally open to interpretation. They may be continually amended to better fit changing circumstances, as well as refined, but they are not approaching any specific end.

4.1. A Note on Xunzi's Religious Sensibility

Homer Dubs, a pioneer in the English-language study of Xunzi,[1] has contended: "Xunzi's chief interest is philosophical, and there is little, if anything, that can be called religious, in his writings" (1966a, xxi). It would be more appropriate to acknowledge that Xunzi's philosophy was deeply religious, but that his religious sensibility was wholly this-world centered.

Xunzi's concerns were practical. And yet, while he held a worldview that is

---

1. Dubs authored the first English book-length study of Xunzi, first published in 1927, which remains a useful introduction to Xunzi's philosophy. He also produced the first English translation of the most important chapters.

fundamentally humanistic, he nevertheless expressed a profound reverence for ritual that was entirely sincere. His conception of ritual propriety is situated in a worldview that may be called religious in the sense described by Jonathan Z. Smith: "What we study when we study religion is one mode of constructing worlds of meaning, worlds within which men find themselves and in which they choose to dwell. . . . Religion is a distinctive mode of human creativity, a creativity which both discovers limits and creates limits for humane existence. What we study when we study religion is the variety of attempts to map, construct and inhabit such positions of power [which enables people to influence their 'situation' and make life meaningful] through the use of myths, rituals and experiences of transformation" (1978, 290–91). In Xunzi's effort to construct a moral world, he emphasized *li* as a complex concept whose scope included ceremonial "rites" and norms of appropriate behavior as well as an attitude that makes certain actions in some sense sacred. *Li* were considered pragmatic devices (*wei* 偽)[2] that gesture at ideals, but not fixed or determinate ones. Robert Campany provides a good description of the practical functions of *li*: "[R]itual serves to train human desires, to express human emotions, to give structure and coherence to human society, to provide a total cultural habitat in which virtue and wisdom can flourish" (1992, 212).

However, too often scholars,[3] upon reading Xunzi's hyperbolic remarks in praise of *li*, attribute to him a view that is overly rigid and insufficiently subtle. The view they present has resonance with sensibilities that seek perfection, finality, and absolute truth. However, traditional Chinese thinkers did not generally hold a worldview that would easily support a rigid absolutism.[4] And Xunzi was no exception. In the course of this discussion of *li*, I will argue against the interpretations of several scholars who suggest that, according to Xunzi, the precise rituals established by sage kings of the past express the fixed and singularly correct solution to humanity's moral predicaments.

One of the benefits of reconsidering Xunzi's conception of *li* in this light is that it reveals an avenue for potential religious expression that would be unavailable to those who identify religion with forms of absolutism they cannot accept. At the same time, it may also address concerns held by those who find the notion of ritual too stifling. Further, if it is right that on Xunzi's view

---

2. I concur with Lao Siguang's assessment of *wei* as both embodied tradition, "inherited cultural accumulations," as well as something to which individual sages continuously make there own contribution. Indeed, the selection of which aspects of tradition to foster in one's own character development suggests these two aspects are inseparable. Lao writes, "Teachers and models, norms of ritual propriety and appropriateness, all are produced by sages. And, sages only then can both make great efforts (accumulating thoughts) of their own, and also inherit cultural accumulations (becoming accustomed to [existing] cultural constructs (*wei*) deliberately)." 師法禮義皆生於聖人。而聖人乃能自作努力 (積思慮)，又能承受文化成積 (習偽故) 者。(1968, 260).

3. In sections 4.3.2 and 4.3.3 below, I focus especially on the views of T. C. Kline, P. J. Ivanhoe, and Bryan Van Norden.

4. The claim that traditional Chinese thought generally is at odds with absolutism is supported by the work of A. C. Graham, Roger Ames, Nathan Sivin, Joseph Needham, and Tang Junyi.

rituals reached their perfect and ultimate form in the rites of the Zhou kings, then the study of Xunzi's thought would be merely an exercise for our curiosity, for nobody would take the idea of a return to these particular ritual practices as a serious and viable course. However, if *li* are understood as ritualized norms of propriety that evolve in communities in response to existing condition and concerns, then the study of this process and its effects, to which Xunzi has provided valuable insights, may be of no small value.

4.2. Confucian *Li:* Code or Disposition?

In our effort to understand *li*, we would do well to reflect on a provocative statement made by Confucius in *Analects* 12.1: "Yan Hui asked about *ren* [the Confucian ideal]. Confucius responded, 'Practicing self restraint and returning repeatedly to *li* is the way to become *ren*. . . .' Yan Hui asked, 'May I inquire about its specific details?' Confucius replied, 'Don't look in a way which is not *li*, don't listen in a way that is not *li*, don't speak in a way that is not *li*, don't move in a way that is not *li*.'"[5] Since Confucius consistently tailored his advice to the needs and level of the person with whom he was speaking, and since Yan Hui was Confucius's most promising and astute follower, we can be confident that he was making an advanced and subtle point.

Commenting on this passage, Patricia Buckley Ebrey writes, "In the first part of this exchange, *li* could be taken to mean propriety or correct behavior in a moral sense. . . . The second part of this exchange shows that *li* was at the same time seen as conformity to an established or external code of behavior regulating every movement, glance, and word" (1991, 17). The point that Confucian *li* includes "propriety or correct behavior in a moral sense" is well taken. However, does the latter part of the passage really imply the existence of an external code with which one must conform in every movement? After all, as Ebrey also observes: "[L]i was also spoken of as a virtue, and scholars like Mencius often listed it with other virtues such as humanity, filial piety, and sincerity. In such cases *li* meant the ethical attitude that leads people to treat others with respect and deference[6]" (31). This aspect, which is too often neglected, is the more important aspect of *li* (and the ultimate goal of its formal aspect) on Confucius's reconstruction of *li*. Further, I would suggest, this meaning pervades even the most ceremonial cases—the fact that norms of proper behavior of various levels of specificity were included in the concept of *li* notwithstanding. When asked about the root of *li*, Confucius answers: "In the observance of ritual propriety (*li*) it is better to err on the side of frugality

---

5. 顏淵問仁。子曰：「克己復禮，為仁。. . .」顏淵曰：「請問其目。」子曰：「非禮勿視，非禮勿聽，非禮勿言，非禮勿動。」

6. It should be mentioned that, on the Confucian view, not everyone is entitled to the same respect and equal deference. The degree of respect and deference one deserves is a function of one's place and role in society.

rather than extravagance, and in mourning it is better to err on the side of grief rather than taking it too lightly."[7] Ames and Rosemont translate the last phrase as: "[I]t is better to express real grief than to worry over formal details" (1998, 83). In the passage in question, while it encourages acting according to *li* at every moment, no specific details are given, despite Yan Hui's asking for them. Is it not precisely the "ethical attitude that leads people to treat others with respect and deference" in every moment, rather than the following of some formalized code, that is being encouraged?

Catherine Bell describes a "sense of ritual" which may clarify what Confucius is promoting. "It is through a socially acquired sense of ritual that members of a society know how to improvise a birthday celebration, stage an elaborate wedding, or rush through a minimally adequate funeral" (1992, 80). She elaborates, "This 'sense' is not a matter of self-conscious knowledge of any explicit rules of ritual but is an implicit 'cultivated disposition'" (98). This is Confucius's *li*,[8] first and foremost—a point we should not lose sight of when we discuss *li*'s more formal aspects.

Echoing Confucius, Xunzi remarks, "One must not abandon ritual and propriety (*liyi*) for even a moment."[9] In this case Xunzi uses the compound *liyi*, ritual combined with a sense of appropriateness. His common pairing of these two concepts suggests a close relation between them, perhaps even an inseparability. Also, there is more context here to guide our understanding. For one thing, the statement is made as a summation of the importance of *yi*, rather than *li*. In addition, it is immediately followed by a description of relational roles, with the implication that ritual appropriateness is effectively fulfilling those roles. For example, "Being able to thereby serve one's parents is called being filial."[10] What is being encouraged, it seems, is the conscientious fulfillment one's various social roles and the responsibilities associated with those roles.

These roles form the exemplary person's ritualized world. *Junzi* never abandon *liyi* because, when they have sufficiently reformed themselves, they become at home in that world to the point where their "inner" feelings and "outer" expressions are in harmony. Xunzi writes: "When refined patterns and emotion are made the inner and outer of each other, that is, the exterior expression and the inner content, and when they proceed in parallel yet as a mixed composite, this is striking the middle course in ritual propriety. Thus, exemplary people . . .

---

7. 林放問禮之本。子曰：「大或問！禮，與其奢也。甯儉；喪，與其易也。甯戚。」(*Analects* 3.4).

8. In addition to *Analects* 3.4, quoted above, the following passages from the *Analects* support this view, especially when considered together: 1.13, 3.3, 3.26, 6.27, 9.3, 11.1, 11.26, 15.18, 16.5, 17.11, 17.13, 20.3. Similarly, Mencius at one point characterizes *li* as "having a reverent and respectful heart-mind." 恭敬之心，禮也。(*Mencius* 6A6). For relevant discussions of the meaning of *li* in early Confucianism, see Sato 2003, 194–208, and 212–14.

9. 不可少頃舍禮義之謂也。(29/9/74; K: 9.16a; W 46; H 259).

10. 能以事親謂之孝。(29/9/74; K: 9.16a; W 46; H 259).

dwell in this mean. Whether walking or running, hurried or in haste, they never leave it. It is their sacred world and palace."[11] Consider this in light of Smith's account of religion: "Religion is the quest, within the bounds of the human, historical condition, for the power to manipulate and negotiate one's 'situation' so as to have 'space' in which to meaningfully dwell" (1978, 291). If we accept such an open account of religion, then Xunzi is a religious philosopher, for it seems that this is precisely the role of ritual propriety in Xunzi's thought.

Xunzi sums up the section just quoted with a line from the *Odes*: "Ritual ceremony, completely according to the standard; laughing and talking, completely appropriate."[12] According to Yang Liang's commentary, "By quoting this he makes clear that, for the person who has *li*, every movement is fitting and appropriate" (Wang 1988, 358).[13] Indeed, Xunzi elsewhere explicitly states that *li* are not fundamentally the specific elements associated with ritual actions but are rather actions and interactions that answer to an aesthetic sense of what is fitting. He quotes a saying that can be found in *Analects* 17.11, "Surely saying 'ritual this, ritual that' is more than talk of jade and silk."[14] Xunzi comments, "If it is not timely and fitting, if it is not respectfully sociable, if it is not cheerfully enjoyed, although it may be beautiful, it is not ritual propriety."[15]

It should be noted that Ebrey recognizes this point: "Although Confucius spoke of conformity to *li*, he expected it to be tempered by reason and custom. Not every detail had to be exactly as in the prescriptions" (1991, 18). Still, she regards *li* as "external and objective codes of behavior." For example, she writes, "Chapter 10 of the *Analects* gives many examples of *li* treated as an external or objective code of behavior. The man who has mastered *li*, for instance, 'When saluting his colleagues he moves his hand to the right or left as needed, while keeping his robe even in front and behind. He quickly advances with dignity'" (Ebrey 1991, 17 n14; quoting *Analects* 10.3; Waley 1938, 146). While the living body of *li* is composed of social norms that may be legitimately viewed as external and in some sense objective, the idea of an external and objective *code* has an unnecessarily rigid ring to it. D. C. Lau uses the word "rules" rather than "code" to a similar effect: "The rites (*li*) were a body of rules governing

---

11. 文理情用相為內外表裡。並行而雜。是禮之中流也。故君子...處其中。步驟馳騁厲 騖不外是矣。是君子之壇宇宮廷也。 (72/19/38–40; K: 19.3; W 96; H 268).

12. 詩曰。禮儀卒度。笑語卒獲。此之謂也。 (72/19/42; K: 19.3; W 96; H 268).

13. 引此明有禮, 動皆合宜。

14. 禮云禮云。玉帛云乎哉。 (96/27/9–10; K: 27.11). While this precise quotation can be found in *Analects* 17.11, the *Xunzi* does not explicitly attribute it to a particular source. Masayuki Sato comments, "The aim of Confucius (or of the author of this passage) is to criticize a situation in which rituals have deteriorated into mere formalities. Therefore, it is not true that the early Confucians were merely professional ritual directors. Rather, they emerged on the historical stage as the interpreters of propriety in rituals according to the moral standards of that time. Indeed, what the early Confucians advocated was not blind adherence to ceremonial regulations, but the volitional practice of social custom on the basis of a person's moral values" (2003, 194).

15. 不時宜。不敬交。不驩欣。雖指。非禮也。 (96/27/9–10; K: 27.11).

action in every aspect of life and they were the repository of past insights into morality" (1979, 20).

Rather than strict rules, the formal aspect of *li*[16] is better thought of as involving norms of varying specificity, grounded in tradition, yet necessarily evolving as a result of individual appropriation over time. It may be that neither Lau nor Ebrey intend to convey anything very different from this.[17] But the language of rules and codes can be, at least, misleading. Worse, as we will see, others have taken this line of thought to the point of attributing an extremely inflexible view to Xunzi.

The passage cited by Ebrey, rather than describing a detailed code of proper behavior to be slavishly followed, may be better understood as containing a depiction of the graceful behavior of one person, namely, Confucius. In their translation of the *Analects*, Ames and Rosemont read nearly all of book 10 under this assumption. The first passage may serve as a representative example, "In Confucius' home village, he was most deferential, as though at a loss for words, and yet in the ancestral temple and at court, he spoke articulately, though with deliberation" (1998, 134). While his behavior stands out as a model, the description of it does not provide a regulation. Cua expresses it well: "particular piece of *li*-conduct displays a 'style of performance' which exemplifies a noteworthy manner of behavior. The slow and unhurried manner in which one eats one's soup, or the cautious way in which one carries oneself in executing a task, betrays a deliberate deportment. . . . And if it has moral import, it is an expression of a cultivated attitude or virtuous disposition which may uniquely reveal the actor's character" (1979, 382).

Is it not admirable conduct, as Cua suggests, rather than a fixed code that sets "standards of inspiration"? Again quoting Cua: "Arguably, Confucius's notion of *junzi* expresses the idea of paradigmatic individuals as exemplary embodiments

---

16. A. S. Cua distinguishes two functions of *li*, one instrumental and limiting, the other expressive and evaluative. He writes, "*Negatively*, as a set of procedures for regulating human intercourse, it directs attention to the problematic nature of man's basic motivational structure, that is, his natural feelings and desires, and its liability to conflict. . . . But *positively*, *li* has the function of nourishing or transforming man's basic motivational structure by way of inculcation of a regard for moral virtues and the development of moral character. A *li*-performance is here no longer a ritualized routine behavior, but a display of moral virtue or virtues relevant to the occasion. It is a moral performance" (1979, 380). These should be seen as two *functions* of *li*, not as two *kinds* of *li*. Indeed, Cua also makes a similar distinction in his analysis of the "delimiting function," "supportive function," and "ennobling function" of *li*. See Cua 1989, 114–223. The first two he considers to be regulative, and the third to be constitutive. However, it is not that some *li* are merely regulative while others are constitutive. They are all to some degree both.

17. The same may be said of Cua, who at times refers to *li* as a "ritual code," and yet he has a flexible understanding of what that means. For example, he writes, "[T]raditional ritual code is essentially a codification of ethical experiences based on *ren* and *yi*. Its relevance to the present, particularly in exigent situations, is a matter of reasoned judgment" (1998, 290). Further, on Cua's interpretation, "Ethical judgments . . . are not only liable to error, but also *revisable* in the light of our historical understanding of an ethical tradition and its prospective significance. In this respect, even if the mind (*xin*) is completely free from *bi* [obsession], its ethical judgments have only the status of plausible presumptions" (1993, 171).

of the spirit and vitality of the tradition. In addition to functioning in moral education, they also serve as living exemplars of the transformative significance of the ideal of the tradition, thus invigorating the tradition. Even more important, for those committed to tradition, paradigmatic individuals serve as points of orientation, as standards of inspiration" (Cua 1998, 241–42). That ritual prescriptions by themselves are insufficient can be seen in Xunzi's statement, "In learning, nothing is as useful as drawing near to the proper people. Rituals and music may be taken as models but they do not offer explanations."[18] Just as "a model cannot stand on its own, and categories cannot apply themselves,"[19] *li* requires interpretation in every performance. Thus a teacher is needed in order to give this interpretation concrete form. Nevertheless, the teacher's example must ultimately become a model of *how to interpret*.

We can gather from the depictions of Confucius in book 10, and throughout the *Analects*, that he was not one to take details lightly. Moreover, on Xunzi's account, "Every word, every subtle movement, may be taken as a model and pattern."[20] But what was the importance of detail in ritualized behavior? Rather than following a code in which details have been painstakingly perfected, Ebrey insightfully observes, "Thinking about the details of ritual provided a way to think about behavior and morality in general" (1991, 220). Or, as Smith remarks, "Ritual is, first and foremost, a mode of paying attention" (1987, 103). Xunzi comes close to making this point himself:

> It is asked: How can all of this [i.e., each person fulfilling their respective role appropriately] be accomplished at the same time? I say: By carefully examining *li*. The former kings of olden days paid careful attention to *li*, and thereby when traveling round the world their movements were always fitting. Exemplary people are reverent but not pressed, respectful but not bound. When poor, they were not tied in knots; when wealthy and honored, they were not arrogant. When they encounter changing circumstances, they carefully examine *li*. . . . The exemplary person's response to change is reasonable, and regularly provides benefits and success without causing confusion.[21]

This passage also exemplifies of how existing translations mislead readers into overly punctilious interpretations. Knoblock's translation of this passage says: "The Ancient Kings minutely observed [*shen* 審] ritual principles." The word "observe" is ambiguous in English. It can mean "to notice" or "pay special attention to," or it can also mean "to adhere to some standard," or "to comply

---

18. 學莫便乎近其人。禮樂法而不說。 (2/1/34; K: 1.10; W 20).
19. 故法不能獨立。類不能自行。 (44/12/2; K: 12.1).
20. 端而言。蝡而動。一可以為法則。 (2/1/31; K: 1.9; W 20; H 250).
21. 請問兼能之奈何。曰。審之禮也。古者先王審禮以方皇周浹於天下。動無不當也。故君子恭而不難。敬而不鞏。貧窮而不約。富貴而不驕。並遇變態。審之禮也。其應變故也。齊給便捷而不惑。 (45/12/21–25; K: 12.3).

with a rule (or something of like-nature)." The character *shen* means: to carefully observe or study and make clear, in the sense of to examine, discriminate, and judge. Thus, translating *shen* as "minutely observed" is not inaccurate so long as "observe" is understood in the first sense. But since the object here is *li*, something which may be taken as rule-like, "observe" here is likely to be understood in the later sense. Thus, the reader is misled into thinking that Xunzi is here claiming that rituals were adhered to in their every detail by the Ancient Kings, when the passage, in fact, asserts nothing of the sort.

4.3. The Status of Ritual in the *Xunzi*

4.3.1. Human Nature and the Origin of Ritual Propriety

Xunzi is most famous (or infamous) for his rejection of Mencius's view that human nature is good. "Original human nature is crude (*xing e*[22])," writes Xunzi, by which he means: we are born with a problematic set of desires and impulses,[23] and thus we need a means of reshaping our motivational structure in order to beautify it. He believed "ritual propriety" (*li* 禮) to be the best means to that end. But it is a means, we will see, which becomes an end in itself.

Xunzi's account of the origin of *li* and its relation to our problematic human nature is given at the beginning of his "Discourse on Ritual Propriety." He writes, "How did ritual propriety (*li* 禮) arise? I say: People are born with desires. If these desires are not fulfilled, [the object of desire] will surely be sought after. If this seeking has no measure or bounds, contention will be inevitable. If there is contention, then there will be chaos, and if there is chaos, there will be difficulty and impoverishment (*qiong* 窮). The ancient kings detested this chaos. Thus they fashioned (*zhi* 制) ritual and propriety (*liyi* 禮義),[24] and

---

22. The slogan *xing e*, often translated "human nature is evil," occurs repeatedly (and only) in the chapter by that name. Xunzi makes explicit his understanding of *xing*: "That which resides in people which cannot be learned and cannot be acquired through work is called *xing*." 不可學不可事而在人者謂之性。 (87/23/12; K: 23.1c; W 158). In another formulation he says, "What is so by virtue of birth is called *xing*." 生之所以然者謂之性。 (83/22/2; K: 22.1b; W 139). Thus it is our "original nature." The character *e*, however, does not mean "evil" in anything like the Christian sense. Sometimes it is translated, somewhat more adequately, with the bland word "bad." It is the opposite of *shan* (good, or morally adept) and of *mei* (beautiful, admirable). Xunzi's evaluation of original human nature is perhaps most accurately described as "crude" or "unadorned" (see section 5.1).

23. For Xunzi, our original desires and impulses are associated with our senses, for example, the eyes and ears are fond of colors and beautiful sounds (K: 23.1a, 23.2a; W 157, 160). However, desires are also situational, we desire warmth when we are cold, rest when we are weary, and food when hungry (K: 23.1e; W 159). Further, original desires are thought to include a general greediness (K: 23.1a, 23.2a; W 157, 161).

24. I have opted for the same translation as Robert Eno for *liyi*, "ritual and propriety," which I take as nearly synonymous with *li*, "ritual propriety." On Eno's view, "The compound is fundamentally a linkage of explicit conventional rules and a more abstract ethical notion, close to 'right.' The linkage is often understood as a way of enlarging the prescriptive range of ritual, allowing individuals to act according to what seems ethically right even if it is not in absolute

thereby made divisions that nurture (*yang* 養) people's desires and provide for their satisfaction."[25]

Xunzi believed that the Mencian conception of human nature—that human nature contained the sprouts of virtues—was dangerously misleading because it encouraged people to overlook the importance of ritual, study, and moral practice in the shaping their character. This compelled Xunzi to oppose Mencius in the strongest of terms on this point and to insist that ritual propriety was of central importance in assuring a harmonious society.

4.3.2. A Critical Review of Kline on Ritual Propriety

As I now begin a critical review of interpretations of the status of *li* in the *Xunzi*, it may be useful to start with a point of, at least partial, agreement. Describing the process of fashioning rituals in early times, Kline writes: "The early sages found themselves in a world in which there were already patterns that could be seen in the movements of the cosmos and the behavior of human beings and animals. Through their cognitive ability to perceive and understand these patterns sages were able to begin fashioning rituals and regulations that brought the human and natural orders into harmony with one another" (2000, 172). Kline refers here to the circumstance in which the "early sages" found themselves. To speak of "early sages" is appropriate, since there was never a "first sage."

Lau has remarked: "[I]t is never very clear whether in Xunzi's view one particular sage king invented morality or a number of sage kings invented it. It would be difficult to know what the other sage kings were responsible for, if only the first was responsible for the invention. It is equally difficult to see how a number of sage kings coming at fairly long intervals could have been jointly responsible for the invention" (2000, 218 n60). While this is a problem that has vexed many interpreters of Xunzi,[26] the conclusion that David Nivison suggests (but does not himself wholeheartedly embrace) seems right. That is, the invention of culture is a product that accumulates over time, a "(perhaps still continuing) *historical process*" (1996, 53).[27] When one abandons the assumption

---

accord with convention" (1990, 273 n71).

25. 禮起於何也。曰。人生而有欲。欲而不得。則不能無求。求而無度量分界。則不能不爭。爭則亂。亂則窮。先王惡其亂也。故制禮義以分之。以養人之欲。給人之求。(70/19/1–2; K: 19.1a; W 89).

26. This question can be traced back at least to Xu Ji (1028–1103), who wrote: "If all human nature in the world is bad, then Yao and Shun, Jie and Zhi also were all [equally] bad. This means that since there have been human beings, there has never been a single person whose nature was good. If this is so, then where do we get his rites and righteousness? Then men he calls sages—how do they become sages?" (Kasoff 1984, 29, Kasoff's translation).

27. On this model, he adds, "the positive moral order is a historical product, perhaps still unfolding, not final" (Nivison 1996, 53). Summarizing one of Nivison's points, Van Norden writes that Xunzi is torn between two positions, one of which is that "the Confucian tradition is the result of a process of historical 'accumulation.'" On Van Norden's view this position "makes it more mysterious how the sages managed to come up with that tradition in the first place" (1996, 6). This is not mysterious from the perspective I am suggesting Xunzi holds. The constructivist

(which we will see is commonly attributed to Xunzi) that "the invention" must be perfect, uniquely optimal, unchanging, and so on, Lau's problem disappears. The second alternative becomes unproblematic, that is, people (in particular "sages") over time are jointly responsible for the invention of constructive artifice (*wei* 偽) such as *li*.

Now, when Kline writes, "The early sages found themselves in a world in which there were already patterns," he is doubly right, for people have always found themselves in a world that was already patterned—in two senses. In one sense, there are regularities in nature, such as the seasons, which exist independent of our picking them out as salient. Also, one is inevitably born into a culture where these regularities are already *in some way*, and to some degree, parsed, explicitly distinguished, or if you will, "patterned." Hall and Ames have expressed the view that "[o]ne appropriates an always-interpreted world through language acquisition and enculturation, and then continues the historical process of world-making. Distinctions, as ad hoc conventions, are always contingent and performative. Thus, as a distinctly historicist thinker, Xunzi makes no appeal to transcendent principles or necessary distinctions" (1995, 208).

When Kline writes that the early sages were able to "perceive and understand these patterns" and on that basis "begin fashioning rituals and regulations," this could simply mean that from understanding the progression of the seasons, the life cycle, and so on, forms of behavior were developed that enabled people to live harmoniously with these forces. This seems both compelling and consistent with Xunzi's thought.[28]

Kline, however, apparently wishes to suggest something stronger than just this. He writes: "The Dao of human beings that is manifest in the ritual and music created by the sages constitutes not simply a pattern of interaction that

---

does not assume a unique solution at which the sages must arrive. There was always a tradition to build on, and there will never be a singular and final exhaustive set of maximally efficient categories or norms. The way of the sage kings sets a standard because it marks a high level of effectiveness. Xunzi is an advocate of building on the tried and true.

28. Xunzi writes, for example, "According with the progression of the four seasons, and apportioning the myriad things, widely benefits the whole world for no other reason than this: it achieves proper divisions and is appropriate (*yi*). . . . A ruler is good at grouping. If the grouping and the guiding discourse (*dao*) are mutually coherent (*dang*), then the myriad things all receive what is suitable to them. [For example] the six domestic animals all will get to grow to maturity, and members of all classes will live out their full life span." 故序四時。裁萬物。兼利天下。無它故焉。得之分義也。. . . 君者善群也。群道當則萬物皆得其宜。六畜皆得其長。群生皆得其命。 (29/9/72–76; K: 9.16a; W 46). Sugimoto Tatsuo comments, "The point is, people engaged in productive activity in accord with the conditions of the four seasons, and nothing other than this could bring forth the benefit of all people. This is precisely [due to] the social order and *liyi* (ritual propriety and appropriateness)." 要するに、人間が春夏秋冬の環境にしたがって、生産活動に従事し、万人の利益を生みだすことができるのは、ほかでもない。社会秩序と礼・義あればこそだ。 (Sugimoto 1996, 88). In other words, Xunzi maintains that what brings benefits to people is a sensible social order supported by ritualized norms appropriately attuned to the environment.

orders the state by keeping people out of conflict. It is not simply a prudential order. It is the proper set of practices and activities that bring human beings into harmony with their own natures as well as the patterns of the rest of the cosmos. The Dao is the moral order. It is the way in which human beings ought to pattern their actions" (2000, 165).

As an indication of how important he takes this thesis to be, Kline writes: "Although this belief in the Dao as the proper pattern of the moral order, as well as the order of the entire cosmos, rarely gets discussed at great length, it cannot be stressed enough for understanding why Xunzi believed that cultivation through ritual was both effective and necessary" (2000, 165). Clarifying the position in question he writes, "[Ritual] embodies not just *a* set of patterns, but *the unique* and most fully harmonious patterns of activity" (166; emphasis his). In support of this view he cites the following passage from Watson's translation: "A man without ritual [*li*] cannot live; an undertaking without ritual cannot come to completion; a state without ritual cannot attain peace" (4/2/9–10; K: 2.2; W 25).[29]

Notice that this passage suggests only that *li* of some sort are necessary, not that there is only one uniquely harmonious set of formal patterns. In fact, this passage occurs near the beginning of the "Improving Yourself" chapter and is preceded by the linking of ritual propriety to the practice of "impartial goodness" (*bian shan*). This is preceded by a discussion of such things as critical self-examination at the sight of someone else's good or bad behavior and discrimination between a true teacher and a flatterer. And it is immediately followed by the same ode we saw earlier in a different context: "Ritual ceremony, completely according to the standard; laughing and talking, completely appropriate."[30] Taken as a whole the conception of *li* depicted here seems rather open, almost to the point of meaning something like "the diligent exercise of sound and sincere judgment." As Arthur Waley long ago remarked: "[I]t was with the relation of ritual *as a whole* to morality and not with the *details* of etiquette and precedence that the early Confucians were chiefly concerned" (1938, 67; emphasis added).[31]

Also, consider the implication of the following passage with respect to Kline's position: "Embody respect with a truly sincere heart. Practice *liyi* (ritual and propriety) with the inner emotion of love for others. When traveling the world, although you may be surrounded by barbarian tribes, everyone will regard you

---

29. 故人無禮則不生。事無禮則不成。國家無禮則不寧。 (4/2/9–10; K: 2.2; W 25). Cf. *Mencius* 7B12, in which Mencius says, "Without *liyi* there will be disorder between superiors and inferiors." 無禮義，則上下亂。 Again, it seems only that *some* reasonably stable set of patterns of deference is required to sustain order.

30. 詩曰。禮儀卒度。笑語卒獲。此之謂也。

31. Note that *li* covers both matters of etiquette and morality. Indeed, Confucians make no clear distinction between the two. Rosemont writes, "To say, then, that an action is in accordance with *li* is to say that it is moral, *and* that it is civil, mannerly, customary, proper, and, in an important sense, religious" (Rosemont 1976, p. 466).

with esteem."[32] On the narrow view of *li* as a singular specific set of rituals, it is hard to reconcile the existence of barbarians with the idea that people need *li* to live. One may argue that barbarians, for Xunzi, are not *ren* (people). However, even with this possibility in mind, the view that *some* forms of *li* are necessary, rather than a privileged specific set, seems like the more plausible alternative. What would barbarians need to do in order to be considered "people"? Would they need to adopt the precise rituals of the Zhou kings just to attain this status? If this were the case, there would be virtually no "people" at all in Xunzi's time (not to mention our own time). *Li* in this passage, as in the one quoted by Kline, probably means appropriate displays of deference and social skills generally rather than any specific set of formalized behavior. Even barbarian tribes, if they are to survive, must develop some patterns of deference, and they are able to recognize such patterns even when they are exhibited in forms other than their own. Thus the point of Kline's passage becomes: some forms of *li*, considered in a broad way, are needed to form a stable society—a much more reasonable claim.

Further, this view of *li* is analogous to Xunzi's view of language. Recall Lee Yearley's observation (quoted in the introduction): "Xunzi's position on moral judgments parallels his position on language. He denies both that language's distinctions have an intrinsic appropriateness and that they convey some stable reality. But he joins those denials with the ideas that language is necessary and that some forms of language, given certain situations, are better than other forms of language for the creation of an orderly society and orderly people" (1980, 476). This could be said of Xunzi's view on the status of rituals as well, especially when viewed broadly. It is necessary that we fashion some devices that formalize behavior in a way that enables us to reform our problematic original nature such that we may live together in peace and harmony. While naming stabilizes constructive patterns in language, ritual propriety is an extralinguistic means to the same end, that is, to pattern the social world with moral efficacy.

Kline quotes two other passages from Watson's translation here as well: "No man who derides true principles [*li* 理 (patterns)][33] in his mind can fail to be led astray by undue attention to external objects. No one who pays undue attention to external objects can fail to feel anxiety in his mind. No man whose behavior departs from true principles can fail to be endangered by external

---

32. 體恭敬而心忠信。術禮義而情愛人。橫行天下。雖困四夷。人莫不貴。 (5/2/22; K: 2.6; W 27). If "barbarians" were able to differentiate rituals that represent the singular specific set of proper rituals (if there were such a thing) from some pretender set, they would be closer to sages than barbarians. More likely, this passage refers to a more general appreciation of appropriate and respectable behavior.

33. I would translate the phrase "No man who derides true principles" as "Those who make light of constructive patterns." In any case, what is doing all the work for Kline's interpretation here is Watson's translation of *li* as "true principles." Knoblock renders it as "rational principles" (K: 22.6d), and Y. P. Mei opts for "moral principles" (1951, 65). See chapter 2 for a discussion of *li* (pattern). See also Cua 1997.

forces. . . . In such a case, a man may be confronted by all the loveliest things in the world and yet be unable to feel any gratification" (W 154–55). And, "If he does not possess ritual principles, his behavior will be chaotic, and if he does not understand them, he will be wild and irresponsible" (W 162). These passages seem to be used in support of the statement that: "to go against the ritual patterns is to try to swim upstream against the Dao" (Kline 2000, 166). This much can be accepted. But the quotations seem also to be used to support the claim: "The patterns of activity set down in the ritual order of the sages provide the optimal patterns of human action in the world. Any deviation results in a loss of efficiency of one's own efforts" (166). I can see no reason to conclude this, even as the passages stand.

Nevertheless, it may be instructive to consider, briefly, the second passage. As I read it: "Without ritual and propriety (*liyi*), there will be chaos. If *liyi* is not understood, there will be confusion and contention."[34] This statement, which occurs in the *xing e* (Original Human Nature is Crude) chapter, is part of a discussion of the condition in which we are born. In that condition, not having our problematic desires and impulses curbed or shaped in any way, we tend toward wrangling and strife. The point is that we need some means of reforming our character, but there is no reason here to conclude that only the specific rituals of the sage kings would be effective.

In a similar passage, Xunzi writes: "People who lack a model are at a loss and uncertain. Those who have a model but do not understand its meaning are ill at ease. When one accords with the model and in addition has a profound understanding of its categories, only then will one's actions be congenial and cordial."[35] On Eric L. Hutton's translation: "If he has the proper model but does not fix his intentions on its true meaning, then he will act too rigidly" (H 256). As justification for Hutton's reading, one could cite Yang Liang, who comments that "'not knowing its meaning' means merely holding fast to the letter"[36] (Wang 1988, 33). The message is that *li* as a virtue is the mean between aimless confusion and punctiliousness.

4.3.3. Ivanhoe, Hansen, and Van Norden

Kline, however, is by no means alone in his view that Xunzi is speaking of a precise set of rituals that had already been perfected. In two influential articles, P. J. Ivanhoe has made claims such as, "Xunzi believed that the society worked out by the former sages provided the one and only way to a happy and flourishing world" (2000, 247 n9) and that only the "particular set of rituals and norms: those of Confucianism" could "provide an optimally satisfying life"

---

34. 人無禮義則亂。不知禮義則悖。 (88/23/35–36; K: 23.2b; W 162).
35. 人無法，則倀倀然。有法而無志其義則渠渠然。依乎法而又深其類。然後溫溫然。 (5/2/36–37; K: 2.10; W 30).
36. (志識也。) 不識其義，謂但拘守文字而已。

(240). His view is based on the notion that there is a design to the world and that the Confucian rites hold some privileged relation to it. He writes, "Xunzi believed the rites showed human beings the unique way to cooperate with heaven and earth for the fulfillment of all three, a way that realized a design inherent in the universe itself" (Ivanhoe 1991, 310; cf. Ivanhoe 2000, 240). Ivanhoe clearly suggests that for Xunzi the Confucian rites are singularly correct and unchangeable. He characterizes them as "unalterable patterns" (1991, 321), and as "immutable" (310), and suggests that Xunzi's ethics is "a form of ethical realism" (2000, 247 n10). As far as the development of rites, the process of evolution is over. "[Xunzi] clearly believed that the sages had brought the process to a successful conclusion and that the Confucian Way provided the unique solution which would be valid for all times" (1991, 318).[37]

Chad Hansen, in contrast, has a complex view including both conventionalist and absolutist elements. On the conventionalist side he writes, "[Xunzi] began to doubt any purely naturalistic basis for values. Values, he argued, were products of cultural tradition, not of nature. . . . He, like Zhuangzi, turned the tables on the antilanguage version of his school and celebrated the unavoidable conventionality of any scheme of values" (1992, 309). While I agree that Xunzi saw values as, at least in part, "products of cultural tradition," I do not endorse the radical conventionalist side of Hansen's interpretation of Xunzi. Values are not all equal, some—such as peace and harmony—are more compelling than others—such as wrangling and strife. Similarly, it is not the case that any ritualized mode of social interaction would be as good as any other. Xunzi recognizes rituals as contingent historical products, but he did not consider them arbitrary.[38] They are evaluated on their efficacy in creating and maintaining a stable and harmonious society.

It should be noted that Hansen sees the absolutist side of Xunzi as more basic. He writes, "But the other Xunzi—the political absolutist—also comes through even in philosophical sections. This theorist is an uncritical absolutist. He asserts the possibility of direct access to the correct *dao*" (1992, 309). Hansen continues, "[Xunzi's] absolutist conclusion . . . uses the doctrine of a privileged preconventional vantage point. . . . [S]ince he looks *outward* with this special mindset, he claims to read the correct *dao* in nature. . . . [T]he doctrine is not pluralism; it is absolutism." (310)[39]

---

37. See section 1.2.1 for more on Ivanhoe's view. Also, recall Paul Goldin's assertion (from section 1.3.1): "There is only one Way. The Sage Kings apprehended it, and their rituals embody it. There is no other Way, and no other constellation of rituals that conforms to the Way" (1999, 73). I took this to indicate a position similar to Kline and Ivanhoe. However, Goldin has indicated (citing Goldin 1999, 147 n. 47) that he "agrees that the rituals of the sages can be amended (or even ignored) as long as one follows the Way."

38. Cua observes, "*Li* as civility or decency expresses, so to speak, conventional wisdom. However, it is important not to consider the conventional character of formal prescriptions as altogether arbitrary in the pejorative sense. . . . Conventions may be criticized and revised" (1985, 11).

39. For a longer version of this quotation, and more on Hansen's view, see section 1.3.2.

In response to the conventionalist side of Hansen's interpretation, Van Norden writes, "As attractive as a conventionalist reading might be in some ways, numerous passages in the *Xunzi* demonstrate that this philosopher is an objectivist and 'monist' about ritual, music, the Way, and at least some aspects of language use" (2000, 120). And, he claims, "Xunzi is an objectivist about values. The practices of the ancient sage kings are, Xunzi holds, uniquely optimal for producing social organizations which are 'correct, well-patterned, peaceful, and well-ordered'" (122). He also writes, "Xunzi does hold that the Way had to be invented, but he holds (rather naively)[40] that the Way of the sage kings is the uniquely optimal way for structuring a society. Xunzi holds that this particular Way is the *one* that does best the many things which such schemes are supposed to do" (121; emphasis in original).

4.3.4. Ritual and Music, Unalterable and Unexchangeable?

In support of their positions, Ivanhoe and Van Norden both cite the following passage.[41] Burton Watson's translation reads: "Music embodies an unchanging harmony, while rites represent unalterable reason" (W 117). Ivanhoe's version, which is "adapted from Watson," is actually significantly different: "Music consists of unchanging harmonies; rites are unalterable patterns" (1991, 318 n). Watson's version is open to interpretation; since it is "reason" that is unalterable, on this reading, one may question whether there is only one fixed way rites could "represent" it.[42] Ivanhoe's reading closes off this possibility, since on his reading it is unambiguously the rites themselves that are declared to be "unalterable patterns." Van Norden's version is similar to Ivanhoe's, it reads: "Music is unalterable harmonies. The rites are unexchangeable patterns"[43] (Van Norden 2000, 120). Together Ivanhoe's and Van Norden's translations present

---

40. We ought to be cautious about rushing to the conclusion that Xunzi, who undisputedly possessed one of the greatest minds of the rich classical Chinese tradition, is simply naïve at the core of his doctrine.

41. Van Norden and Ivanhoe also both site this passage: "The Way is the proper standard for past and present" (Van Norden 2000, 120; cf. Ivanhoe 1991, 318; W 153). In addition, Van Norden's list of quotations also includes, "In the world there are not two Ways. The sage is not of two minds" (adapted from W 121). See sections 1.3.1 and 1.5 for detailed interpretations of these passages. Suffice it to say here that the point of the second passage is a practical one: having two competing moral doctrines (*dao*), Xunzi believes, is destabilizing. And, the gist of the first passage is that "*Dao* is proper *balancing*."

42. Knoblock's translation is also somewhat ambiguous. It reads, "music embodies harmonies that can never be altered, just as ritual embodies principles of natural order that can never be changed" (K: 20.3). What is it "that can never be changed," rituals or the principles of natural order that they embody? While this translation would seems to suggest that it both, one could understand it to say that it the principles of natural that are unchanging, while leaving open the possibility that the embodiment may be open to change. The Chinese text reads: 且樂也者。和之不可變者也。禮也者。理之不可易者也。 (77/20/33; K: 20.3; W 117).

43. Translating this phrase differently, Cua comments: "We are told, for example that '*li* is what reason cannot alter.' But to lay stress on this point without regard to other remarks on personal cultivation and the moral basis of social distinctions is to do a great injustice to Xunzi's ethics" (1979, 378).

both elements of the "fixed uniqueness" view discussed in chapter 1. The rites are fixed (unalterable) and represent a unique solution (unexchangeable with any other set of patterns). However, depending on how this passage is translated and interpreted, it does not necessarily imply a belief in a fixed set of specific and uniquely optimal rituals. Before suggesting an alternative reading, there are some general points I would like to make.

First of all, one must keep in mind that *li* is a broad category which includes detailed ceremonial procedures. As Ebrey observes, "In many contexts writers use *li* to refer to the rules for such details as the placement of objects during ceremonies, with no suggestion that they invested these details with great moral significance. This side of the polarity could also be expressed in the Chinese term *yi* [儀], 'form, etiquette, ceremony'" (1991, 31). It is this aspect of *li* that seems to be at issue here.

In addition, Confucius's position on changes to ceremonial practice may be helpful to consider. On the one hand, if a ritual called for a *gu* drinking vessel, then using some other vessel would not do (*Analects* 6.25). Once a rite is fashioned, a person performing the rite is not at liberty to casually alter it. Just as a particular tune fails to be that tune if you change the notes, a ritual ceremony fails to be that ceremony if you change the patterns. However, Confucius did allow for ceremonial rites to evolve and change. It always falls on the exemplary person to validate alterations. Recall Confucius's remark: "A hemp cap is called for by *li*, but nowadays a silk one is worn as a matter of frugality. On this matter I follow the common practice. To bow before ascending is called for by *li*, but nowadays people bow after ascending. This is arrogant. Although diverging from the common practice, I bow before ascending."[44] Regarding this passage Masayuki Sato explains:

> The term *li* in a narrow sense denotes obsolete regulations that had been indiscriminately followed from ancient times. Yet, in the time of Confucius various different social customs prevailed and their incongruity with the pre-existing regulations was recognized. In this passage Confucius does not overtly acknowledge the widely accepted social customs of his time as *li*. This implies that the early Confucians considered a person's own moral standard to be essential in deciding whether he would observe a customary regulation or not. In other words, the early Confucians started to question the appropriateness of blindly following social custom in their argumentative framework regarding ethical discourse. (2003, 194)[45]

---

44. 麻冕，禮也；今也純，儉，吾從眾。拜下，禮也；今拜乎上，泰也。雖違眾，吾從下。 (*Analects* 9.3).

45. Sato also notes that in the *Yanzi chunqiu*, "the author creates a fictitious dialogue between Yan Ying and Confucius who was questioned by his disciple about Yan Ying's violation of *li*. Yan Ying's explanation of this is that the procedure for *li* can be changed, suiting the actual requirement of the situation. According to the text, Confucius has been impressed by Yan Ying's insightful answer" (Sato 2003, 213; *Yanzi chunqiu* 5.21). The *Yanzi chunqiu* is thought to have

Confucius, by (in one case) following the change in custom, validates it because it has a rationale. Confucius's actions also illustrate the point that "ritual activities, *in their doing*, generate distinctions between what is or is not acceptable ritual" (Bell 1992, 80; emphasis mine).[46]

Analects 2.23 also implies a view of *li* as evolving. There, Confucius says: "The Yin dynasty was based on the ritual patterns (*li*) of the Xia, what was added and subtracted can be known. The Zhou dynasty is based on the ritual patterns of the Yin, what was added and subtracted can be known. If there is a dynasty which inherits Zhou culture, although a hundred ages may pass, it can be known."[47]

I expect Xunzi's position is not different from that of Confucius in this regard. As we already noted, Xunzi's common pairing of *li* with *yi* (appropriateness) suggests that he took the exercise of ritual propriety as inseparable from the use of a sophisticated sense of what is appropriate for the circumstances. Further, that Xunzi believed in a living tradition is evident from his statement: "If true kings were to arise, they would certainly revitalize old names and create (*zuo*) new ones."[48] The Japanese scholars Abe Yoshio and Murase Hiroya agree that for Xunzi *li* can legitimately evolve. Abe writes, "At any rate, since the authority of these later kings is something that one should recognize as a projection of the former kings, one can acknowledge that for Xunzi the new *li* established by the later kings have the same dignity as the *li* of the former kings."[49] And, Murase reasons, "Based on the accumulation of thought and experience, and having considered the actual situation, sages established norms of ritual propriety (*liyi*). Assuming this, if norms of ritual propriety, which were established in this way, lose their compatibility with the actual situation due to a change of circumstances, then they may always be modified by the same procedure, and one would expect no objection."[50]

---

been compiled from the writings of the Jixia Academy, of which Xunzi was a prominent member. See Sato 2003, 211–17.

46. *Li* may be thought of as being continuously negotiated through action in the following sense: "[O]rdinary actors find themselves in a world of practical actions having the property that *whatever* they do will be intelligible and accountable as a sustaining of, or a development or violation, etc. of, some order of activity. This order of activity is, as Garfinkel puts it, 'incarnate' in the specific, concrete, contexted and sequential details of actors' actions. . . . It is through these same properties that the actors' actions, to adapt Merleau-Ponty's phrase, are condemned to be meaningful" (Heritage 1984, 110; emphasis in original). However, not everybody's actions have equal weight.

47. 殷因於夏禮，所損益，可知也；周因於殷禮，所損益，可知也。其或繼周者，雖百世，可知也。 (*Analects* 2.23; cf. Ames and Rosemont 1998, 81).

48. 若有王者起。必將有循於舊名。有作於新名。 (83/22/11–12; K: 22.2a; W 141).

49. いずれにせよ、荀子はこの後王の権威は先王の投影として承認すべきだというのだから、後王によって制定される新礼は、先王の礼と同等の尊厳を有するものと認められる。 (Abe 1964, 61).

50. 聖人は、思索と経験の蓄積をもとに、現実を考慮して礼義の規範を制定したのである。とすれば、かくて制定された礼義の規範も、もし状況の変化によって実情への適合性を失うならば、同じ手続きによっていつでも変更されて差しつかえないはずである。 (Murase 1986, 62).

As for *li* outside the scope of formal ritual, Xunzi goes as far as to assert that norms governing the most basic relations should be continually refined: "Distinctions which serve no purpose, and observations on matters which are not pressing, should be discarded and not mastered (*zhi*). But as for the appropriate relation between ruler and ministers, the close relations between father and son, and the respective roles of husband and wife, cut and polish them every day and do not give up."[51] The character *zhi* 治 has the meaning here of "to study" or "research extensively," thus "master." But we should also keep in mind a common meaning that covers the senses of: to order, to arrange, to manage, to govern.[52] Useless distinctions, in contrast to important ones, need not be attended to in the sense of extensively studied and also in the sense of being judiciously organized and continuously fine-tuned. That is, important distinctions, especially the roles, attitudes, and rituals that relate to the most important and paradigmatic relationships must be continuously evaluated, re-evaluated, shaped, brought into order, and maintained. As Ames and Rosemont contend, "Full participation in a ritually-constituted community requires the personalization of prevailing customs, institutions, and values. What makes ritual profoundly different from law or rule is this process of making the tradition one's own" (1998, 51). Confucians well recognize that: "Ritualization will not work as social control if it is perceived as not amenable to some degree of individual appropriation" (Bell 1992, 222).[53]

So far I have argued merely that Confucius allows for rituals to change, that Xunzi elsewhere seems to allow it, that it would make his position on ritual propriety consistent with his position on names, and that it makes better sense theoretically. But, perhaps, Xunzi is not a loyal follower of Confucius, he is inconsistent, and his theory is unsophisticated. Before we draw those conclusions, let's consider if the passage in question could be read differently.

Graham's translation of the passage reads as follows: "'[M]usic' is the un-alterable in harmonising, 'ceremony' is the irreplaceable in patterning. Music joins the similar, ceremony separates the different" (Graham 1989, 261). Here both music and ceremony are active, they are establishing standards, rather than conforming to them. Though unconventional, one must admit that Graham's

---

51. 無用之辯。不急之察。棄而不治。若夫君臣之義。父子之親。夫婦之別。則日切瑳而不舍也。 (64/17/37–38; K: 17.7; W 85).

52. Sato provides the following useful characterization of *Zhi* 治: "As a verb, it means 'to deal with well' (*zhisang* 治喪, *zhiqi*, 治棲 *zhiqi*), 'to control' (*zhishui* 治水) or 'to rule' (*zhiren* 治人, *zhiguojia* 治國家, *zhitianxia* 治天下). With this nuance, moral acts such as *liyi* ([the sense] of respectfulness and righteousness) could be *zhi*-ed (奚暇治禮義哉) [*Mencius* 1A7]" (2003, 120–121 n92).

53. Cf. Confucius's comment in *Analects*, 2.3: "Lead them with legalistic government, keep them in order with punishments, and the common people will avoid trouble but have no sense of shame. Lead them with *de* (charismatic virtue), keep them in order with *li* (ritual propriety), and they will develop a sense of shame and furthermore will reform themselves." 子曰：「道之以政，齊之以刑，民免而無恥；道之以德，齊之以禮，有恥且格。」 The notion of reforming oneself implies personal appropriation.

reading does a better job than the standard reading could in revealing a link with the second sentence—harmonizing is joining together, while patterning is making distinctions.[54] Just as the passage "people cannot live without *li*" does not imply that there is one specific set of rituals without which people cannot live, but rather that some form of patterning appropriate behavior is necessary for any society to survive (see section 4.3.2), this passage can be taken to assert there is there is no substitute for ritual propriety; it is an invaluable and irreplaceable mode of patterning a moral world. However, this is not to deny that Xunzi thought the rites developed by the sage kings were particularly good, and that he would encourage people to follow them.

4.3.5. *Ritual Propriety and the Order of the Cosmos*

In support of their above mentioned views, Van Norden and Ivanhoe both also cite the following passage, offering Watson's translation:

> Through rites Heaven and earth join in harmony, the sun and moon shine, the four seasons proceed in order, the stars and constellations march, the rivers flow, and all things flourish. . . . When they [i.e., the rites] are properly established and brought to the peak of perfection, no one in the world can add to or detract from them. (Van Norden 2000, 120; cf. Ivanhoe 1991, 317; W 94)

Rosemont has warned against making too much of this passage. He writes, "[It] is the only one of its kind, and is flatly incompatible with those other of Xunzi's writings in which the sage-kings are praised for having *produced* the *li*. . . . Indeed, a good case could be made for maintaining that it was partially *because* they were man-made that Xunzi held the *li* in such high esteem" (1971, 212; emphasis in original). Rosemont cites Derk Bodde, who writes:

> The mystical tone of this passage, however, accords poorly with Xunzi's usual humanistic outlook. Indeed, at the very beginning of the same chapter in which it appears (Dubs, p. 213), Xunzi gives an entirely rationalistic explanation of the origin of the *li*, saying that they were originally instituted by the early kings in order to put an end to human disorder. On the other hand, the passage is reminiscent of certain metaphysical interpretations of the *li* found in such Confucian compilations as the *Liji*, or Book of Rites.[55] As a matter of fact, it happens to be one of several passages in the *Xunzi* which also appear almost verbatim either in the *Liji* or the closely analogous *Dadai Liji*. The thesis has already been advanced, on grounds

---

54. Understood in this light, the passage may be taken as another example of how Xunzi tends to think in terms of mutually supportive structures rather than foundations. As Masayuki Sato describes it, "[L]i and music are not only complementary, but also indispensable to each other: music needs *li* to settle all different factors into order; *li* needs music to make this order harmonious" (2003, 366). See also Cook 1997.

55. Bodde cites Fung 1952, 343–44.

other than those given here, that all or most of such passages do not actually come from Xunzi's hand at all but have been incorporated at a later time into the work now bearing his name from these ritualistic texts, rather than the other way round as traditionally assumed. (Bodde 1953, 78 n27)

These considerations notwithstanding, let's assume the passage is genuine. I offer a slightly extended version:

> The earth and sky accord with each other according to *li*. The sun and moon, by *li*, shine [in alteration], just as the four seasons proceed in order, and the stars traverse the sky. The rivers and streams flow according to patterns of *li*, and the myriad things flourish. Likes and dislikes are moderated by *li*, and pleasure and anger thereby suit the circumstances. Through *li* subordinates become deferential and superiors become insightful. Though the myriad things transform, they do not bring disorder. Not to concentrate on *li* would be a cause for sorrow. Has not ritual propriety reached great heights (*zhi* 至)? Establishing and exalting it and making it the ridgepole, nothing in the world can add to or subtract from this.[56]

The character *zhi*, which means, "to arrive," on the one hand, and "the utmost," on the other, may be thought of in the combined sense of "to have reached a pinnacle." Watson chose to translate it as "peak of perfection," which seems to imply there was singular ultimate end. But it is an open question, relative to this passage, whether other great heights are possible.

Note that Knoblock's translation of the last part of the passage is superficially similar to the one offered above, but there is a significant difference. His version reads, "Establishing them and exalting them, make of them the ridgepole, and nothing in the world can add to or subtract from them." On this reading the *content* of the rites cannot be changed, whereas on the proposed reading the point is simply that there is nothing better or more important than making ritual principles the centerpiece of one's ethical development. The text just says "nothing [or 'no one'] can add or subtract." So either interpretation seems possible. A freer translation could read: "Nothing in the world is better than establishing and exalting ritual propriety, making it the ridgepole."

As for the sun and the moon, the elegance and orderliness of the movements of the heavenly objects are a fitting metaphor for the aesthetic component of *li*, as in the following passage: "In the heavens there is nothing so bright as the sun and the moon. . . . Among people there is nothing so bright as ritual and propriety. If the sun and the moon were not high, their light would not shine with fiery awesomeness. . . . If ritual and propriety are not applied in a state,

---

56. 天地以合。日月以明。四時以序。星辰以行。江河以流。萬物以昌。好惡以節。喜怒以當。以為下則順。以為上則明。萬物變而不亂。貳之則喪也。禮豈不至矣哉。立隆以為極。而天下莫之能損益也。(71/19/26–29: K: 19.2c; W 94).

its achievements and due fame will not be clearly apparent."[57] While Xunzi's veneration of *li* can have a cosmic tone, he recognizes the object of his esteem as intelligently constructed "artifice," that is, the product of conscious activity (*wei* 偽).[58] And though he regards the development of ritual propriety as an unparalleled cultural achievement, in both beauty and significance, culture is at the same time a work of art always in progress. As Abe observes, "This theory of *li* being made by the sages does not amount to an explanation of the ultimate origin of *li*, but we can recognize the sages as formulators of *li* that have been formulated along with the times."[59]

4.4. Mourning and Universalism

There are other passages that could be cited in support of more rigid views of *li* like those held by Ivanhoe, Van Norden, Kline, and others. One passage in particular stands out as requiring comment: "What is the three year mourning period? I say: It is balancing the emotions and establishing refined patterns (*wen* 文). By doing so it adorns society and provides a venue for distinguishing the intimate and the distant, as well as the eminent and the humble. It can neither be increased nor decreased. Thus it is said that it is a method which ought not to be changed without a suitable (*shi*) [alternative]."[60] This translation differs from other published translations. Knoblock, for example, follows Yang Liang in reading *shi* 適 (suitable, appropriate) as *di* 敵 (match, equal). Based on this alteration of the text, he translates the last line as "they are methods that are matchless and unchanging." On the one hand, this change may seem allowable since it appears to result in not much more than an echo of the previous sentence, which says, or seems to say, that the term of mourning can neither be increased nor decreased. However, despite the implications of taking that sentence literally, I'm not sure that the concluding line doesn't really amount to something closer to: "How great indeed is this method." After all, the reasons given, while providing a reasonable defense of the process, do not justify the claim that twenty-five months[61] is always an exactly perfect time period. Of course, his argument was never intended to be a deductive proof, but rather a largely rhetorical defense. However, if the argument is considered in such

---

57. 在天者莫明於日月。... 在人者莫明於禮義。故日月不高。則光暉不赫。... 禮義不加於國家。則功名不白。(64/17/40–42; K: 17.9; W 86).

58. See Cua 1979 for a discussion of the "moral dimension," "aesthetic dimension," and "religious dimension" of *li*.

59. この場合の聖人制礼の論は、礼のそもそもの起源を説明することにはならないが、時代とともに制定されて行く礼の制定者として、聖人を認めることが可能なわけである。(Abe 1964, 61).

60. 三年之喪何也。曰。稱情而立文。因以飾群別親疏貴賤之節。而不可益損也。故曰。無適不易之術也。(74/19/93–94; K: 19.9a; W 105–106). David Wong first suggested to me that this passage needed to be addressed.

61. The "three-year" mourning period was actually twenty-five months, that is, into the third year.

a light, why not the conclusion as well? The conclusion is, really, "follow the ritual!" Absolutist inferences to Xunzi's worldview here would probably not be justified. And, although the role of *shi* in this passage is not entirely clear, we always do well to give privilege to an unamended text.

It should be noted, also, that Xunzi considers it particularly important to take care with the rites associated with mourning. He writes, "Ritual propriety is being cautious in the management of life and death."[62] Or, as Watson renders the same passage, "Rites are strictest in their ordering of birth and death" (W 96). Much of his chapter on *li* focuses on the rites of mourning. And it would be fair to say that, for Xunzi, with matters regarding the transition from life to death, one must be particularly circumspect. Thus, an observer of the rites is not at liberty to make an exception of himself in the manner of his observance most especially in the case of mourning. But as for whether the ritual itself may evolve as a result of further considerations and changing circumstances, when we consider Xunzi's characterization of the purpose of mourning rites, we find nothing to exclude this possibility. For example, Xunzi writes, "The funeral rites are for nothing other than this: To illuminate what is appropriate in both death and life. And, sending off the dead with grief and reverence, finally to bury them."[63] That is, funeral rites are artifice developed to facilitate the handling of an emotional circumstance in a way that gives form to appropriate displays of emotions and to enable people to come to terms with what has occurred. It is edifying for the ritual participants and observers alike.

Reflecting on statements regarding mourning rites, such as "the sacrificial rites originate in the emotions of remembrance and longing,"[64] Nivison concludes that *li*, for Xunzi, has a universal scope. He writes: "[Xunzi's view] was a view large enough for him to see human customs, 'rites', norms, as both products of human invention, and so 'conventional', and yet as 'universal.' They had to happen, come to be, in more or less the form they have, sooner or later; and the fact that we see they are man-made does not insulate them from our commitment to them: their 'artificiality' thus in no way renders them not really obligatory and normative" (2000, 185).[65] However, though the rites may be

---

62. 禮者謹於治生死者也。(72/19/42–43; K: 19.4a; W 96). Cf. "Ritual propriety is being cautious with respect to the auspicious and inauspicious, so that they don't obstruct each other" 禮者謹於吉凶。不相厭者也。(72/19/54; K: 19.4c; W 98).

63. 故喪禮者無它焉。明死生之義。送以哀敬而終周藏也。(74/19/89–90; K: 19.7b; W 105).

64. Watson's translation (W 110), quoted in Nivison 2000, p.184. 祭者志意思慕之情也。(75/19/117; K: 19.11).

65. In another formulation Nivison writes, "Xunzi argued that language, understood as names for things, is artificial, having been invented and decreed by the sage kings to satisfy human and administrative needs; yet he also thinks the language we have is right, and deplores the confusions of the sophists who treat names as merely conventional. He thought that the sage kings likewise created 'rites and norms,' i.e., the ordinary moral rules and standards of civilized society; and yet he also thinks that these rules and standards are universally binding on us and are not mere conventions" (Nivison 2000, 176). The constructivist position is between, on the one hand, Nivison's "right" language and "universally binding" moral rules, and, on the other hand,

said to "originate" in natural emotional responses, on Xunzi's account, specific ritual form is not dictated by these responses. Essentially, our emotions are the "origin" of the rites in the sense of being what the rites have to deal with. Rather than a fixed set of universally applicable rituals, *li* are products of the always on-going practice of conscious activity. Xunzi states plainly, "Ritual and propriety are produced by the conscious activity (*wei*) of sages.[66] They are not products of people's original nature."[67] Rituals are fashioned in response to our nature but may be tailored to circumstances.[68] Further, there is no reason to assume that on Xunzi's view only one design could be fitting.

Interpreting *wei*, Jonathan W. Schofer writes, "Conscious activity as a part of learning includes studying texts, practicing ritual, being conscious of good and bad qualities in oneself and others, following the instructions of a teacher, associating with good and learned people, and concentrating on attaining the qualities exhibited by a Confucian sage" (2000, 70). On this view, which I endorse, conscious activity is necessarily situated. That is, it is tied to tradition, draws inspiration from social and educational affiliations, and culminates in insights had in to relation one's study and moral experience. Quoting Schofer again, "Xunzi states explicitly that rituals, the principles embodied in ritual, and the process of conscious activity are not 'natural,' that is, they are not part of people's innate or spontaneous nature. The ancient sages created rituals and their underlying principles as a potter molds pots out of clay" (72). Note that this metaphor[69] does not well suit the theory that there is only one unique solution to our moral problems. Clay may be fashioned into various shapes and forms. Not all would be equally useful or elegant, but neither is there a single privileged uniquely optimal form. On the contrary, each pot is a singular aesthetic expression, which may be evaluated as anything from crude to elegant.

---

a conventionalism in which both distinctions made in language and moral norms are "arbitrary." For more on Nivison's views, see sections 1.2.2 and 1.5.

66. In Chinese (both classical and modern) time and number are not indicated grammatically (i.e., verbs are not conjugated and there are no articles corresponding to "a" or "the," nor is there typically a singular/plural distinction). Thus, if number, definiteness, and time are not specified, one has to interpret from the context. Often it is not entirely clear, for example, whether a phrase should be translated "the sages made" or "sages make." The differences in the implications that flow from such choices are often significant.

67. 凡禮義者。是生於聖人之偽。非故生於人之性也。 (87/23/22–23; K: 23.2a; W 160).

68. Characterizing Xunzi's view of morality, Takeuchi Yoshio states: "Morality is not based on our natural constitution, it is something artificial which rectifies and ornaments our nature, that is, it is *wei* (artifice)." 道徳は天性に本づく行でなく、性を矯飾する人為的のもの即ち偽である。 (1936, 105). Robert Campany has a more balanced view: "[O]n the one hand, ritual belongs to the realm of *wei* or conscious activity and not that of *xing* or innate nature, but on the other hand, to the extent that ritual is patterned on the structure of, and can have real effects on, the course of nature itself, it takes on a 'natural' dimension (no longer a mere human artifice) which lends it greater power in the eyes of Daoist opponents" (1992, 223 n38). It is fair to say that *li* is in some sense patterned on nature. Indeed, *wei* itself is not *mere* human artifice. All forms of constructive artifice must be responsive to conditions, including natural ones.

69. The potter metaphor, along with similar ones, occurs twice in almost identical form in book 23, *xing e*, 87/23/23–25, 89/23/51–53; K: 23.2a, 23.4a; W 160, 164.

Xunzi expresses the relation between nature and artifice such as *li* in the following passage: "Thus I say: Original nature (*xing*) is the root and beginning, the unadorned raw material. *Wei* (artifice/conscious activity) is the flourishing abundance of cultural patterns. If there was no original nature, then there would be nothing to which *wei* could add. If there was no *wei*, original nature would not be able to beautify itself."[70] Note that beauty is an aesthetic quality not suggestive of a singular privileged instantiation.

Xunzi sees our original nature as problematic, and the rites are part of a solution that evolves through the cumulative efforts of exemplary individuals' intellectual and moral efforts. Nivison himself quotes the passage: "Heaven and earth are the beginning of life, rites and norms are the beginning of order, and the gentleman is the beginning of rites and norms" (2000, 184; W 110–11). Norms and rites, though designed to be "fitting" given our nature, are products of the ongoing interpretation of the exemplars of a tradition. The extended passage reads as follows: "The heavens (*tian* 天) and the earth are the beginning of life. Ritual and propriety (*liyi* 禮義) are the beginning of good government (*zhi* 治). The exemplary person (*junzi* 君子) is the beginning of ritual and propriety. Acting on them, stringing them together, increasingly emphasizing them, and bringing about a fondness for them, is the beginning of the exemplary person. Thus, nature and the earth produce the exemplary person, and the exemplary person applies patterns (*li* 理) to earth and nature. . . . If there were no exemplary people, nature and the earth would not be patterned."[71] There is a virtuous cycle that connects the rise of ritual propriety and self-cultivation. Through following *li* and modeling one's teacher, one develops not only a habit of, but also a fondness for, acting in accordance with *li*; that is, one develops the virtue of ritual propriety. For Xunzi, people who develop this virtue sufficiently also acquire a kind of practical wisdom, or sense of appropriateness *yi*, which allows them to skillfully apply *li* in novel circumstances. While the novice is expected simply to follow a model, the exemplary person's example sets the standard to be followed. The evolution of *li* is a natural consequence of the personal appropriation and interpretation of exemplary people over a period of time.

Interpretation, however, takes place within the context of understood norms. These norms have a basis both in their reasonableness, and their conventionality. Xunzi characterizes the three-year mourning period as a compromise, a middle course sufficient to serve its purpose. At the same time, it was a way of *setting* a fixed time when even the most dutiful should say "enough is enough" and return to a normal life. "The former kings and sages settled the matter by establishing a middle course, fashioning a fixed term. Once it adequately

---

70. 故曰。性者本始材朴也。偽者文理隆盛也。無性則偽之無所加。無偽則性不能自美。(73/19/75–76; K: 19.6; W 102; Goldin 1999, 77; Graham 1989, 251).

71. 天地者生之始也。禮義者治之始也。君子者禮義之始也。為之貫之。積重之。致好之者。君子之始也。故天地生君子。君子理天地。. . . 無君子則天地不理。(28/9/64–66; K: 9.15; W 44–45).

achieves ornamentation and reasonableness, mourning should finally come to an end."[72] Just as in Xunzi's doctrine of *zhengming* (attunement of names) it is "inappropriate" to use names differently from their established meanings, the mourning period was not to be "increased nor decreased" because it had been "set" as a *reasonable convention*. Its rationale is explained as follows: "At the point when a change in emotion shows in one's countenance sufficient thereby to differentiate the auspicious from the inauspicious, and to clarify the distinction between the eminent and the humble, and the nearness or distance of relation, then the period of mourning should come to an end."[73] But this rationale does not dictate a specific time period; so there is a degree of convention necessarily involved. Thus other peoples may be thought to be able to reasonably set different norms.

In fact, Xunzi explicitly discusses and approves of differences in ritual implements and protocol. When the extent of the success of kings Tang and Wu was called into question by those who argued that those kings were unable to extend their influence to the regions of Chu and Yue (where rituals were practiced differently), Xunzi defended Tang and Wu by advancing the view that the details of ritual, rather than being universal, should be fitted to one's circumstances. He writes:

> Why would they necessarily be uniform? The people of Lu use cups, the people of Wey use vats, and the people of Qi use containers made of hide. When the soils, land, and inherent qualities of the topography are not the same, it is impossible that their vessels and implements should not be differently prepared and ornamented. Accordingly, the various states of Xia have similar obligations for service to the king and similar standards of conduct. The countries of the Man, Yi, Rong, and Di barbarians perform similar obligatory services to the king, but the regulations governing them are not the same.[74]

Also, Xunzi twice uses the image of fording a river to describe the relation between rituals and the way.[75] He likens rituals to markers that enable people

---

72. 先王聖人安為之立中制節。一使足以成文理。則舍之矣。 (75/19/103; K: 19.9c; W 107; H 271). In lines directly preceding this passage, Xunzi rhetorically asks whether we should follow depraved people who forget their parents immediately, or whether we should follow those who are so cultivated that they would go on mourning without limit (Xunzi may be being sarcastically critical of the practices of some Ruist schools, as is suggested by Knoblock).

73. 故情貌之變足以別吉凶。明貴賤親疏之節。期止矣。 (73/19/67–68; K: 19.5b; W 101; H 269).

74. 豈必齊哉。故魯人以擔。衛人以柯。齊人用一革。土地刑制不同者。械用備飾不可不異也。故諸夏之國同服同儀。蠻夷戎狄之國同服不同制。 (67/18/47–49; K: 18.4; translation adapted from Knoblock).

75. Xunzi writes: "Those who ford rivers indicate the deep spots, allowing others to avoid falling in. Those who bring order to the common people indicate the sources of disorder, enabling others not to fall into error. Rituals are the markers. The former kings used rituals to indicate the sources of the world's disorder. To abandon ritual now is to remove the markers. Thus, the common people are confused and misled, and fall into misfortune and disaster. That is why punishments

to manage their way across the river while avoiding the deep spots. By focusing on this metaphor, we can understand how Xunzi can have both a traditionalist attitude and a worldview that allows for the possibility of pluralism. While he advocates a return to following the way marked by the successes of the sage kings, his image does not suggest that there are no other ways, or that the way outlined will remain absolutely constant. In fact, he characterizes rituals as markers that help people avoid pitfalls, not as a singular course.

The rites of mourning are not justified by virtue of some privileged relationship to our emotions (and thus by extension to the universe).[76] Rather, they are justified by their consequences, how effectively they help us deal with our situation and our emotions regarding it. Their specific forms are the result of a contingent historical process. While they are intended to be advantageous, they are not deduced. And though they may be judged "appropriate" or "inappropriate" for a time and place, they need not be considered inevitable or universal.

The social anthropologist A. R. Radcliffe-Brown has suggested the following theory (which he finds expressed in the Xunzi)[77]:

> [A]n orderly social life amongst human beings depends upon the presence in the minds of the members of a society of certain sentiments, which control the behaviour of the individual in his relation to others. Rites can be seen to be the regulated symbolic expressions of certain sentiments. Rites can therefore be shown to have a specific social function when, and to the extent that, they have for their effect to regulate, maintain and transmit from one generation to another sentiments on which the constitution of the society depends. (1952, 157)

He elaborates:

> The view taken by this school of ancient [Confucian] philosophers was that religious rites have important social functions which are independent of any beliefs that may be held as to the efficacy of the rites [e.g. whether bamboo vessels buried with the dead would be usable].[78] The rites gave regulated expression to certain human feelings and

---

are so numerous." 水行者表深。使人無陷。治民者表亂。使人無失。禮者其表也。先王以禮表天下之亂。今廢禮者是去表也。故民迷惑而陷禍患。比刑罰之所以繁也。 (96/27/10–11; K: 27.12). Cf. 64/17/48–49; K: 17.11; W 87.

76. Interpreting a passage from the *Yijing*, Nivison writes, "[T]he explanation for 'rites and norms' must be the basic structure of the universe." He quotes this passage to suggest that the view he attributes to Xunzi is a way of thinking "obvious to 4th and 3rd century China" (2000, 185). See also section 4.7 below for similar views expressed by other scholars.

77. "It is most explicit in the teachings of Xunzi . . . and in the *Book of Rites*" (Radcliffe-Brown 1952, 157).

78. Xunzi writes, "If one prays for rain and it rains, what does this mean? I say it means nothing. It is just like when one does not pray, yet it rains anyway. . . It is not that one thinks one will get what one seeks through these means; they are to ornament the occasion. Thus, exemplary people regard them as ornaments, while the people regard them as miraculous. Regarding them as ornaments is auspicious, regarding them as miraculous is inauspicious." 雩而雨。何也。曰。

sentiments and so kept these sentiments alive and active. In turn it was these sentiments which, by their control of or influence on the conduct of individuals, made possible the existence and continuance of an orderly social life.[79] (1952, 160)

Notice the mutually supportive, rather than foundational, relationship between rites and sentiments, for it is by their "influence on the conduct of individuals" that sentiments contribute to the reinforcement, and sometimes modification, the rites. Rituals and sentiments are mutually shaping.

The perspective assumed here is (at least potentially) pluralist. That is, even if Xunzi did not know about or take an interest in the possibility of other flourishing cultures, the underlying worldview is nevertheless open to pluralism. Radcliffe-Brown would seem to concur. He writes, "In so far as religion has the kind of social function that the theory suggests, religion must also vary in correspondence with the manner in which the society is constituted" (1952, 160–61). Further, while the theory suggests conservativism, it does not negate the possibility of cultural evolution. Indeed, it implies that as conditions change rites may need to evolve in order to maintain their social function. Confucius's attitude toward the silk cap illustrates this. While the constitution of society, and the religious practices found in it, are mutually shaping, sustained efficacy does not require permanent stasis. The fact that both Confucians and Daoists revere the *Book of Changes* (*Yijing*) is but one indication that early Chinese thinkers were generally united in their recognition that, fundamentally, change *is* the order of things.

4.5. A Reasonable Traditionalism

Xunzi valued stability and harmony, and he believed uniting the people around a single moral order was the only practical way to achieve this. His worldview, however, included no absolute standard with which he could ground a unifying moral discourse. All he really needed was an acceptable standard, not an absolute one. He needed it to be stable, but not immutable. He needed it to be unifying, but not universal. Tradition provided an acceptable unifying standard. But the standard also had to be a good one. Selective traditionalism isolates successful periods, and the common elements of those might be thought to

---

無何也。猶不雩而雨也。... 非以為得求也。以文之也。故君子以為文。而百姓以為神。以為文則吉。以為神則凶也。(64/17/38–40; K: 17.8; W 85).

79. Similarly, Cua writes, "For Xunzi, the rites of mourning and sacrifices have a deep significance, not as an embodiment of religious beliefs, but as a profound expression of our attitude toward human life as a whole. The beginning and the end of our life may be depicted as extreme points of a line. These rites are especially important in *li*-performance, for they betray the spirit of human life itself that is lived in the intermediate regions" (1979, 387). While these rites do not express "religious" beliefs in the sense of "supernatural" beliefs, the sentiments which give rise to them (and which they support in turn) may count as religious on the more open interpretation of religion discussed near the beginning of this chapter.

continue to provide success. But Xunzi went further and attempted to show *why* they were effective. He explained the reasonableness of traditional ritual practices; he articulated their rationales (*li* 理, patterns).

Describing the intellectual climate of the time, Ebrey writes: "*[L]i* were man-made and therefore alterable. From the time of Xunzi at least, scholars were aware that rituals were not god-given but had been created by human beings; they also realized that rituals carried meanings and wanted them to carry ethically desirable meanings. This intellectual framework provided possibilities for invention" (1991, 221).

At the same time, Ebrey writes,

> Xunzi was a rationalizer, but he was not a reformer: all of the existing practices should be continued because they could all be explained in rational ways once one understood that they were based on human nature and the patterns of heaven and earth. Xunzi's concern to prove the rationality of each step of the rituals suggests that he saw his secular attitude as a potential threat to the objective, external authority of the rites. He did not want people to infer that because the rites were social creations they could be easily curtailed or ignored. He wanted established traditions preserved as much as the punctilious ritualists did. (1991, 28–29)

Overall, Ebrey's characterization is balanced and reasonable, but it overstates the case to say that Xunzi rationalized each step. In our discussion of the three-year mourning period we saw that Xunzi's reasoning provided a rationalization for having norms for mourning, and not just any norms, but ones that were carefully conceived. But the justifications fell short of showing that only those precise norms would do the job. Cua observes, "[Xunzi's] principal preoccupation pertains to the rational justification of *li* rather than specific rules of proper conduct" (1979, 391 n4). Nevertheless, the thrust of Ebrey's characterization seems right. There is conservativism in Xunzi that cannot be denied. Still, it is conservativism more consistent with a constructivist worldview than a rationalist one.

Chen Jingpan's characterization of Xunzi's rationalizations expresses it well: "Xunzi tried to give new rationalistic interpretations of the traditional beliefs in God, Heaven, Earth, spirits, and the religious ceremonies. He gave new and different meanings to them, while still retaining the use of those terms and practices. He justified their existence not because of their objective realities or truths, but because of their subjective usefulness or expediency" (1954, 372).

In another formulation, Ebrey provides a sensible account of Xunzi's conservativism without having to attribute to him an overly rigid system of rituals based on an implausible worldview. She writes:

> The fundamental features of the rites were tied to enduring moral truths unaffected by social change. For people of all social stations to participate in the same overall

structure was a way to integrate them into a common moral system, leading to social and political harmony. Change was inevitable, but slowing it down was better than speeding it up. . . . Efforts to adapt rites so that they could match current social arrangements or sentiments were justified by a desire to preserve the true core of the rites by whatever expedient would work, not by any notion that rites ought to change. (1991, 218)

Ebrey's characterization of rites as being tied to "enduring moral truths" seems apt. Xunzi writes: "If something did not change throughout the period of the hundred kings, this is enough to consider it a connecting thread of the way. One should respond to the ups and downs of history with this thread. If one applies constructive patterns to this thread, there will not be disorder. But if one does not understand it, one will not know how to respond to changing circumstances."[80] Throughout changing conditions, people's (undeveloped) problematic set of desires and emotions remain more or less the same. The aspects of *li* that effectively foster harmony throughout changing circumstances may be considered the "true core" of the rites. But the image of correspondence with a single rational universal structure is inappropriate, as is the language of absolutism, realism, and objectivism.

4.6. Ritual Propriety as an Intrinsic Value

Turning to a point of general agreement, consider Ivanhoe's remark on the process by which the rites move from being regarded as something with merely instrumental value to something seen as having great intrinsic value:

Confucian rites . . . redirect, regulate, and refine the desires, embellish the search for satisfaction, and ultimately enhance the satisfaction we experience. Because the rites prevent disorder, lead to the satisfaction of our desires, and extend and enhance our satisfaction, they have great *instrumental* value. But Xunzi claims that as one cultivates a deeper understanding of the rites, one begins to see them as *intrinsically* valuable practices worthy of profound respect and complete devotion. At the highest stage of moral awareness [that of a sage] the collective rites, the Confucian Way, become an end unto themselves. (1991, 310)

In a similar vein Schofer writes, "An important part of learning is that people come to value the process, the objects of their study, and the forms they practice as inherently good" (2000, 71). Xunzi seems to be aware of dynamics such as the movement from extrinsic to intrinsic motivations. "*Li* is nurturing. The exemplary person, having received his nourishment [from *li*], also cherishes its

---

80. 百王之無變。足以為道貫。一廢一起。應之以貫。理貫不亂。不知貫。不知應變。 (64/17/46–47; K: 17.11; W 87).

distinctions."[81] But being aware of it *as a dynamic* enables one to conceptually step out of it and observe that this dynamic, of coming to see certain forms as "inherently good," could have occurred differently. The forms have some objective validity in being responsive to our nature, as well as maintaining a sufficient level of both coherence and comprehensiveness, while always being tied to an ever-progressing tradition. And, one who follows *li* learns to love them, comes to take them as intrinsically valuable, and in this process develops a compelling character (*de* 德). This is enough to justify them. They do not require any deeper or more fundamental grounding.

When Xunzi is speaking as one who has gone through this transformational process himself, he speaks of the rites as the true believer he is. But he is also capable of stepping back and taking a more removed stance. He is not being contradictory; he is just speaking from two perspectives that are both available to him. Here I am in agreement with Yearley, who writes, "Astute Confucians who follow Xunzi must always be aware that both the affirmation of their way of life and their ease in it arise from their choice to become what they now are. They conditioned themselves both to be the sort of people they now are and to feel the surety they now do" (1980, 479). Their confidence in and commitment to the *dao* that they practice and advocate does not require a philosophical stance that regards the status of rituals as fixed and singular. Yearley sums this up well:

> Xunzi cannot argue that people should become Confucians on the grounds that Confucianism represents the one eternally true way, the only way that reflects what people really are and what the universe really is. Nevertheless, his most basic reason for asking people to become Confucians remains intact: if you become a Confucian you will become—or stand a good chance of becoming—an admirable person. Xunzi's main argument for choosing to become a Confucian rests on the existence of Confucians who live the kind of life that others would like to live. Unlike the choice to become, say, a Christian, no belief element is involved here, no sense that you must believe the universe is set up in a certain way. (1980, 479)[82]

4.7. Conformity and the Role of Ritual in Forming Values

Some interpreters of Xunzi disagree with Yearley's assessment. They believe that in Xunzi's philosophy the Confucian rituals have a privileged status precisely because the universe is set up a certain way, that is, rituals embody a true moral

---

81. 故禮者養也。君子既得其養。又好其別。 (70/19/5–6; K: 19.1b–c; W 89).

82. For more on Yearley's position, see "An Overview of the Argument" in the introduction to this book.

order somehow embedded in the deep structure of reality. This can be seen in the following remarks by Ivanhoe, Eno, Schwartz, and Munro:

> Only the Confucian Way can insure that the needs of all are met, because it alone accords with the inherent structure of the universe itself. (Ivanhoe 1991, 311; cf. section 1.2.1)

> This analogous structure between natural and ethical worlds allows the *Xunzi* to make an implicit but clear claim to the effect that ritual *li* embody intrinsic principles of ethical existence fundamentally equivalent to principles of natural existence, or '*li*' [pattern]. Ritual *li* are, in essence, the extension of natural principles into the human sphere. (Eno 1990, 152; cf. section 2.3)

> [T]he "objective" order of society embodied in *li* [ritual propriety] and law is also on some level embedded in the order of Heaven and . . . in fashioning the human order the sages do not freely invent but actually make manifest a universal pattern somehow already rooted in the ultimate nature of things. (Schwartz 1985, 316; cf. section 2.1)

> [F]or Xunzi, man's task is to establish the social distinctions that have their counterparts in the natural hierarchical order. (Munro 1969, 39).

Similarly, Scott Cook bases his view of rituals as "static" on the notion that they are thought to correspond to the inviolable order (*xu* 序) of nature. He writes, "The static force through which ritual derives its power of differentiation is defined by the term *xu* 序, an ordering achieved purely by virtue of the static and unchanging relationships that exist in the natural world. The foremost of which is the unalterable status of Heaven and Earth." (1997, 32). Ritual, in his view, as a means of differentiation, is an "essentially negative force" (21). Cook writes, "[R]itual is conceived primarily in the negative—as an essentially externally imposed means by which may be internalized differentiation and restraint for the purpose of preventing transgressions and providing the framework that makes mutual support possible" (25). *Li* is viewed in an almost cynical light as a "method of control." Further, the adoption of ritual practice is based on an implicit "threat": "violation of ritual bounds permits no escape, for it is a violation of the natural 'laws' under which human society operates, and the transgressor must ultimately succumb to the inevitability of those laws" (19–20).

While Cook acknowledges that the result of ritual is positive, he insists on characterizing it in negative terms. For example, he writes, "Ritual . . . is a force which contributes just as much [as music] to the achievement of positive goals, but does so in a way that is seen as negative, static, and passive . . . " (1997, 32). Again, he stresses, "[H]owever much we may wish to emphasize the social fulfillment of individual roles and ritual duties as a means by which the individual may partake in the harmonious existence of society, the fact remains that ritual, considered in and of itself, is characterized by differentiation and restraint[83]" (21).

However, that rites are a means of differentiation does not mean that they are "negative, static, and passive" or that they are better understood as constraining rather than as enabling. Bell's general analysis of ritualizaion is useful here.

> The ultimate purpose of ritualization is . . . nothing other than the production of ritualized agents, persons who have an instinctive knowledge of these schemes embedded in their bodies, in their sense of reality, and in their understanding of how to act in ways that both maintain and qualify the complex microrelations of power. Such practical knowledge is not an inflexible set of assumptions, beliefs, or body postures; rather, it is the ability to deploy, play, and manipulate basic schemes in ways that appropriate and condition experience effectively. It is a mastery that experiences itself as relatively empowered, not as conditioned or molded. (1992, 221)

With regard to Cook's emphasis on *li* as "restraint," we should keep in mind that while deference and respect play large roles in ritual propriety, Xunzi says that *li* not only cuts back what is too long in our original nature, but also extends what is too short.[84] In addition, Xunzi criticises not only those who say we need to get rid of desires, but even those who merely say we need to reduce our them, suggesting that such people just do not understand how desires can be satisfied (K: 22.5a; W 150). His solution amounts to acting according to intellegence rather than instinct. This need not be thought of in a negative light, even as a means. Analogously, ritual propriety is not best characterized as restrictive, as if ritual propriety was chiefly concerned with prohibitions. Rather, norms of ritual propriety are forms through which we can act effectively.

Li are often interpreted as the embodiment of the way. Indeed, this is in one sense accurate: they give concrete form to the vague ideal of a system that produces and sustains social harmony. But primarily, in the Confucian context, while they may be said to "give form," rituals neither correspond nor conform. They do something; they perform. That is, for example, a bow may be a show

---

83. Cook's insistence that ritual is primarily about "restraint," or "constraint," seems to have as its basis an interpretation of the character *jie* 節 as "regulation, or restraint" (1997, 19). See section 5.1 for a discussion of Sato Masayuki's account of *jie* as "moderation" and "to modify." Cook also interprets *caoshu* 操術 as "method of control" (1997, 20 n50). Knoblock's rendering of "holding on to the method" (K: 3.10), where *shu* (method, skill, art) refers to adept use of Confucian principles (such as "being respectful"), seems more apt.

84. "Ritual propriety cuts off what was too long and extends what was too short. It decreases where there was a surplus, and increases what was not enough. It brings out a decorative pattern for love and respect, and is the beauty of accomplishments sprouting forth and appropriateness being put into practice." 禮者斷長續短。損有餘。益不足。達愛敬之文。而滋成行義之美者也。(73/19/63–64; K: 19.5b; W 100; H 269).

of deference (whether to someone present or to a distant ancestor), but as such it is adding content to the situation, not representing or conforming to something outside of it. It is *presenting* oneself as exemplary. Ritual actions may gesture at a vision of an ideal, but they don't reflect a determinate moral way implicit in nature of the world—nor in "reason," the order of some other transcendent world, or any other absolute ground for that matter. The idea that rituals might correspond to the true nature of the world is outside the scope of concern for the early Confucians. A ritual's meaning, for Confucians, is in its pragmatic effects.

Ritual's power to produce these effects, at least in part, comes from its suggestiveness. And rituals become more suggestive as they become further removed from the normal course of things. Smith observes, "Ritual is a means of performing the way things ought to be in conscious tension to the way things are. Ritual relies for its power on the fact that it is concerned with quite ordinary activities placed within an extraordinary setting, that what it describes and displays is, in principle, possible for every occurrence of these acts. But it also relies for its power on the perceived fact that, in actuality, such possibilities cannot be realized" (1987, 109).[85] Thinking about it in this way, Confucius was described fittingly as "the one who knows it is impossible, but acts it out anyway."[86]

Ebrey voices a similar theme, "Rituals need not reflect actual social circumstances: they can function most powerfully when they create images of a 'true' order at considerable odds from the actual social order" (1991, 219). It is not entirely clear what Ebrey means here by a "true" order, but given her account of Confucianism generally it is unlikely she means "the true," singular, ideal order in anything like the Platonic sense, but rather *an* ideal. That is, when rituals are incongruent with the existing social situation, they may gesture powerfully at a possible better way. Again quoting Smith, "From such a perspective, ritual is not best understood as congruent with something else—a magical imitation of desired ends, a translation of emotions, a symbolic acting out of ideas, a dramatization of a text, or the like. Ritual gains force where incongruency is perceived and thought about" (1987, 109–10).

Just as the attunement of names (*zhengming*) is an assertion of ethical distinctions in language, ritual provides modes of moral motivation through the assertion of value distinctions within participatory settings. "Acting ritually is first and foremost a matter of nuanced contrasts and the evocation of strategic, value-laden distinctions" (Bell 1992, 90). "Ritual is, above all, an *assertion* of difference" (Smith 1987, 109; emphasis mine). Both in attuning names and in interpreting ritual through practice, ideals are postulated. To the degree that

---

85. Commenting on this statement, Sam Gill notes, "The impossibility of achieving perfection 'in actuality' is precisely why ritual must be understood as a genre of play" (1998, 298 n23).
86. 是知其不可而為之者 (*Analects* 14.38).

rituals and moral language represent, they represent a vision, not a reality that is already present—neither in this world nor in some other. And to the degree they conform, they conform to the needs of the social circumstances. Thus, Xunzi writes, "Those who apply their moral aptitude to harmonize with others are called 'compliant.'"[87]

"Compliance" in this sense cannot escape change, because one always needs to interpret the situation and make one's compliance fitting. On the other hand, change requires conformity as a medium to take place. As Anthony Giddens noticed, "properties of society are fundamentally *recursive*" (1981, 171). Using language as an example, he explains:

> When I utter a grammatical sentence, I draw upon various syntactical rules of the English language in order to do so. But the very drawing upon those rules helps reproduce them as structural properties of English as recursively involved with the linguistic practices of the community of English language speakers. The moment (not in a temporal sense) of the production of the speech act at the same time contributes to the reproduction of the structural qualities that generated it. It is very important to see that "reproduction" here does not imply homology: the potential for change is built into every moment of social reproduction (as a contingent phenomenon). (Giddens 1981, 171–72)[88]

With the following suggestive comment, Cheng Chung-ying reveals an implication this has for our understanding of Confucian conformity. He writes:

> The notion of propriety (禮 *li*) is the notion of social norms and ethical rules which should always have applications to actual human relationships. Propriety was tested and found by the sage-kings to be conducive to peace, order, and the realization of human good. Therefore individuals should try to conform to *li* in their conduct. *This conformity is not passive, but active*. It is the beginning of active participation in a civic and social life from which individuals derive satisfaction, and through which they will achieve self-control. (Cheng 1969, 6–7; emphasis added)

Cheng does not elaborate further on the meaning of *active* conformity. He could merely mean to take action to conform to *li* just the way it is. But a more radical distinction may be made here. As we actively participate in civic society and social life, *li* is continuously negotiated and interpreted. There is a mutual shaping that goes on between the specific content of *li* and the people who perform it

---

87. 以善和人者謂之順。(4/2/11; K: 2.3; W 25; H 254).
88. Giddens concludes, "[T]here can be no theoretical defence for supposing that the personal encounters of day-to-day life can be conceptually separated from the long-term institutional development of society. The most trivial exchange of words implicates the speakers in the long-term history of the language via which those words are formed, and at the same time in the continuing reproduction of that language" (1981, 173).

as they actively seek to maintain an appropriate conformity to evolving norms and negotiate their "way" through the flux of circumstance.

In this chapter I have characterized Xunzi's conception of ritual propriety as a contingent human product that is always open to further evolution. It is the role of sages and exemplary people, in particular, to manage the continual patterning of ritual propriety. In the next chapter I turn to the other side of the above-mentioned "mutual shaping," that is, how artifice—such as norms of ritual propriety and morally attuned language—shape exemplary people.

Artifice and Virtue: Getting from *E* 惡 to *De* 德

5

This chapter addresses the relation between Xunzi's theory of moral development and his underlying worldview. The main purpose is to show how Xunzi's understanding of virtue and moral development dovetails with his positions, as I have characterized them, on ritual propriety, the attunement of names, the relation between *li* (理 patterns) and *lei* (類 categories), and his view of *dao* (道 the way) in general. Further, the analysis implies that a society of legal institutions is incomplete without mechanisms to facilitate moral cultivation, for morally cultivated people are necessary to continually interpret and apply the various norms and standards of society in a constructive way. With this in mind, let us briefly retrace some of the major points we have discussed so far.

First, a constructivist assumes that the patterns and categories that inform our perceptions of the world are, in part, contingent products of an always-ongoing cultural tradition. As the work of history is never complete, cultural constructs must always be intelligently managed. And, a Confucian constructivist is, as a manager, also an artisan. In Xunzi's words, 心也者道之工宰也。 "The heart-mind is the craftsperson and steward of the way" (82/22/40; K: 22.3f; W 147).

In addition, names-concepts (*ming* 名), according to Xunzi, "have no intrinsic appropriateness."[1] He takes the contingent nature of cultural artifice, such as words and their associated meanings, as an urgent call to diligence. One form of this diligence, in Confucian language, is *zhengming* (正名), the attunement of names. The management of names and the categories, relations, and values they signal is of fundamental importance for Xunzi, as it was for Confucius. In various ways Xunzi indicates that the wise and morally cultivated use their developed sense of appropriateness to articulate constructive patterns. Further, he says directly that, were sages to arise again, they would not only revitalize old names, but create new ones as well.[2] Craftspeople such as potters and carpenters are offered as metaphors for sages, whose products, in addition to names, include *liyi* (禮義 ritual and propriety), *yue* (樂 music), as well as laws and standards (K: 23.2a; W 160; cf. K: 23.4a; W 164).

---

1. See section 3.4 for my translation of the extended passage, and see section 3.2 for a discussion.

2. "If true kings were to arise, they would certainly revitalize old names and create new ones." 若有王者起。必將有循於舊名。有作於新名。 (83/22/11–12; K: 22.2a; W 141).

Over time, sages developed an effective set of social institutions.[3] These institutions, though regarded as great achievements worthy of reverence and study, are nonetheless ultimately social constructs designed to facilitate peace and social harmony, and as such are subject to alteration. Xunzi sees names and categories as well as patterns of ritual propriety as always evolving, as exemplars strive to achieve and maintain social harmony in the midst of changing circumstances. As Fung Yu-lan notes, "[I]n Xunzi's cosmology no such thing as objective Principle is postulated. Hence rites, standards of justice, and morality generally are simply conceived of as man-made artifacts designed to serve human existence" (1953, 670).

In this chapter, I will describe Xunzi's conception of the process of self-cultivation in a way that further reveals his thoroughgoing constructivist outlook. I will begin with a discussion of Xunzi's negative evaluation of initial human dispositions, proceed to his theory of how we may acquire new dispositions through a process of continual accumulation of instructive and productive habit forming experiences (that is, learning experiences), and then consider the nature of the end result, an admirable character. Finally, I will suggest a social-political implication of this view.

5.1. Original Human Nature and Constructive Activity

Xunzi is notorious for his slogan *xing e* (性惡), generally translated as "human nature is evil." The slogan, while it may indeed be Xunzi's own words,[4] does not straightforwardly express his position, especially in its familiar English translation.[5] "Original human nature is problematic," would be a more accurate description of his view. As Masayuki Sato puts it: "[W]hen Xunzi characterized human instinct by the term '*e* 惡' (evil), he did not mean evil as an intrinsic attribute of human beings, rather as a cause of social disorder" (2003, 251).

In Kodama Rokurō's interpretation, human nature is crude, or unadorned.

---

3. David Nivison explains: "It is reasonable to suppose that this process of *ji wei* 積偽 (Xunzi's term: literally, 'accumulation of [the result of] intelligent action') will take not just one lifetime but centuries (and the work of many 'sages')" (1996b, 53; brackets in original). The passage referred to is: *Xunzi* 88/23/50–56; K: 23.4a; W 164. As Kim-Chong Chong describes it: "Cumulative effort (*ji* 積) is an essential part of *wei* or human artifice. . . . But consistently it can also refer to the cumulative efforts of exemplary people and the fostering of ritual processes over time to curb the indulgence of certain motivational states, as well as to refine and transform them into more noble feelings and emotions" (2003, 223). This "accumulation" or "cumulative effort" applies both to social norms as well as to the character of individual people, each side assisting the other.

4. Reasons to suspect that the slogan may be an interpolation include its relative isolation. In the *Xunzi*, the phrase *Xing e* occurs only in the chapter that is named as such. For a short discussion whether *xing e* is an interpolation, and its place in Xunzi's philosophy, see Munro 1969, 77–78.

5. Both Watson and Knoblock translate the chapter title as: "Man's Nature is Evil." Similarly, Dubs renders it: "The Nature of Man is Evil." Hutton improves on this slightly: "Human Nature is Bad."

He writes: "At the root of Xunzi's thought, when we think about the fact that he considered the basic character of humans to be plain and without affectation, the real substance of Xunzi's theory of human nature, rather than the common view of it as a 'human nature is evil theory,' we consider it more appropriate to express it as 'human nature is plain or crude' (*seiboku setsu* 性朴説)."[6] Endorsing Kodama's interpretation, I use the word "crude" as a stand-in for *e* 惡, which has a range of senses from ugly to detestable. For Xunzi, our original nature is ugly and detestable because it is unrefined, or crude, and acting on undeveloped emotional impulses leads to undesirable consequences. It is difficult to find a fully adequate translation for *e*, but the following case can be made in favor of "crude." *Shan* 善 means good, or good *at*, that is, adept, especially *morally* adept—and praiseworthy for it. *Mei* 美 means beautiful and admirable. *E*, as an antonym of *shan* and *mei*, implies being unattractive, morally inept, and thus detestable. The word "crude" implies these senses as well. However, the main reason the word "crude" has been chosen is because it best captures Xunzi's view of *xing* as expressed in the *xing e* chapter and elsewhere.[7] The word "crude" describes a state of something prior to refinement, thus suggesting the possibility of improvement. Other translations—especially "evil"—risk misleadingly implying that people are incorrigibly bad.

Indeed, focus on the slogan too often results in an unfairly pessimistic, "glass is half empty," caricature of a philosopher who was trying to help people learn how to improve themselves and lead more fulfilling lives. His prescription involved using our intelligence to create and maintain structures (*wei* 偽) that would enable desires to be largely satisfied, partly by reforming those desires. As Roy Perrett describes Xunzi's position, *xing e* "means only that our natural desires, if uncultivated, will lead us to act in ways that cause social disorder. This claim is quite compatible with his claim that education and culture, which proceed from human nature, can have a morally transforming effect upon us" (2002, 315–16).

---

6. 荀子の思想の根底に、かれが人間の本性を素朴な飾り気のないものであると考えていたことを思えば、荀子の人間本性論の本質は、通説の「性悪説」にかえて、「性朴説」なる語で表現するのが最も適当であると考えるのである。(Kodama 1992, 19). Kodama also writes, "The division between basic nature and learned nature expounded by Confucius, '[People] are close by nature, but distant by learning' (*Analects* 17.2), is nothing but the division between *xing* and *wei* in Xunzi. Consequently, on the basis of the structure of Xunzi's theory of human nature, we submit that the phrase 'Human nature is *e*, its goodness is *wei*,' quoted at the beginning of this chapter, should be interpreted as 'the basic nature of human beings becomes bad easily, nature which has become good is reformed nature.'" 孔子が「性相近也、習相遠也」（論語・陽貨）と説く本性・習性の分はとりも直さず荀況のいう性偽之分である。ゆえに荀況のかかる人性論の構造に立って、本稿は性悪篇冒頭の「人之性悪、其善者偽也」の語を「人間の本性は悪になりやすい。性が善になったのは矯性である」と解釈すべきであると提起するものである。(Kodama 1973, 89). This last phrase also reinforces a point I make in section 5.2 below: *wei* is not only artifice (i.e., manmade) but also reformed nature, that is, a made-person.

7. See, for example, the quotation near the end of this section where *xing* is characterized as the "unadorned raw material" (材朴). See also the quotation in footnote 75 which speaks of "raising and adorning one's emotional nature" (橋 [撟] 飾其情性).

While Xunzi characterizes *xing* (性 original nature) as something we have by virtue of birth,[8] he nevertheless holds that people's *character* can change and grow. Indeed, his philosophy is designed to show how we can improve ourselves. As many scholars have pointed out, the substantial disagreement between Xunzi and Mencius regarding the goodness of human nature was not so great. According to Ōmuro Mikio, for example, "While [Xunzi] concludes that human nature is *e* [crude], he agrees with Mencius' doctrine of the goodness of human nature at its root. At least, one piece of evidence is the optimistic ethical doctrine that if one accumulates virtue by means of ritual propriety, even the ordinary person on the street may be cultivated into a sage."[9] It is not that Xunzi had a fundamental disagreement with Mencius over whether people, when properly nurtured, can develop virtues. They both thought this. They both also would agree that an improper upbringing could result in pettiness, or worse. Xunzi's point was that moral cultivation requires hard work, not merely following our natural dispositions. Our original desires and emotions, which Xunzi takes as the content of *xing*, are such that if we follow these we will wind up creating a truly ugly situation for others and ourselves.[10] For this reason, constructs such as norms of ritual propriety are needed. Xunzi writes: "People are born with desires. If these desires are not fulfilled, they are certain to be sought after. If this seeking has no limit or bounds, contention is inevitable. If there is contention there will be chaos, and chaos leads to ruin (*qiong* 窮). The ancient kings detested this chaos. Thus, they fashioned (*zhi* 制) ritual and propriety (*liyi* 禮義), and thereby made divisions which nurtured and cultivated (*yang* 養) people's desires, and provided for their satisfaction."[11] The project is to fashion a social system in which we may all find greater satisfaction.

Though he criticized Zhuangzi for only seeing part of the big picture, Xunzi

---

8. Xunzi describes *xing* as follows: "*Xing* is something given by nature. It cannot be learned nor acquired through work." 凡性者。天之就也。不可學不可事。(87/23/11; K: 23.1c; W 158; H 285). He also writes: "What is so by virtue of birth is called *xing*." 生之所以然者謂之性。(83/22/2; K: 22.1b; W 139; H 278).

9. 人間の性は悪だと断定しながら根底において孟子の性善説に一致する、すくなくとも礼義によって積善すれば、路傍の凡人も聖人に教化できるという楽観的な道徳論もその一証である。(Ōmuro 1967, 115; See K: 8.11 & K: 23.5a; W 166–67; and introduction). Ōmuro's paper was written using some traditional-style kanji. They have been converted to standard modern ones.

10. See the opening lines of the *xing e* chapter (K: 23.1a; W 157).

11. 人生而有欲。欲而不得。則不能無求。求而無度量分界。則不能不爭。爭則亂。亂則窮。先王惡其亂也。故制禮義以分之。以養人之欲。給人之求。(70/19/1–2; K: 19.1a; W 89). Echoing this passage, regarding music Xunzi writes: "The ancient kings detested this chaos. Thus they fashioned the sounds of the Ya and the Song in order to guide [the people]." 先王惡其亂也。故制雅頌之聲以道之。(76/20/3; K: 20.1; W 112; Cook 1997, 3). Scott Cook concludes, "[I]t is clear that Xunzi conceives ritual and music as two complementary *tools* that do, in fact, ultimately bring great benefit to society in terms of establishing and maintaining social order and harmony" (1997, 15; emphasis added). While I agree with this instrumentalist reading of Xunzi, I do not share Cook's almost cynical view of how the ruler is to use these tools (see section 4.7).

fully understood and appreciated the significance of Zhuangzi's fundamental insight into the conventional aspect of language and social norms. He also saw how this insight could be useful to Confucianism, rather than a repudiation of it. Since names, categories, and norms are not absolutes, they can be shaped and reshaped as needed and appropriate.

Xunzi uses the character *wei* 偽 to refer to social devices devised to encourage and facilitate moral growth and social harmony. Itano Chōhachi comments: "The relation between *xing* and *wei* is the relation between the natural (*tian*-given) and the artificial (man-made), in other words, the relation between the natural and the human. Xunzi's *xing e* theory is based on distinction between *xing* and *wei* as well as the different roles of nature and humanity."[12] Just as people—through well-ordered social arrangements—make the most out of the conditions that *tiandi* (nature) provides, it is incumbent upon people—through intelligently directed diligence—to make the most of themselves. Morality is what we do with what we are naturally provided. Despite his assertion of different roles for nature and people (*tian ren zhi fen* 天人之分),[13] Xunzi never abandons the idea of continuity between the natural and the human (*tian ren he yi* 天人合一).[14]

Consider the following assertion: "Morality is man-made, and is included in what [Xunzi] calls 'artifice' (偽 *wei*)."[15] *Wei* is conscious activity or the products thereof, thus "artifice" is a common translation. It can be conceived of as that which is constructed to serve the Confucian goal of social harmony. It is "constructive activity"[16] and the resulting "constructs." In other words, *wei*, for Xunzi, is a web of mechanisms designed to curb harmful behavior and to encourage, facilitate, and guide the development of productive habits and beneficial desires. In all this, however, one must work with the materials on hand. That is, human nature cannot be ignored in the constructive process.

Among the most important types of *wei* is *li*, ritualized roles and responsibilities. Equally critical, and integral to his project, is the idea of *zhengming*.

---

12. 性と偽との関係は、天与のものと人為的なものとの関係すなわち天と人との関係であって、荀子の性悪説は性偽の分に、さらに天人の分に基づくものである。(Itano 1995, 270).

13. See 62/17/5–7; K: 17.1–17.2a; W 79–80.

14. Kodama also argues that Xunzi holds both *tian ren he yi* as well as *tian ren zhi fen* (see Kodama 1992, 78). But while Kodama and I seem to share a common understanding of *tian ren zhi fen*, his interpretation of *tian ren he yi* is quite different from the characterization I have given it.

15. This is from Kakimura and Azuma's Japanese translation of Fung Yu-lan's *History of Chinese Philosophy*, and is subtly different from Derk Bodde's English translation. His reads: "Morality is something made by man, and so is called 'acquired'" (1953, 286). Bodde's rendering of *wei* as "acquired" is supported by arguments I make below. Bodde's translation is also more faithful to the original (see Feng 1961, 357), but Kakimura and Azuma's version gives it an interesting twist. 道徳とは人為的なもので、いわゆる「偽」に属するのである。(1995, 423).

16. This reading of *wei* was first suggested to me by an anonymous reader of an early version of chapter 2. Recently, A. S. Cua has also used "constructive activity" as a translation of *wei*. See Cua 2003, 170, 193 n98.

Names, and the categories to which they point, are socially defined artifice. Institutions, rites, terminology, and so on ought to be designed to further the satisfaction of our desires by forming a structure wherein we can develop a set of virtues which will allow us to satisfy our (new) desires. These new "desires," what one has learned to be fond of, resemble values more than they do our original desires.

The idea that human nature is *e*, understood in terms of base original desires, has often led interpreters to the idea that Xunzi thought we ought to suppress or restrain our desires.[17] But Xunzi's view stresses intelligent guidance rather than simple suppression. He writes, "Those who say that order depends on first getting rid of desires, having no way to guide desires, are distressed by their mere presence. Those who say that order depends on reducing the number of desires, having no way of moderating (*jie* 節) desires, are distressed that there are so many."[18] Reflecting on the meaning of *jie* here may aid our understanding of Xunzi's attitude toward desires. According to Sato, although *jie* often means "moderation," it can (even at the same time) mean "to modify," as in the phase *le jie liyue* 樂節禮樂, "to take pleasure in modifying one's behavior by ritual and music."[19] Roger Ames and Henry Rosemont render this phrase: "the enjoyment found in *attuning* oneself to the rhythms of ritual propriety (*li* 禮) and music (*yue* 樂)" (1998, 197; emphasis added). Attunement is a particular kind of modification, one that seeks to achieve a harmonious balance. Sato also understands *jie* to have this sense. In the natural realm, he explains, "*jie* denotes a balanced condition, an appropriate mixture of nature's ingredients" (2000, 21). Xunzi is saying that desires can be directed so that they harmonize with the environment. While it is true that some impulses will need to be suppressed during a period of training, the emphasis is on re-forming our character such that our new desires can be fulfilled.

Xunzi was an optimist. He believed that, starting with a selective[20] revival

---

17. Fung Yu-lan, for example, quotes the following passage from Xunzi: "The necessary beginning of knowledge is to consider that desires are permissible and so to guide (but not wholly repress) them . . ." (Fung 1952, 290, Bodde's translation) 以為可而道之。知所必出也。 (85/22/64; K: 22.5b; W 152). Yet, Fung's interpretation emphasizes restraint rather than guidance. "The desires need not be wholly eliminated, but only need to be kept in proper restraint by the mind. . . . This [empty unified and quiescent] mind sets up a 'standard' (*quan* 權) or 'balance' (*heng* 衡), with which to place a restraint upon the desires" (Fung 1952, 290, 292).

18. 凡語治而待去欲者。無以道欲而困於有欲者也。凡語治而待寡欲者。無以節欲而困於多欲者也。 (85/22/55–56; K: 22.5a; W 150; D 293; H 282).

19. See Sato 2000, 24. The quotation is from Sato's translation of *Analects* 16.5.

20. As evidence that this was selective, consider Xunzi's remark describing people who devote themselves to understanding the ways of the ancient kings: "Sagacious, they alone clearly perceive and elucidate wherein the former kings achieved it, and wherein they lost it. They know a state's conditions of peace and those of peril, its good and bad, as clearly as distinguishing white from black." 曉然獨明於先王之所以得之。所以失之。知國之安危臧否。若別白黑。 (46/12/40; K: 12.5). Cf. Knoblock's translation: "Fully understanding, only he elucidates how the Ancient Kings succeeded and wherein they failed. He would recognize the signs of danger and of security, of good and of bad, in the government of a state as easily as one distinguishes black from white."

of the successful ways of the past, it would be possible to once again construct a peaceful and flourishing society in which there is a virtuous cycle linking the constructs that facilitate moral growth and the people who manage these constructs. "Ritual propriety is that by which one's person (*shen* 身) is attuned (*zheng* 正).[21] A teacher is the means by which ritual propriety is attuned."[22]

But Xunzi worried that the Mencian conception of *xing* and the notion *xing shan* 性善 (human nature is good) would obscure the role of *wei* (constructive activity and the moral artifice it produces). On the Mencian view, all that is needed to become virtuous is to nourish one's "natural" tendencies. The critical functions of ritual propriety and moral language would not be adequately appreciated, he feared, if this view held sway. Further, Xunzi saw that a standard of efficacy, that is, of what works in practice, is needed for evaluating social norms, and that such a standard would not seem so compelling if people thought they could simply take their natural inclinations as reliable guides for moral development, and that this would be enough to ensure a harmonious society. In addition, while the Mencian view might leave one in doubt regarding the importance of the sages, their role is clear from a Xunzian perspective. Conscious activity, devising mechanisms that will work to facilitate moral development and produce a harmonious society, is what the sages involved themselves in—designing and instituting workable artifice.[23]

All this, however, is not to say that *xing shan*, as Mencius defined those terms, is *false*. Whether it is true or false is never really the question.[24] Rather, the problem Xunzi has with Mencius is that conceiving things in Mencian terms hinders the project of building a better society. Let's consider the most relevant passage. Xunzi writes:

This passage suggests that the ancient kings were fallible and that, in reconstructing the way, those who study the ancients well can separate what was effective from what was not and build on those successful parts.

21. As explained above, *jie* (moderation, to modify) can be understood as a kind of attunement, that is, modification that moderates, seeking a harmonious balance. *Zheng* (to make proper) may likewise be understood as a kind of attunement, namely, an adjustment that coordinates something with an appropriate standard.

22. 禮者所以正身也。師者所以正禮也。 (5/2/37; K: 2.11; W 30).

23. Cua observes, "Xunzi does explicitly state that the sages are responsible for the existence of *li* [propriety] through conscious or productive activity (*wei*)" (1985, 69).

24. Donald Munro has written, "What were important to the Chinese philosophers, where questions of [ultimate] truth and falsity were not, were the behavioral implications of the statement or belief in question" (1969, ix). I have added the word "ultimate" to Munro's claim to distinguish this issue from the question of pragmatic truth—whether something can be effectively put into practice—which is a different matter, and an issue very important to Xunzi. If Munro's claim (as I have qualified it) is right, then we may expect Xunzi's theory of virtue to be somewhat open—virtuous character being a matter of constructive efficacy, rather than ultimate truth—as I argue below that it is. I would also extend Munro's claim to cover not only statements and beliefs but also words and their meanings. *Zhengming*, attuning names, is better understood as an ethical task than as an epistemological one.

Theories are valued for coherent distinctions and conforming to experience. Sitting, one discusses it. Rising,[25] one is able to set it up (*she* 設). Extending it, one is able to carry it out (*shi* 施) and put it into practice. Now, Mencius says, "Human nature is good." This is both incoherent and fails to conform to experience. Sitting, one may discuss it,[26] but rising, one is unable to set it up, and extending it, one is unable to carry it out and put it into practice. How could it not be colossal mistake? If human nature is good then we may cast aside the sage kings, and ignore ritual propriety and appropriateness. But if our original endowments (*xing*) are crude, then, along with the sage kings, we place value in ritual propriety and appropriateness.[27]

Xunzi concludes that we should understand *xing* in such a way as to make clear the importance of sages and the social artifice they create. Although one can *talk* about it differently, as Mencius did, this way of conceiving things hinders our efforts to realize social goals.

Therefore, in keeping with his conception of *zhengming* as the articulation of constructive concepts that forward the project of achieving a better world, Xunzi reconstructs the concept of *xing*. He defines it in a way he believed would be useful.[28] He then contrasted it with *wei* (constructive activity/artifice) in a way that enabled him to raise *wei* while lowering *xing* saying, "People's original nature is crude. Their goodness is a product of *wei*."[29] To define *xing* such that it makes sense to call it "crude" allows him to emphasize the importance of creating structures to sometimes curb our desires, and sometimes to allow

---

25. *Qi* 起 is likely doing double duty here. It clearly means "rise," in opposition to the previous phrase involving merely sitting. But equally it means *chuxian* 出現, "arise" in the sense of "appear" or "emerge" as well as *chansheng* 產生 "produce; engender" or "emerge; come into being." It also means *jianzao* 建造 "build; construct; make." So, the meaning is that a theory should be constructed such that it is able to stand, that is, that it will work in practice.

26. One might think that since Xunzi says that Mencius's view is incoherent, that is, that it lacks distinctions which fit together (無辨合), he should say here that "sitting, one *cannot* discuss it intelligibly." But given his emphasis on the inseparability of knowledge and practice, incoherence is precisely being able to say it convincingly while not being able to actually make it work in practice; the distinctions don't fit in a way that is effective.

27. 凡論者貴其有辨合有符驗。故坐而言之。起而可設。張而可施行。今孟子曰人之性善。無辨合符驗。坐而言之。起而不可設。張而不可施行。豈不過甚矣哉。故性善則去聖王息禮義矣。性惡則與聖王貴禮義矣。(88/23/44–47; K: 23.3b; W 163; H 288–98). Notice how the usage of the characters employed here have evolved. In modern Mandarin, *she* 設 is used for *jianshe* 建設 "build, construct," and for *sheji* 設計 "design, plan." And, *shi* 施 "execute, carry out" is used for *shigong* 施工 "construction."

28. On the other hand, although Xunzi *does* define *xing* differently from Mencius, their contrasting evaluations of *xing* is not due *simply* to differences in definition. Chong uses Xunzi's distinction, between merely having a capacity and actually being able to do something, to convincingly argue that there is a real difference in their positions. On Mencius's view, our innate moral qualities (or "capacities") translate directly to actual moral abilities. On the other hand, while Xunzi also accepts that at least some of our innate capacities and tendencies may be "congenial" to moral development, he argues that they do not thus constitute actual moral abilities. "He [Xunzi] argues specifically against Mencius that these desires and emotions do not come to us in a morally packaged way, but require nurturance and guidance through the rites" (Chong 2003, 226–27).

29. 人之性惡。其善者偽也。(86/23/1; K: 23.1; W 157).

for their fulfillment in synergetic ways. At best, these structures enable us to transform our desire such that the new desires (no longer considered part of *xing*) cannot be frustrated,[30] and such that their fulfillment becomes beneficial to society. In a less antagonistic moment, Xunzi spells out the respective roles of *xing* and *wei* as follows: "Original nature (*xing*) is the root and beginning, the unadorned raw material (本始材朴). *Wei* (artifice/conscious activity) is the flourishing abundance of cultural patterns. If there were no original nature, then there would be nothing to which *wei* could add. If there were no *wei*, original nature would not be able to beautify itself."[31]

Since *wei* as artifice comes from *wei* as conscious activity, it seems that people are the source of these constructs. Indeed, numerous passages also indicate explicitly that it is through the creative activity of people, in particular exemplary people and sages, that a moral world is constructed.[32] Xunzi writes, for example:

A tradition says: "Order is produced by exemplary people."[33]

Constructs[34] constitute the flow of order, but they are not its wellspring. Exemplary people are the wellspring of order.[35]

"The way" is not the way of *tian* 天, neither is it the way of the earth. It is that by which the people are led; it is the path of exemplary people.[36]

---

30. Rosemont makes a similar point. "[B]y shifting attention away from material goods Xunzi increases the probability—especially among the literati—that goals will be reached and desires satisfied. . . . [E]very budding official can achieve his goal if he desires to win fame as a moral exemplar, or write poetry, hear good music, or contemplate the beauty of a ritual state sacrifice" (2000, 12). Cf. K: 29.8.

31. 故曰。性者本始材朴也。偽者文理隆盛也。無性則偽之無所加。無偽則性不能自美。 (73/19/75–76; K: 19.6; W 102; Graham 1989, 251). Cf. *Analects* 3.8, which likens *li* to the applying of color to an unadorned face.

32. Chen Daqi's interpretation of Xunzi makes the same point. "Ritual propriety, appropriateness, and moral standards for governing a country and cultivating one's moral character, these begin from exemplary people, or are produced by sages. They are what people themselves invent and establish, not something existing naturally." 治國修身的禮義法度，始自君子，生於聖人，是人們自己所發明而創設的，不是自然存在的。 (1954, 5). See Chen 1954, 4–5, for a list of relevant passages, and section 1.1 for more on Chen's position.

33. 傳曰。治生乎君子。 (26/9/14–15; K: 9.2; W 36 and 52/14/13; K: 14.2).

34. I've translated *xie shu* 械數 simply as "constructs." *Xie* 械 means apparatus, and *shu* 數 has several meanings centering around numbers, amounts, and counting. Probably as an extension of this, *shu* also means "rule, norm" as well as "method, art" (See GSR: 123r). Knoblock interprets the metaphor here to mean that *xie* and *shu* are the consequences of order. I believe that idea of *liu* 流 (stream, flow) expresses more then mere result, constructs form the substances of order as well as being the result of the creative process of exemplary people.

35. 故械數者。治之流也。非治之原也。君子者。治之原也。 (44/12/10–11; K: 12.2).

36. 道者非天之道。非地之道。人之所以道也。君子之所道也。 (20/8/24; K: 8.3). Cf. Graham's translation: "The Way is not the Way of Heaven, nor the Way of Earth, it is what man uses to make his way, what the gentleman adopts as the Way" (1989, 242–43).

Tian can generate things but cannot articulate distinctions among them. The earth can support people but cannot order them. The myriad things of the whole world, and all living people, await sages, and only then are they apportioned.[37]

Thus, the earth and nature produce exemplary people, and exemplary people apply patterns to earth and nature. . . . If there were no exemplary people, the earth and nature would not be patterned.[38]

Xunzi is equally clear regarding *how* people are able to create constructive social distinctions: by virtue of *yi* 義, a developed sense of appropriateness. He writes:

How are we able to put social divisions into practice? I say it is *yi*. If *yi* is used in forming divisions then there will be harmony.[39]

If a sincere mind applies a sense of appropriateness (*yi*) then there will be constructive patterns (*li* 理).[40]

[The exemplary person's] social relations are characterized by categories which follow from a sense of appropriateness (*yi*).[41]

Moral categories, and the roles and responsibilities that go along with them, as contingent products of sages and exemplary people, provide no absolute standards. Rather, important distinctions, roles, and norms must be continually refined.[42] So too must a person's character. Here I concur with Lee Yearley, and it is worth recalling a statement cited in the previous chapter:

Xunzi cannot argue that people should become Confucians on the grounds that Confucianism represents the one eternally true way, the only way that reflects what people really are and what the universe really is. Nevertheless, his most basic reason for asking people to become Confucians remains intact: if you become a Confucian you will become—or stand a good chance of becoming—an admirable

---

37. 天能生物不能辯物也。地能載人不能治人也。宇中萬物。生人之屬。待聖人然後分也。 (73/19/78–79; K: 19.6; W 103).

38. 故天地生君子。君子理天地。. . . 無君子則天地不理。 (28/9/65–66; K: 9.15; W 44–45).

39. 分何以能行。曰義。故義以分則和。 (29/9/71; K: 9.16a; W 45–46).

40. 誠心行義則理。 (7/3/27–28; K: 3.9).

41. 其交遊也。緣義而有類。 (45/12/27; K: 12.3).

42. Recall the passage quoted in section 4.3.4: "Distinctions which serve no purpose, and observations on matters which are not pressing, should be discarded and not mastered. But as for the appropriate relation between ruler and ministers, the close relations between father and son, and the respective roles of husband and wife, cut and polish them every day and do not give up." 無用之辯。不急之察。棄而不治。若夫君臣之義。父子之親。夫婦之別。則日切瑳而不舍也。 (64/17/37–38; K: 17.7; W 85).

person. Xunzi's main argument for choosing to become a Confucian rests on the existence of Confucians who live the kind of life that others would like to live. (Yearley 1980, 479)

5.2. *Wei* as Acquired Character

Something important is obscured when *wei* is construed as "artifice" or "constructs"—as if they are merely external. Yang Liang 楊倞, in the earliest extant commentary on the *Xunzi*, notes:

> *Wei* 偽 means *wei* 為 [to do or accomplish, to be or become] and *jiao* 矯 [to straighten, rectify, correct; to raise high]. It is to straighten/raise up one's original nature. Things which are not natural tendencies but rather accomplished by people, are all called *wei* 偽. Thus, the character composed of *ren* 人 [a person] beside *wei* 為 [to become] is also an associative compound character [that is, a character formed from the meaning elements of other characters].[43]

Wei indicates that by which one straightens one's nature, and the straightened nature as well. In other words, while *wei* 偽 indicates something manmade (人為), it equally means making (為) a person (人). That is, while *wei* is indeed constructive activity and its products, its principal product is a transformed person.[44] Moral norms and concepts are important, even critical, but nonetheless secondary.

Consider the following passage: "The sages Yao and Yu and exemplary people are valued for being able to transform their original nature and being

---

43. 偽，為也，矯也，矯其本性也。凡非天性而人作為之者，皆謂之偽。故為字「人」傍「為」，亦會意字也。 (Wang 1988, 434). While the interpretation of *wei* 偽 as deriving its meaning from the combination of *ren* 人 (person) and *wei* 為 (make) traces back at least to Yang Liang's commentary (818 CE) and is commonly found in contemporary Chinese and Japanese writings on Xunzi (see, for example, Lao 1968, 258, Lin 1978, 39, Nagao 1999, 100; Murase 1986, 50–51; and Kaizuka 1961, 172), not all experts agree with it. For one thing, the forms *wei* 偽 and *wei* 為 were not consistently distinguished at the time when Xunzi was writing. However, Xunzi clearly uses *wei* as a technical term. Thus, we can expect that *he* used it consistently. We do not know whether or not he used the *ren* radical. But it would have made sense for him to have done so, given *wei*'s use as a technical term. In any case, the *ren* radical is present in the text as it has been handed down, suggesting that this usage had resonance with early interpreters. And, given that it makes a good deal of sense within his theory, the account given is at least a plausible hypothesis.

44. Explaining Xunzi's remark "one's goodness is *wei*" (其善者偽也。), Chen Daqi writes, "*Wei* is artifice, and it is also conduct. . . . *Wei* is artifice which cultivates, it is equivalent to what is called personal character in modern psychology" 偽即是人為，亦即是行為。. . . 偽是人為所養成的，相當於現代心理學上所說的人格。 (1954, 57). Both the interpretations of *wei* as constructs and *wei* as acquired character can also be found in the Japanese literature on Xunzi. For example: "Ritual propriety and division of roles are constructions (human products) of sages." 礼分は聖人の偽 (人間の制作) である。Nishi 1969, 43). And, on the other hand, "Sages, transforming original nature into acquired character (*wei*), established ritual propriety." 聖人が性を化し偽を起して礼を定めた。(Abe 1964, 61).

able to give rise to *wei*. As *wei* emerges, *liyi* is produced. Thus the *liyi* of the sages and their accumulation of *wei* is like a potter producing pots."[45] The image of a potter making pots may give us the false impression that the object is external, but similar metaphors, such as the following from the *Daxue* (Great Learning) show that this kind of metaphor applies reflexively to the character of the artisan. The *Daxue* comments on a passage from the *Book of Songs*, which says: "The refined person, like cutting and filing, like carving and polishing."[46] The comment reads: "'like cutting and filing' is learning the way; 'like carving and polishing' is self-cultivation."[47]

Also consider Xunzi's distinction between *xing* and *wei*: "Ritual propriety and a sense of appropriateness (*liyi*) are the products of sages. They are what people become capable of through learning; they are what people can accomplish through work. What resides in people and cannot be learned or acquired through work is called *xing*. What resides in people that they are capable of through learning and can accomplish through work is called *wei*. This is the distinction between *xing* and *wei*."[48] Here Xunzi is clear that *wei* is something which resides in us, it is the part of our character that we can self-mold.

With this in mind, let's consider how we might best interpret the following passage: "Someone may ask, 'If original human nature is crude, where do ritual propriety and a sense of appropriateness come from?' I would reply that they are produced by the constructive activity (*wei*) of sages."[49] Watson translates *wei* here as "conscious activity," while Knoblock renders it "acquired nature." Our discussion so far implies that they each capture one dimension of the meaning. I have said that *wei* means both conscious activity and its products—especially the effect on one's character. Xunzi writes, "What the mind deliberates and is able to put into motion is called *wei* 偽 (conscious activity).[50] Deliberations accumulate and one is able to become practiced in them, after this is accomplished, it is [also] called *wei* 偽 (acquired character)."[51] In the passage in question we can see how *wei* may carry these meanings vaguely, rather than ambiguously. As I have argued, sages and exemplary people are responsible for constructive artifice by virtue of their *yi*, their developed sense of appropriateness. *Yi* is a way of being.

45. 凡所貴堯禹君子者。能化性能起偽。偽起而生禮義。然則聖人之於禮義積偽也。亦猶陶埏而生之也。 (89/23/55–56; K: 23.4a; W 165, H 289).

46. 有斐君子。如切如磋，如琢如磨。 (*Daxue* 3.4).

47. 「如切如磋」者，道學也；「如琢如磨」者，自脩也。 (*Daxue* 3.4).

48. 禮義者。聖人之所生也。人之所學而能所事而成者也。不可學不可事而在人者謂之性。可學而能可事而成之在人者謂之偽。是性偽之分也。 (87/23/11–13; K: 23.1c; W 158; H 285).

49. 問者曰。人之性惡。則禮義惡生。應之曰。凡禮義者。是生於聖人之偽。 (87/23/22; K: 23. 2a; W 160; H 286; D 305).

50. Cf. Munro's translation: "By *wei* is meant the direction of one's sentiments as a result of the mind's reflections" (1969, 80).

51. 心慮而能為之動謂之偽。慮積焉能習焉而後成謂之偽。 (83/22/4; K: 22.1b; W 139–40).

It is the virtue of consistently exercising one's hard earned practical wisdom. Ritual propriety is not born directly from the cogitations of the sages, but out of their exemplary actions. Thus, Knoblock's "acquired nature" is perhaps the more instructive translation. It is the persuasive force of the acquired character of sages, of their developed virtues in action, which gives rise to appropriate social norms. Rendering *wei* as constructive activity here preserves the ambiguity (or, rather, vagueness). Both considered judgment and virtuous action are integral to forming social norms in a productive way, and Xunzi does not make a clear distinction between the two—indeed, for him, the two are one.

Itano makes clear the integral relation between thought and action as it relates to *wei*: "*Wei* is the work of the heart-mind such as conduct that is the product of thoughtful deliberation, or work that is fulfilled by virtue of accumulation of thought. In other words, *wei* is people's self-conscious conduct or the product thereof."[52] *Wei* is "self-conscious *conduct*" and the dispositions acquired by the continual exercise of such conduct.

On Murase Hiroya's interpretation of Xunzi's theory of moral development, active and independent personal molding of one's character is likened to the role of humans taking advantage of what is given in the natural environment. "In 'A Discussion of *Tian*,' [Xunzi] advocates 'different roles for *tian* and people' and emphasizes the independence and activeness of humans toward external nature. And, in this chapter, ['Human Nature is Crude'] he clarifies the 'different roles of *xing* (original human nature) and *wei* (artifice)', and he clears the way for people's independence and activeness toward their own internal nature."[53] Independence and activeness in self-cultivation implies the result will be a personal achievement unique to oneself. As I will argue in the following sections, just as there are better and worse institutions people might devise to organize society and to take advantage of the propensities of nature—but no single ultimate set, similarly, while there are better and worse ways to develop one's character, there is no single best set of disposition or personality, no single best complete character.

5.3. The Accumulation of Character

In the preceding chapter, I argued that, for Xunzi, social constructs such as norms of ritual propriety are products of historical accumulation as each generation builds on, refines, and adapts existing norms according to their own interpretations and in consideration of current needs. Accumulation applies to self-cultivation as well as to building social constructs. The constructiv-

---

52. 心の働き例えば慮が加わってなされる行為、または慮が重なって成就する仕事が偽である。換言すれば人間の自覚的な行為ないしその所産が偽である。 (Itano 1995, 267).

53. 「天論篇」では「天・人の分」を唱え、外的自然に対する人間の主体性・能動性を力説した荀子は、ここでは「性・偽の分」を明確にし、自己自身の内的自然に対する人間の主体性・能動性に道を拓こうとする。(Murase 1986, 58).

ist position, in fact, is reinforced by the centrality of personal accumulative cultivation.

Several passages describe Xunzi's view of virtue as a result of a process of accumulation. For example, he writes: "Whether one is able to become a sage like Yao or Yu, or a tyrant like Jie or robber like Zhi, or a craftsman or artisan, or a farmer or merchant, this resides solely in the accumulation of the forces of circumstance, what one concentrates on and what one puts aside, and habits and customs."[54] By focusing on what we want to be, setting aside our natural inclinations, and developing habits through the practice of *li*, we accumulate desirable dispositions. The result is an ever-increasing propensity (*shi* 勢) to become capable of further moral development. By taking appropriate action, one can transform one's dispositions. Again quoting Xunzi: "Being a teacher and a model is achieved by an accumulation. It is not something received from one's original nature, which is insufficient by itself to establish order. Although 'original nature' is something we are unable to do anything about, there can be a transformation. Although 'accumulation' is not something that we possess, we can do something about it. Original nature is transformed by establishing a process and becoming accustomed by practice."[55]

Xunzi offers several metaphors for this transformation: "Wood as straight as a plumb line may be bent into the shape of a wheel, with a curvature as true as a compass. Even if it is dried in the sun, it will not return to its former straightness, because the bending process has made it like this. Thus, if wood is marked

---

54. The passage goes on to state that, "If one becomes a Yao or a Yu, then one normally will be settled and secure, and honored. If one becomes a Jie or Zhi one is normally in danger and will suffer disgrace. If one becomes a Yao or Yu then one is normally content and at ease." 可以為堯禹。可以為桀跖。可以為工匠。可以為農賈。在執注錯習俗之所積耳。...為堯禹則常安榮。為桀跖則常危辱。為堯禹則常愉佚。 (10–11/4/45–48; K: 4.9; I am reading 執 as 勢 and 錯 as 措) See also 10/4/41–42; K: 4.8.

Note that Knoblock also uses the word "normally" for the first two occurrences of *chang* 常 (constant, enduring, usually), though he opts of the stronger "constantly" in the third instance. While the word "constantly" is open to either a strict or loose interpretation, *chang* does not mean "always" in a strong sense. That *chang* allows for exceptions is made clear by the immediately preceding passage, which reads: "Putting *ren*, *yi*, and *de* into practice is the normal (*chang*) method of achieving peace and safety. Even so, it is not necessarily the case that there will be no danger." 仁義德行常安之術也。然而未必不危也。 (10/4/41–42; K: 4.8). Also, the frequency indicated by *chang* is context sensitive. Xunzi even uses the word *chang* when he says that, in all eras, eclipses and other anomalies are relatively common (*chang*) (63/17/31; K: 17.7; W 84; Machle 1993, 111). See Machle 1993, 114, and Cua 2003, 191–92 n85, for more on the meaning of *chang* in the *Xunzi*.

55. 而師法。所得乎情。非所受乎性。不足以獨立而治。性也者。吾所不能為也。然而可化也。情也者。非吾所有也。然而可為也。注錯習俗。所以化性也。 (24–25/8/108–10; K: 8.11). I am following Knoblock, who is following Yang Liang, in reading *qing* 情 as *ji* 積 "accumulation." See Knoblock 1990, 289 n105. Cf. "Accumulated soil makes a mountain, and wind and rain flourish as a result. Accumulated water makes an abyss, and flood dragons are born in it. Accumulated good acts makes virtue or moral power (*de*), and in this way one obtains a god-like clarity as a matter of course, and the sagely mind is prepared." 積土成山。風雨興焉。積水成淵。蛟龍生焉。積善成德。而神明自得。聖心備焉。 (2/1/17–18; K: 1.6; W 17–18).

with a plumb line, it will become straight; if metal is put to a whetstone, it will become sharp; if the exemplary person studies broadly and examines himself daily, his wisdom will become illuminating and his conduct will be without fault."[56]

Xunzi's point here is not about making something conform to a singular privileged form, rather he is stressing that the original character of a thing can be transformed into a product with resilient new features. T. C. Kline explains this process well:

> Xunzi conceives of cultivation as analogous to the bending and steaming and squaring involved in crafts. A craftsman takes raw material and shapes it into the desired form. The finished product does not grow out of the form of the raw material. Rather it is shaped and molded by the intentional activity of the craftsman. . . . This is not to say that the properties of the material itself can be ignored. To be successful the craftsman must understand the properties of the raw material and as far as possible work with the grain as opposed to against it. (2000, 157)

In the case of moral development, the raw material consists of human endowments, limitations, and potentials. Thus, in devising workable constructs one must consider how they will resonate with people who try them out. Xunzi reasons:

> Humans are born with the firm dispositions of an inferior person. If they lack a teacher and a model, they will see only personal profit. . . . Consider: if one had never tasted the meat of grain-fed animals, and rice and fine millet, but only beans, pulse leaves, husks and chaff, then one would consider this sufficient. If one were then suddenly presented with portions of fine meats, rice and millet, splendidly displayed, one would gaze at them with a look of horror and say: "What strange things are these?" But since the smell does not disturb the nose, the taste is sweet to the mouth, and eating it puts the body at ease, anyone would abandon the original diet and take up the new one.[57]

This passage shows a kind of naturalistic objective standard at work in Xunzi's thinking. We are so constituted that some experiences tend to be reinforcing. When we apply ourselves to a constructive way, Xunzi is suggesting, we will find it to be satisfying, and sustaining. He writes, "Those who follow proper categories are called fortunate, those who go against them are called hapless.

---

56. 木直中繩。輮以為輪。其曲中規。雖有槁暴。不復挺者。輮使之然也。故木受繩則直。金就礪則利。君子博學。而日參省乎己。則智明而行無過矣。(1/1/1-3; K: 1.1; W 15).
57. 人之生固小人。無師無法則唯利之見耳。. . . 今使人生而未嘗睹芻豢稻粱也。惟菽藿糟糠之為睹。則以至足為在此也。俄而粲然有秉芻豢稻粱而至者。則瞲然視之。曰。此何怪也。彼臭之而無嗛於鼻。嘗之而甘於口。食之而安於體。則莫不弃此而取彼矣。(11/4/49-55; K: 4.10).

This is called *tian*'s regulation."[58] It is because of *tian*—the way things hang together and the propensities of nature—that constructive categories prove themselves beneficial. This is why it is called *tian*'s regulation.

Categories, however, are human constructs. People who structure their lives based on categories devised and promoted by sages are likely to benefit—but not because they are acting in accordance with a uniquely true view of the way things are. Rather, they will benefit because the categories that give shape to their lives where formulated by sages with precisely that end in mind. While the idea of a sage devising categories is not logically incompatible with the idea that those categories accord with a singular metaphysical truth, such a conclusion is unnecessary. That is, it is not necessary for Xunzi to hold that there is one true picture of the world in order for him to appreciate that there are propensities in nature and in human nature, and that we can use our insights into these in ways that promote virtues and foster a society in which all may find a greater share of contentment.

5.4. Perfection and Uniqueness: Excellence in One's Own Way

I turn now to a consideration of the nature of virtue itself. Eric L. Hutton's recent (2001) translation of various sections of the *Xunzi* is in some ways an improvement over previous ones. At times, however, his translation is misleading regarding what it is to be an achieved person, one who has developed an admirable character. Translating *de* 德 as "Virtue" with a capital "V,"[59] which suggests some connection with the divine or with an absolute reality of some kind, is emblematic of a realist understanding of virtue, and his use of words such as "perfect" and "complete" suggest a closed conception of human moral potential. For example, he translates a section near the end of the first chapter, "Exhorting Learning" (*quanxue* 勸學), as follows: "Make it perfect and complete, and only then is it truly learning. The gentleman knows that whatever is imperfect and unrefined does not deserve praise" (Hutton 2001, 252). Shortly after this, the chapter concludes, in Hutton's translation, as follows: "When one has grasped Virtue, then one can achieve fixity. When one can achieve fixity, then one can respond to things. To be capable both of fixity and of responding to things—such a one is called the perfect person. Heaven shows off its brilliance,

---

58. 順其類者謂之福。逆其類者謂之禍。夫是之謂天政。(62–63/17/12–13; K: 17.3a; W 81).

59. Hutton has informed me that translating *de* as "Virtue" with a capital "V" was not his own decision, it was made by the editors of the collection (P. J. Ivanhoe and Brian Van Norden). Further, Hutton believes that it was not intended to signal any association with the divine. Nevertheless, the effect remains—especially in combination with the all-too-common translation of *tian* as "Heaven," with a capital "H."

earth shows off its breadth, and the gentleman values his perfection" (252). This may give the impression that there is some perfect way for a person to be, and that when one achieves this state one no longer changes or grows—one has achieved "fixity."[60]

Since Xunzi contrasts human nature being crude or ugly with *wei* (constructive artifice)—*li* (norms of ritual propriety) in particular—being beautiful, it would make sense for him to also suggest that *li*, and the person well versed in it, is "consummate." That is, the accomplished person achieves an *aesthetic* perfection (if we are to use this word at all), and thus one that is nonexclusive and nonfinal. Below I will consider the argument for nonexclusivity, that is, that there is no uniquely privileged way for a person to be consummate. For the moment, I will concentrate on establishing that for Xunzi moral development never reaches a state of finality or completion.

The first words of "Exhorting Learning" (and thus of the entire text) read: "Exemplary people say: Learning must never cease."[61] Later in the chapter more detail is given:

> Where does learning begin, and where does it end? I say: Regarding its method, it begins with reciting the classics and ends with studying ritual propriety. Regarding developing a sense of appropriateness, it begins with becoming a scholar-official and ends with becoming a sage. When one has accumulated one's strength for a long time, then one is ready to begin. Learning continues until death and only then stops. Thus, the method of learning has an end, but it is never appropriate to abandon it. To do it is to be human; to abandon it is to be a beast.[62]

What is true of Xunzi's idea of individual moral development is likewise true of his ideal of cultural development. There is no completed culture any more than there is ever a completed person.

Now, retranslating the two passages in question reveals an alternative understanding of Xunzi's message here, one both more consistent with Xunzi's thought overall, and with the purpose of the chapter stated in its title and opening sentence—exhorting people to continually learn and improve:

---

60. Based on an informal correspondence with Hutton regarding an earlier version of this chapter, I have come to believe that my disagreement with him on this point turns out to be more a matter of what is the appropriate language to express more or less similar ideas, than it is a substantial difference in interpretation. For, it seems, that what Hutton means by "fixity" is really just resolve, that is, steadfastness in one's commitment to pursuing the way. I would stress, however, that the language of "fixity" when combined with that of "perfection," and the idea of achieving capital V "Virtue," especially in the context of someone who has been characterized as a realist, objectivist, and absolutist, regarding various other aspects of his worldview, can be at least misleading.

61. 君子曰。學不可以已。 (1/1/1; K: 1.1; W 15).

62. 學惡乎始。惡乎終。曰。其數則始乎誦經。終乎讀禮。其義則始乎為士。終乎為聖人。真積力久則入。學至乎沒而後止也。故學數有終。若其義則不可須臾舍也。為之人也。舍之禽獸也。 (2/1/26–28; K: 1.8; W 19; H 250; D 36).

Completely integrate one's learning, put it fully to use, and only then is one learned. Exemplary people know that what is neither whole (*quan* 全)[63] nor pure (*cui* 粹)[64] is not sufficient to be deemed beautiful or admirable (*mei* 美).[65]

> Only when one is steadfast in moral integrity (*decao* 德操)[66] can one be resolute (*ding* 定). When one is resolute, only then can one be responsive and adaptable (*ying* 應). Such people are called an accomplished people (*chengren* 成人). The value of the heavens is seen to be its brightness; that of the earth is seen to be its breath; what exemplary people value is their wholeness (*quan* 全).[67]

On this reading, these passages do not suggest a terminal point in moral development.

Let's turn now to the second point, which I promised to discuss, that to be an achieved or accomplished person is to be admirable (*mei*) in one's own unique way. Consider the following short passage: "Those who are subtle are the most achieved people (*zhiren* 至人)."[68] Watson and Knoblock both translate *zhiren* as "perfect man" (Knoblock goes as far as to capitalize this). Hutton improves on this only slightly; eschewing sexist language, he renders it "perfected person."

Consider what the idea of subtlety implies. Can subtlety be characterized in terms of specific kinds of dispositions with particular directions and degrees? Does it not rather suggest that truly achieved people, each in their own enigmatic way, exhibit a kind of effortless activity (*wuwei* 無為) arising from a developed character uniquely fitting for both the enduring aspects of morality as well as their own personal traits and personality? It is more likely closer to the latter. Achieved people are not all alike. They are each subtle in their own way.

For example, Xunzi characterizes Confucius as follows: "Confucius was

---

63. *Quan* 全, which is often translated as "complete," means "whole." In this passage it is a wholeness that implies being fully *integrated*. Once one has achieved integrity, one is ready to be a model. But, unlike the word "complete," this does not at all imply that the work is over—indeed here it suggests that the work has only begun.

64. That this passage is concerned with integrity is further supported by considering that *cui* 粹 (pure) can be a loan for *cui* 萃 (gather together). In either case really, but more clearly in the case of "gather together," the idea of integrity is implicit. I have used the standard translation "pure" with some reservation. The English word "pure" has several meanings, most of which are misleading in this context. It is the sense of "unmixed" that is intended, implying consistency of conduct as well as congruence between theory and practice, that is, invariably following one's considered sense of propriety.

65. 全之盡之。然後學者也。君子知夫不全不粹之不足以為美也。 (3/1/45–46; K: 1.13–14; W 22; H 252; D 40).

66. The preceding sentence defines *decao* as "following this [i.e., learning] in life, following it until death." 生乎由是。死乎由是。夫是之謂德操。 (3/1/49–50; K: 1.14; W 23; H 252; D 41). Note that learning (*xue* 學) is not limited to book learning in this context. The inseparability of knowledge and practice makes learning the rough equivalent of self-cultivation, or moral training.

67. 德操然後能定。能定然後能應。能定能應。夫是之謂成人。天見其明。地見其光。君子貴其全也。 (3/1/50–51; K: 1.14; W 23; H 252; D 41).

68. 夫微者至人也。 (81/21/55; K: 21.7d; W 133; H 278).

ren 仁[69] and wise, and moreover was not obsessed. His study of an eclectic variety of doctrines and arts is sufficient to rank him among the former kings. [Appropriating them into] a single school, he achieved an encompassing way. He promoted it, and put it to use, without being obsessed by old customs.[70] Thus, he had transformative power (*de*) on par with the duke of Zhou, and acquired fame equal to that of the three kings. These are the fortunes of not being obsessed."[71] Confucius is described here not as someone who met some specific preexisting standard, but someone who developed his own way, and an inspiring character.

Jonathan W. Schofer has made the following instructive observation: "A discovery model of attaining virtue is based on ontological notions that people have a 'fundamental nature' or 'true self' that is covered or obscured. In a discovery model, attaining virtue consists in touching or realizing that true self. The person thus *discovers* a true essential self. Xunzi's view of how people attain virtue is clearly not a discovery mode" (2000, 71). One would expect broad agreement here, that Xunzi does not offer *this kind* of discovery model. There does seem, however, to be another kind of discovery model at work in some interpretations of Xunzi that I would question. Regarding ritual propriety, for example, Benjamin Schwartz writes, "[I]t would appear that what the ancient sages did in bringing the order of society into existence was not invent an arbitrary system of *li* but 'discover' it by a process of arduous reflection" (1985, 301–2). Similarly, Xunzi's position may be taken to be that while we do not discover who we really are, we do discover the best way for us to be. Virtues, on this model, like the unique set of specific rites that lead to them, would still turn out to be discoveries.[72] There would seem to be, on this model, a predetermined *ideal* that, through ritual practice, we may come to realize.

Similarly, in the context of a discussion of Xunzi's thought, Graham has written, "Morality has the pattern (*li*) by which it is knowable by thought; man

---

69. *Ren* can be considered a combination of *zhong* and *shu*, doing one's utmost in the service of others. It includes exhibiting an array of virtues. See the glossary for more on the meaning of *ren*.

70. Morohashi, citing this passage, defines *cheng ji* as: "Something established as a custom. Old custom." 習慣として出来上ったもの。古いならはし。 He is following Yang Liang, who comments, "*cheng ji* means old custom." 成積，舊習也。 This passage occurs in the context of a criticism of other philosophers for being blinded by their main concern. For example, Mozi was so obsessed with the practical use of things (*yong* 用) that he did not appreciate cultural refinement, and Zhuangzi was so blinded by the propensities of nature (*tian* 天) that he failed to appreciate the role of people. The meaning of this passage is that Confucius, on the contrary, indeed stressed the value of ancient customs, but he was not blinded by or obsessed with them. That is, he was also cognizant of other relevant considerations: the role of nature as well as that of humans, the importance of utilitarian considerations as well as cultural refinement, and so on. Thus, this passage strongly suggests that interpretations of Confucianism that imply blind obedience to tradition are suspect.

71. 孔子仁知且不蔽。故學亂術足以為先王者也。一家得周道舉而用之。不蔽於成積也。故德與周公齊。名與三王並。此不蔽之福也。 (79/21/26–28; K: 21.4; W 126; H 274).

72. Schofer does not address the issue of this kind of discovery model explicitly, and there is no clear indication of whether he would endorse or reject it.

has, presumably in his nature, the equipment by which, although his desires run the other way, it is possible for him to know it" (1989, 249).[73] According to the model of moral development being presented here, on the contrary, moral wisdom for Xunzi is gained through a process of habituation and is not a product of detached rational thought.[74] For Xunzi, moral development goes through stages that involve following the model of exemplary people and acquiring from that experience an appreciation for the rites and a fondness for acting virtuously.[75]

As Schofer also points out, a "development model" in which virtues develop in a way analogous to plant growth does not fully capture Xunzi's view since he uses images of external standards as the means of reforming one's character, such as a straightening board being used to straighten wood (see Schofer 2000, 71–72). It warrants comment, however, that these means are not entirely external. Murase makes the point that one does not rely on external standards alone in reforming one's character. He writes:

> For Xunzi, "human formation" means transforming one's internal nature (the raw material)—which is given as a simple possibility—by infusing artificial operations, and in this way realizing human values (the flourishing of cultural patterns). However, the artificial operations that are at work in this case are not just actions from the outside like education; they also include one's own inner operations, the main organ of which is the heart-mind. In other words, it is not the case that Xunzi is talking about human formation as leaving out the active thinking operations of the heart-mind.[76]

---

73. See section 2.1 for more on this and similar ideas.

74. For Xunzi, moral insight is not derived solely from reason, or pure reflection. As Schofer points out, "Conscious activity is not simply a matter of reflection. In fact, Xunzi sees pure reflective thought as having little value for learning" (2000, 70). Xunzi writes, "I once spent an entire day thinking, but it was not as good as a mere moment of learning." 吾嘗終日而思矣。不如須臾之所學也。 (1/1/6; K: 1.3; W 16; H 249; cf. *Analects* 15.31 and 2.15).

75. "When one emulates those of outstanding character and one's purpose is firm, when one is fond of cultivating oneself according to what one has been taught, thereby raising and adorning one's emotional nature . . . such a person may be called a sincere and magnanimous exemplary person." 行法至堅。好脩正其所聞。以橋[撟]飾其情性... 如是則可謂篤厚君子矣。 (22/8/57–59; K: 8.7). "Their purposes settle comfortably on the public good; their conduct settles comfortably in self-cultivation. They thoroughly understand the guiding principle of categories. Such people may be called 'Great Confucians.'" 志安公。行安脩。知通統類。如是則可謂大儒矣。 (25/8/122; K: 8.12).

76. すなわち荀子にあっては、人間形成とは、単なる可能性として与えられている内部の自然（本始材朴）に人為的作用を加えてこれを変革し、そこに人間的価値性（文理隆盛）を実現することであるが、その際、ここに働く人為的作用には、教育のような外部からの作用だけでなく、「心」を主体とする自己内部の作用も含まれている。つまり荀子は「心」の能動的な思慮作用を抜きにして人間形成を語っているわけではないのである。 (Murase 1986, 50). Cf. Lao Siguang: "This is nothing more than taking the establishment of *liyi* to reside in people's effort and their own conscious effort, thus [Xunzi] illustrated it using the analogy of a craftsman making a utensil. The earth and wood await people to turn them into utensils (*chengqi* 成器) with great effort, that is, relying on external transformative forces to turn them into utensils.

On Xunzi's conception, "inner" and "outer" are interpenetrating and complementary. The so-called "external" means are, after all, artifice (*wei*). As such, they are the product of conscious activity—which cannot be construed as entirely external. Indeed, Murase's points dovetails with this one: it is constant (re-)interpretation ("the active thinking operations of the heart-mind") which always-ongoingly determines, reaffirms, and adjusts these allegedly "external" standards.

Speculating on why Xunzi did not offer any detailed account of individual virtues, Schofer writes, "he [Xunzi] does not want people to think that they can have a clear sense of what virtue is without re-forming themselves through ritual and study" (2000, 84). This seems consistent, for example, with Xunzi's emphasizing that there is no short cut to learning. "If there is no dark and dogged will, there will be no shining accomplishment; if there is no dull and determined effort, there will be no brilliant achievement."[77] Notice that in Xunzi's characterization of learning there may be "shining accomplishments" and "brilliant achievements," but there is no suggestion of a final end. It is likewise with the attainment of virtue—and with the construction of culture for that matter. Schofer speculates, "Perhaps Xunzi is afraid that if he were to give focused attention to human excellence itself, he would lead people to think that they know what virtue is before they reach a state where they are truly able to have that knowledge" (2000, 84). Given Xunzi's conception of the unity of knowledge and practice, it would indeed be impossible to have "knowledge" of virtues without embodying them in one's conduct. Xunzi writes, "One should study until one puts it [the way] into practice. To practice it is to have clarity."[78] In addition, considering the view of *li* presented in the previous chapter, we may speculate that virtues, likewise, have no determinate form; there is nothing fixed of which one might have knowledge. That is, perhaps, Xunzi does not outline the specific characteristics of virtues because the cultivated and subtle person, who becomes truly authoritative, becomes the author and reinterpreter of virtue, rather than attaining some predestined form of it. In other words, through ritual practice, study, and in other ways doggedly striving to cultivate oneself, one develops, not the *knowledge* of what virtue *is*—in the sense of a

---

Since Xunzi uses this as an analogy for people, people must wait for an external transformative force thereby to turn them into [people of] *liyi*. Even so, from where does this external force originate? Xunzi again takes it as coming from 'people', but in this case 'people' simply pertains to 'sages.'" 此仍不過以為人在自覺努力中創建禮義，故以工人為器喻之。土木待人之努力而成器，即依外來之改造力量而成器。荀子以此喻人，則人須待外來之改造力量以成禮義矣。然而此外來力量源自何處，荀子又以為仍來自「人」，不過此種「人」係「聖人」而已。 (Lao, p. 260). Note that *chengqi* 成器 also means "growing up to be a useful people."

77. 是故無冥冥之志者。無昭昭之明。無惛惛之事者。無赫赫之功。 (2/1/21–22; K:1.6; W 18). Watson's translation.

78. 學至於行之而止矣。行之明也。 (24/8/102–3; K: 8.11). Cf. "Completely integrate one's learning, put it fully to use, and only then is one learned." 全之盡之。然後學者也。 (3/1/45–46; K: 1.13; W 22; H 252).

specific set of definable virtues—but rather the ability to act effectively in ways that are worthy of admiration and emulation.[79] This is, in essence, to have *de* 德, moral power.

Schofer does outline some "specific virtues such as oneness, having broad intentions, being respectful, and subtlety" (2000, 85). It is perfectly appropriate and potentially illuminating for us to look back at Xunzi's work and try to clarify what Xunzi's own view of some set of virtues may have been, as Schofer has done with his explication of "oneness" as a preservative virtue, and "subtlety" as a virtue characteristic of a sage.[80] Nevertheless, that Xunzi had his own interpretation of virtues does not commit him to the view that there is only one real, exclusively legitimate, specific set of virtues, and that he got it right for everywhere and all time. That is, while he does employ a conception of virtues, we need not ascribe to him a *worldview* that would support absolutist claims about them. In fact, describing one who has attained particularly clear insight, Xunzi goes as far as to ask rhetorically, "So extensive, so expansive, who know his limits? So broad-minded, so boundless, who knows his virtue? Boiling and bubbling, from one to another, who knows his form?"[81]

It should not be too surprising that those who are morally cultivated never stop changing and growing, and responding in innovative ways to new circumstances. After all, considering Confucius's own moral struggle, we may readily infer that the exemplary person never gives up trying to become better. In addition, Xunzi's assumption that there may be more than one way to be virtuous is consistent with Confucius's teaching. For example, when asked by Zilu about the accomplished person (*chengren* 成人), Confucius suggests that there is more than one possible description of such a person, saying: "People who

---

79. Schofer acknowledges that fully cultured people use their own judgment, "their own sense of 'proper order.'" He writes, "The sages' excellence, or 'brightness,' is internal. They follow their desires and their own sense of 'proper order;' they no longer have to rely on external guides and prods, such as teachers and a burning stick, to know and do what is good. In other words, the sages have fully acquired virtuous dispositions" (2000, 81). However, this statement seems ambivalent regarding the question of whether an exemplary person's "own sense of proper order" will necessarily always yield the same knowledge of what is good, and result in identical virtuous dispositions.

80. The classification of subtlety as a virtue is questionable, since subtlety is a more holistic concept then traditional virtues are. If we take a broad view of what count as a virtue, uniqueness itself may be considered a virtue. The opening passage in the *Zhongyong* may be interpreted to suggest this: "[E]xemplary persons are ever concerned about their uniqueness." 故君子慎其獨也。 (Ames and Hall's translation, 2001, 45, 89).

81. 恢恢廣廣。孰知其極。睪睪廣廣。孰知其德。涫涫紛紛。孰知其形。 (80/21/43–44; K: 21.5e; W 129). Knoblock, following commentaries, suggests reading: 睪 as 嶧, 廣 as 曠, and 涫 as 滾. Cf. the following passage from the *Zhongyong*: "The *Book of Songs* says, 'Moral power (*de* 德) is light as a feather,' but a feather still can be classified (*lun* 倫). 'What permeates the sky above has neither sound nor scent.'—an accomplishment indeed." 詩曰：「德輶如毛。」毛猶有倫。「上天之載，無聲無臭。」至矣！ (*Zhongyong* 33). Fu Yunlong and He Zuokang interpret the last bit tagged on at the end (*zhi yi* 至矣) as "This is the best description of virtues" 這才是對品德的最好形容。 (1996, 107). The suggestion seems to be that *de* 德 (virtue, or moral power) resists classification.

are as knowledgeable as Zhang Wuzhong, as free from desires as Gongzhuo, as brave as Bian Zhuangzi, as skilled in the arts as Ranyou, and are cultivated by means of ritual propriety and music, surely they can be considered accomplished people." He continues: "Must accomplished people today necessarily be like this? At the sight of profit, those who think of what is appropriate, at the sight of danger, those who would offer their lives, when in want for a long time, those who do not forget the words they lived by in better times, they surely may also be considered accomplished people."[82] The *Analects* also records several passages in which, rather than asserting a fixed classification of prescriptions and prohibitions, Confucius says that he considers things case by case.[83] These considerations bolster Cua's claim that *dao*, as an ideal way of life, "is more like a theme to be developed in the concrete setting of human life than a norm that contains specific precepts of content" (1998, 274 n19).

Speaking of the virtue *ren* 仁 in Confucianism generally, Cua makes a similar point, clarifying his distinction between an "ideal theme" and an "ideal norm." He writes, "*[R]en* is more an ideal theme, a standard of inspiration, than an ideal norm. The realization of *ren* will thus be manifested in an individual's style or manner of performance and/or style of life. As an ideal theme, *ren* is a quasi-aesthetic vision that provides a point of orientation. It is expected that the achievement of *ren* as an ideal theme will be a polymorphous exemplification, especially in the lives of paradigmatic individuals"[84] (1998, 233). As a "theme" this ideal accommodates differing exemplifications. The theme itself may be thought of as being composed of these differing exemplifications, and thus is subject to movement since the sum of specific personalizations will vary over time.

Ames and Rosemont use different language, saying there is "no ideal." Indeed, the language of "ideals" can be at least misleading. Nevertheless, the description they offer does not seem to be at odds with the intent of Cua's "ideal theme." They write, "Given that *ren* denotes the qualitative transformation of a *particular* person, it is further ambiguous because it must be understood relative to the specific concrete conditions of that person. There is no formula,

---

82. 子路問成人。子曰：若臧武仲之知，公綽之不欲，卞莊子之勇，冉求之藝，文之以禮樂，亦可以為成人矣。曰：今之成人者何必然？見利思義，見危授命，久要不忘平生之言，亦可以為成人矣。 *Analects* 14.12. It is ambiguous in both descriptions whether a person must have all or just one of the stated qualities to qualify as accomplished. It is unambiguous, however, that a person qualifying under either description would be considered accomplished. Further, the characterizations are nonexhaustive—they are merely examples of clear cases.

83. Here I am thinking particularly of *Analects* 2.14, 4.10, and 18.8.

84. Expressing the manner in which the *junzi* serves as a "standard of inspiration," Cua also writes, "Arguably, Confucius's notion of *junzi* expresses the idea of paradigmatic individuals as exemplary embodiments of the spirit and vitality of the tradition. In addition to functioning in moral education, they also serve as living exemplars of the transformative significance of the ideal of the tradition, thus invigorating the tradition. Even more important, for those committed to tradition, paradigmatic individuals serve as points of orientation, as standards of inspiration" (1998, 241–42).

no ideal. Like a work of art, it is a process of disclosure rather than closure, resisting fixed definition and replication" (1998, 50).

Those aspiring to moral cultivation take a worthy teacher as their standard. The teacher, in order to be "worthy" of being an example to others, must be morally admirable. Nevertheless, the standard the teacher offers could be called, to use Cua's words, "a standard of inspiration." The teacher provides a concrete interpretation worthy of emulation, though ultimately to emulate is not the same as to copy. The teacher's actions always involve an interpretation of what is called for in a situation. Thus to truly emulate the teacher, the student must also learn to interpret.[85] If this depiction is accurate, though this process takes place in the context of existing norms, these norms themselves are not the standard to which one conforms. One cannot conform to an uninterpreted abstract standard, but one can model the concrete interpretation of these standards exhibited by a moral exemplar. It is the role of exemplary people to continually interpret norms and standards.

In a recent article comparing Aristotelian and Confucian virtues, Nicholas F. Gier opines, "Aesthetic order focuses on the concrete particulars so thoroughly that there can be no substitution and no interchangeability. This applies to a work of art as much as to a person of great virtue" (2001, 291). Gier offers the following reformulation of Gaozi's famous woodworking analogy,[86] noting that he believes that Xunzi would embrace the new version:

> Woodworkers always look for certain features in the wood they select, sometimes choosing certain patterns in the wood's grain or even a knot around which there are sometimes beautiful swirls. In this alternative reading of Gaozi's analogy, the person of vice would be like the woodworker who works against the grain and destroys the beauty of the original forms. The virtuous person, on the other hand, works with the grain of her own nature, respecting its innate patterns, and makes herself into a thing of moral beauty. (294)[87]

---

85. *Analects* 15.36 suggests that, at least in some situations, an individual's own interpretation can override even his or her teacher's: "Facing *ren* 仁 [an opportunity to exhibit the highest virtue] do not yield even to your teacher." 當仁，不讓於師。

86. "Gaozi said: 'Nature is like a willow. Appropriateness is like cups and dishes. Making a virtuous person with a sense of appropriateness out of human nature is like making cups and dishes from a willow.'" 告子曰：「性猶杞柳也，義猶桮棬也；以人性為仁義，猶以杞柳為桮棬。」 (*Mencius* 11.1).

87. Mencius suggests that, according to Gaozi's position, one must do violence to one's willowlike nature in order to become virtuous. Xunzi, however, though he does take our original nature to be crude, is quite optimistic about our ability to develop it. And, though he suggests that this will take strenuous effort, it is done in consideration of human aspirations, potentials, and even some of our natural feelings such as "remembrance and longing" (see W 110; K: 19.11). Thus, Xunzi would likely reject Mencius's characterization. Indeed, Xunzi recasts the reformation of one's character as adornment. See 22/8/57, cited in footnote 75, and 73/19/75, cited in section 5.1 above.

Gier makes clear that the resulting set of virtues would and should be unique to each person rather than corresponding to some specific set of privileged dispositions. He writes, "The virtue-ethics approach is . . . to develop a unique ensemble of behaviors, dispositions, and qualities that lead to human excellence" (300). Note that it is not that we must develop *the* unique ensemble that leads to human excellence, but rather an ensemble unique to each of us.

> In contrast to the father who tells his son "Be just like me," a contemporary Confucian (following the craft analogy) would say "Be your own person" and develop a unique ensemble of character traits, moral dispositions, and behaviors. Confucius might have said: "Don't be just any old mug, be a gem!" Or a contemporary Confucian would say: "Don't be a chip off the old block, but carve your own nature." It is significant to observe that we sometimes use the word "gem" to describe a person of good character. (297)

If there is a privileging of some trait in this depiction, it is that of always making a conscientious effort to personalize one's self-cultivation.

It is clear that Xunzi believed that our problematic original nature can and should be transformed to allow people and society to flourish. Moreover, he believed, we can and should construct categories and practices that facilitate this. While we would expect a person who had achieved noteworthy success in self-cultivation to be admirable in many ways, it is not clear that Xunzi believed that there was a privileged conception of precisely what such a person would be like. As Chen Daqi remarks, "*Wei* is not the same in everyone."[88] I would add (or perhaps merely clarify) that not only are there differences between those more morally developed and those less so, but *wei* is not even the same in various moral exemplars—or even in the same individual at different times. Further, the categories that describe the virtuous person would be, after all, constructs;[89] and as such, they would be subject to continuous reinterpretation, reevaluation, and reappropriation.

5.5. Political Implications

Xunzi's theory suggests a mutually supportive relationship between good government and virtue. Good government fosters cultural artifice—such as norms of ritual propriety and constructive distinctions in language, as well as appropriate music, laws, and standards—that create fertile conditions for the

---

88. 偽不是人人所同的。 (Chen 1954, 58–59).

89. As T. C. Kline observes, Xunzi recognizes virtuous dispositions as products of *wei*. Referring to virtuous motivation, as contrasted with our original desires, Kline writes, "This new motive is explicitly described as a result of deliberative activity 偽 *wei*. It is definitely not a naturally occurring state of mind, emerging from human nature" (2000, 161).

development of virtue. At the same time, the virtuous person must construct and sustain this cultural artifice. The latter part of this relation is expressed in Xunzi's descriptions of the insufficiency of good policies, or laws (*fa* 法), and the need for good people to interpret and administer them. Xunzi writes:

> Exemplary people are vital for uniting the way (*dao*) with law (*fa*). They must not be neglected for even for a short time. If they are acquired there will be order; if they are lost there will be chaos. If they are acquired there will be peace and security; if they are lost there will be danger. If they are acquired [the state] will survive; if they are lost it will perish. Thus, there are cases in which there were good laws, and yet there was chaos. But I have never heard of a case, from ancient times to the present, of their being exemplary people and yet chaos. A tradition says, "Order is produced by exemplary people; chaos is produced by inferior people." This expresses my point.[90]

Xunzi also writes:

> There are disorderly rulers, not disorderly states. There are orderly people, not orderly laws and norms (*fa*).[91] The methods of the archer Yi are not lost, yet such an archer does not appear generation after generation. The laws and norms of the sage king Yu [of the Xia dynasty] still exist, yet the Xia could not continue its rule. Thus, laws and norms cannot stand alone. Categories cannot apply themselves. If there are good people, then [the state] will survive. If there are no good people then it will be lost. Laws and norms are the starting point of orderly government. Exemplary people are the wellspring of these laws and norms. Thus, if there are exemplary people, this is sufficient for a vast state, even if laws and norms are omitted. But if there are no exemplary people, then although a state may be equipped with laws and norms, it will misstep in the application of priorities, and its inability to cope with changing circumstances will suffice to result in anarchy.[92]

---

90. 君子也者。道法之摠要也。不可少頃曠也。得之則治。失之則亂。得之則安。失之則危。得之則存。失之則亡。故有良法而亂者有之矣。有君子而亂者自古及今未嘗聞也。傳曰。治生乎君子。亂生乎小人。此之謂也。 (52/14/11–13; K: 14.2; Sato 2003, 337–38 and 410).

91. Cf. Knoblock's translation (K: 12.1): "There are lords who produce chaos in their states, but there are no countries that are naturally chaotic; there are men who can bring order about, but there is no model that will produce order." This spells out the point better than the more literal yet cryptic version given in the main text. It is analogous to the point that Xunzi makes at the beginning of the *tian lun* chapter ("A Discussion of *tian*"). Rather than being the work of *tian* (i.e. natural propensities associated with "the heavens"), it is the action people that gives rise to fortune or misfortune; similarly, laws by themselves cannot assure order, appropriate interpretation and implementation of those laws are also necessary.

92. 有亂君。無亂國。有治人。無治法。羿之法非亡也。而羿不世中。禹之法猶存。而夏不世王。故法不能獨立。類不能自行。得其人則存。失其人則。法者治之端也。君子者法之原也。故有君子。則法雖省。足以偏矣。無君子。則法雖具。失先後之施。不能應事之變。足以亂矣。 (44/12/1–4; K: 12.1).

A similar sentiment is expressed in the *Zhongyong*: "The orders issued by King Wen and King Wu written on bamboo strips were effective only when there were wise and virtuous officials. If there were no wise and virtuous officials, the orders would not have been effective."[93]

Although Xunzi clearly percieves a role for law,[94] his praise of legalism is severely limited. He writes, for example, "[The legalist state of Qin] concurrently possesses numerous positive qualities in the greatest possible degree, yet if one measures it by the success and fame of a true king, it is far inferior. Why is this? Because of the dearth of Confucians."[95]

What is most important for good government is good people, and since people's original set of desires are problematic, a society needs mechanisms (*wei* 偽) that will encourage and facilitate moral development. Confucius recognized that law was not the best means to achieve this: "Lead them with [legalistic] government, keep them in order with punishments, and the common people will avoid trouble but have no sense of shame. Lead them with *de* (charismatic virtue), keep them in order with *li* (ritual propriety), and they will not only develop a sense of shame, but will reform themselves."[96] After one has reformed and oneself, and cultivated one's virtue sufficiently, one is prepared to be of service in govenment, and participate in cultivating cultrual constructs. Xunzi writes,

> What I refer to as *renyi* (comprehensive virtue and a sense of appropriateness) is the opportunity for the greatest of opportunities. This comprehensive virtue and appropriateness is that by which good government is cultivated (*xiuzheng*). . . . [The triumphs of Tang and Wu] were a result of their prior conduct and habitual cultivation [i.e., of their own moral qualities and of good government].[97]

As Sato points out, "[T]he term *xiuzheng* 修政 in the Confucian intellectual tradition is analogical to '*xiushen* 修身' (self-cultivation). It is in this analogical link that we can see why moral values and policy implementation are directly combined in Xunzi's statement" (2003, 271). Good govenmental policies, in order to be effectively administered, need to be cultivated by those who have also cultivated a moral sense and character.

---

93. 哀公問政。子曰：文武之政，布在方策。其人存，則其政舉：其人亡，則其政息。 (*Zhongyong* 20, Fu Yunlong and He Zuokang's translation, p. 61).

94. See the latter part of section 1.2.1, and the corresponding footnotes. See also *Xunzi* book 9, *wang zhi* 王制 ("Kingly Regulations"), especially K: 9.12–9.13; W 42–43.

95. 兼是數具者。而盡有之。然而縣之以王者之功名。則倜倜然其不及遠矣。是何也。則其殆無儒邪。 (61/16/67–68; K: 16.6).

96. 子曰：「道之以政，齊之以刑，民免而無恥：道之以德，齊之以禮，有恥且格。」 (*Analects* 2.3; cf. *Analects* 13.6 and 13.13).

97. 吾所謂仁義者。大便之便也。彼仁義者所以脩政者也。... 皆前行素脩也。 (56/15/73–77; K: 15.3; Sato 2003, 270).

When it comes to managing a myriad changes, adjudicating[98] the myriad phenomena, nurturing (*yang*) the myriads of common people, and simultaneously governing the whole empire, those of comprehensive virtue (*ren ren* 仁人) are the best (*shan* 善). Their wisdom and planning are sufficient to manage the changes; their virtue and generosity are sufficient to pacify the common people; and the resonance of their moral power (*de*) is sufficient to transform them. If such people are obtained, there will be order; if not, there will be chaos.[99]

Xunzi repeatedly stresses the need for people of exemplary character, whose moral authority is sufficient to inspire, and whose judgment is sound enough to intelligently interpret existing policies as well as extend tradition appropriately to cover new situations. Most importantly, this system of governance, which requires good and wise people to manage it, must be so constituted as to continually produce such people. From a Confucian perspective, it is norms of ritual propriety and morally attuned language, more than laws, that are essential for this task to be effectively sustained.[100]

5.6. Conclusion

Classics like the *Xunzi* do not interpret themselves. Thus, just as every act of ritual propriety necessarily involves the exercise of judgment and discretion—which must be in some degree personal—so too any explication of the philosophy of Xunzi involves an interpretation from which the interpreter cannot hope to fully extract him- or herself. All significant Confucian thinkers, while representing Confucius, have at the same time added to, emended, or otherwise embellished Confucius's ideas, and the traditional understanding of those ideas.[101] Indeed, it is this contribution that makes them significant.

In arguing for a constructivist understanding of Xunzi, I attempt to make a contribution of my own. However, interpretation does not occur in a vacuum; and the *Xunzi* is not a blank slate. Thus, I have tried to tie my interpretation as closely to the text as possible, and have offered my criticisms of competing interpretations based on close readings of key passages, as well as some appeals to authorities—a valid Confucian move. My purpose was not to prove that

---

98. I follow Knoblock and Yang Liang in reading *cai* 材 as *cai* 裁, and endorse this reading. The meaning of *cai* 裁 comes from the idea of cutting cloth. It is made up of *zai* (to cut) and *yi* 衣 (clothing). Karlgren defines *cai* 裁 as "to cut out cloths," "regulate, moderate," and "decide" (GSR: 943c').

99. 治萬變。材萬物。養萬民。兼制天下者。為莫若仁人之善也。夫故其知慮足以治之。其仁厚足以安之。其德音足以化之。得之則治。失之則亂。(33/10/30–32; K: 10.5).

100. This point has contemporary relevance, as it is largely this concern that motivates the so-called East Asian challenge to human rights—but that is a topic for another time.

101. Even Confucius himself, though he modestly claimed to be a mere transmitter and not an innovator (*Analects* 7.1), also remarked, "[Those who] rekindle the old with an understanding of the new, one may take them as teachers." 溫故而知新，可以為師矣。(*Analects* 2.11).

Xunzi was a constructivist, but rather to propose a manner of understanding Xunzi that has advantages over competing interpretations and represents a more compelling philosophical position, one that is philosophically viable both from contemporary Confucian perspectives and from contemporary Western ones.

Simply stated, the view is as follows: *Dao* signifies a broad vision of a way to achieve and maintain a harmonious and stable social reality, given the propensities of nature and human nature. However, rather than being a closed or determinate conception, its very breath contributes to its openness in the sense that all matters must be taken into consideration, including those which are historically contingent—and thus instantiations of the way may vary according to the particulars of ever-emerging situations. Patterns and categories are malleable interdependent social devises that are judged according to their practical success and mutual coherence. Naming properly (*zhengming*) is solidifying morally efficacious categories into language. Norms of ritual propriety are social patterns of deferential conduct conducive to social harmony. These are the embodiments of *dao*, continually negotiated through exemplary action; they form, at the same time, the basis for constructive discourse regarding the direction of the way.[102] They are both the means by which a person develops virtue, and the product of people who have been in this way cultivated.

There is a parallel between the continual process of learning, as one cultivates constructive habits, and the selective traditionalism involved in the evolution of norms of ritual propriety and other constructs. Traditions, like people, can and should grow and improve. However, the mechanisms that facilitate that growth are not fully separable from the substance of the growth. For instance, exemplary people, in their role as teachers and models, provide the means for others to become exemplary, and, at the same time, they represent culminations-in-progress of the very process of moral cultivation that they facilitate. Similarly, tradition provides a ground for reconstruction, while, at the same time, it is the evolution of constructs—through the continual interpretation of exemplary people—that composes (and continually recomposes) the tradition.

---

102. "If they respect ritual propriety only then can one speak meaningfully with them about the direction of the way. If their disposition is considerate only then can one speak meaningfully with them about the patterns of the way. If their demeanor is deferential only then can one speak meaningfully with them about transmitting the way." 故禮恭而後可與言道之方。辭順而後可與言道之理。色從而後可與言道之致。 (3/1/41–42; K: 1.12; W 21).

Glossary of Key Terms

In the list of glosses immediately following the character, quotation marks indicate common ones that I do not necessarily endorse, while italics indicates those recommended for consideration.

Dao 道 "The Way," a way, or path, *a holistic guiding moral discourse*. Eric Hutton describes *dao* as "an overall conception of how to live upon which deliberation focuses" (2002, 372). He suggests that *dao*, like Aristotle's *eudaimonia*, is "incapable of being completely captured in any set formulation" (373).[1] Hanfeizi, a student of Xunzi,[2] characterizes *dao*, saying: "As for what the Dao essentially is, it is undefined and unshaped, it yields with the times, it and the order of things correspond to each other."[3]

 Dao is an encompassing ethical doctrine that is conceptually coherent and composes a living tradition. It resonates with and is capable of uniting all levels of society, and effectively facilitates the achievement of cultural and human values such as peace, harmony, and joyful community life. *Dao* is the name for this vague ideal and for an effective path to it. It does not indicate a determinate, yet ineffable, metaphysical reality to be understood and conformed to. *Dao* is a way simultaneously followed and extended by exemplary people.

De 德 "Virtue," excellence, inner power, moral charisma, *compelling moral character*. Arthur Waley suggests that, depending on the situation, one may translate *de* as: moral force, character, or prestige (see Waley 1938, 33). Xunzi explicitly contrasts *de* with physical power: "The exemplary person uses moral power (*de*); the petty person uses physical power (*li* 力)."[4] Xunzi elsewhere explains, "Exemplary people achieve a compelling moral character

---

1. Hutton quotes Aristotle: "In matters of conduct and matters of what is beneficial (*ta sumpheronta*) there is nothing fixed, just as there is neither [anything fixed] in matters of health. And since the overall account is like this, even more so there is no exactness to be had in the account of things in individual cases, for they fall under neither art (*technē*) nor precepts, but instead it is necessary for those taking action to consider what is appropriate to the moment, just as it also holds in medicine and navigation" (Hutton 2002, 356, quoting *Ethica Nicomachea* 1104a3–10).

2. Hanfeizi and Li Si were Xunzi's two most famous students. Embarrassingly, they both became legalist. Although it is unknown just how close their contact with Xunzi actually was, many scholars believe Hanfeizi's philosophy was significantly influenced by Xunzi.

3. A. C. Graham's translation. 凡道之情，不制不形，柔弱隨時，與理想應。(*Hanfeizi*, chap. 20; Graham 1990, 60).

4. 君子以德。小人以力。(33/10/36; K: 10.6).

(*de*). Though silent, they serve as an analogy. Though not bestowing gifts, they are held dear. Though showing no anger, they have influential power stemming from their prestige."[5] *De* is a compelling moral force so potent that it is regarded a transformative (K: 10.5; cf. *Analects* 12.19).

E 惡 "Evil," bad, ugly, detestable, *crude*. *E* is simultaneously the opposite of *shan* (good, or morally adept) and of *mei* (beautiful, admirable). For Xunzi, *xing e* 性惡 amounts to: "original human nature is crude and unadorned." The gist of the "*xing e*" chapter, rather than "human nature is evil," can be stated more accurately as "original human nature is problematic." (See section 5.1)

Fa 法 Laws and norms, a standard, method, or *model*. *Fa* can have a meaning similar to penal law. On the other hand, more positively, it can indicate a model, in the sense of the conduct of a person who sets a standard worthy of emulation. It can also mean "method" as in "The methods (*fa*) of the archer Yi are not lost" (44/12/1–4; K: 12.1). These meanings are related, and often more than one is implicated to some degree. Herrlee G. Creel provides a useful characterization. He writes:

> The character *fa* has a whole series of meanings, which are closely related to the special nature of the Chinese idea of law as being that of a model, and as including not only what we regard as law but also many things that we would regard as merely regulations. This series might be represented as follows:
>
> model—method—technique—rule—regulation—law.
>
> There is a logical progression. A model is the pattern for the method of following it. Technique is method made more precise and formal. A rule describes an aspect of putting technique into practice. A regulation is a formalized rule. A law is a regulation established by authority, and often enforced by sanctions. This progression is not a series of steps, but rather a scale of infinite gradations, like a spectrum. (1974, 147–48)

He 和 *Harmony*. "The etymology of the term is culinary. Harmony is the art of combining and blending two or more foodstuffs so that they mutually enhance one another without losing their distinctive flavors" (Ames and Hall 2001, 65). *He*, not surprisingly, is also associated with music; in addition to meaning harmonious music, according to Karlgren, it can also mean to tune instruments, as well as "respond in singing" (GSR: 8e). It has the sense of to mix or to blend and is in this sense related to *he* 合, which not only means "to combine" but also suggests that the combination should be

---

5. 君子至德。嘿然而喻。未施而親。不怒而威。 (7/3/29–30; K: 3.9b; Cf. K: 16.2).

fitting. *He* 和 further implies mildness, and tranquility. The task of realizing a stable harmonious society is the heart of the Confucian project.

Junzi 君子 "Gentlemen," "superior man," noble person, *paradigmatic individual, exemplary person*. Confucius is responsible for altering the meaning of this term from denoting political status to indicating moral status. That is, what had meant mere prince, literally the son (*zi* 子) of a lord (*jun* 君), was altered to mean one worthy of high station by virtue of moral achievement. For Xunzi, as for other Confucians, *junzi* may be reasonably glossed "exemplary person,"[6] for the *junzi* is one who fulfills the critical role of teacher and model in Xunzi's moral scheme. Xunzi writes:

Sages speak volumes and make classifications; *junzi* speak seldom but serve as exemplary models (*fa* 法).[7]

The learning of the *junzi* enters through his ears, adheres to his thoughts and feelings (*xin* 心), spreads to his four limbs, and is embodied in his actions. Every word, every subtle movement, may be taken as a model and pattern.[8]

Junzi measure themselves with a stretched cord [i.e., strictly]. . . . Thus, they may be taken as a model worthy of emulation everywhere.[9]

Junzi achieve a compelling moral character (*de*). Though silent, they serve as an analogy. Though not bestowing gifts, they are held dear. Though showing no anger, they have influential power stemming from their prestige.[10]

The last quotation is reminiscent of Confucius's remark: "The moral power of the exemplary person is the wind; that of the petty person is grass. When the wind blows over the grass, it will surely bend."[11] This statement occurs in the context of Confucius encouraging a ruler to be good (*shan*) and govern properly, for in so doing he would be a model for the people. However, *junzi* are supposed to be modest about all this (see 107/31/13–14; K: 31.2).

Paul Goldin's translation of *junzi* as "noble man" is a clever attempt to suggest both the earlier political meaning as well as the later moral meaning. However, it does not directly reveal the function of *junzi* as moral

---

6. Ames and Rosemont have used this phrase "exemplary person" to translate *junzi* in their *The Analects of Confucius: A Philosophical Translation*. Similarly, A. S. Cua uses the phrase "paradigmatic individual." For a defense of the characterization of a *junzi* as a "model" in the *Analects*, including an etymology of the word, see Hall and Ames 1987, 182–92.

7. 故多言而類，聖人也。少言而法，君子也。 (16/6/22–23; K: 6.9).

8. 君子之學也。入乎耳。箸乎心。布乎四體。形乎動靜。端而言。蝡而動。一可以為法則。 (2/1/30–31; K: 1.9; W 20; H 250).

9. 故君子之度己則以繩。. . . 故足以為天下法則矣。 (14/5/47–48; K: 5.7).

10. 君子至德。嘿然而喻。未施而親。不怒而威。 (7/3/29–30; K: 3.9b).

11. 君子之德風，小人之德草。草上之風，必偃。 (*Analects* 12.19).

exemplars. In addition, when Confucius changes *junzi* from a political and hereditary concept to a moral one, the concept *junzi*, at least arguably, loses its gender.

Lei 類 "Type," category, *analogical grouping*. Its more basic meaning is resemblance, in the sense of being similar or analogous. It can also be used as "roughly." Though it can mean a "type" of thing or event, as Robert Eno notes: "When we view the text as a whole, it is apparent that the terms 'type' (*lei*) and 'distinction' (*bian*) are used to refer less to objective entities than to situations, behavior, and value" (1990, 146). For example: "A model (*fa*) cannot stand on its own, categories (*lei*) cannot apply themselves."[12] And, "If there is a law (*fa*), carry it out. If there is not, decide (*ju* 舉) according to analogical extension (*lei*)."[13] In addition, according to Karlgren, *lei* can mean, "discriminate" in the sense of "determine a category" (GSR: 529a).

Li 理 "Principle" of organization, rationale, *pattern*. Expressing reservations about the translation "principle," A. S. Cua writes: "[G]iving a rationale for anything *x* may well be just an emphasis upon the significance or appropriateness of *x* within a particular context of discourse, and this does not entail the use of a context-independent notion such as the notion of principle" (1985, 24). Cua also raises questions about the translation of *li* as "pattern." He writes, "[W]e need to have some clear answers to such questions as 'What sort of pattern?' 'Are these patterns natural or artificial—that is, products of human invention?' 'If they are natural, how do we go about finding them?'" (1997, 201). These are good questions. But trying to answer them does not necessarily mean abandoning the word "pattern."

David Hall and Roger Ames describe the origin of the character as follows:

> [I]n its earliest occurrence, *li* conjures up the image of "dividing up land into cultivated fields *in a way consistent with the natural topography*." [Book of Songs, 210.] It refers to the pathways that permit access to the fields under cultivation. The *Shuowen*, a Han dynasty Chinese lexicon, inspired perhaps by the fact that *li* is classified under *yu* 玉, the "jade" signific, suggest that "dressing or polishing jade" and the "veins or striations within the jade" are its most fundamental meanings. Significantly, the dressing of jade requires craftsmen to conform their creative expression to those possibilities resident in the natural striations of the stone. In fact, the best lapidary is the one whose art maximizes the richest possibilities of the stone itself. As Tang

---

12. 故法不能獨立。類不能自行。(44/12/2; K: 12.1).
13. 其有法者以法行。無法者以類舉。(26/9/13; K: 9.2; W 35). Note that *ju* 舉 has the senses of "to choose" and "to promote," and thus the passage suggests room for discretion. Cf. "[Sage ministers] draw inferences from the categories by analogical extension and connect things with comparable cases in order to handle those cases for which there is no paradigm in the model." 推類接譽以待無方。(49/13/5; K: 13.1), Knoblock's translation.

Yi in his analysis of *li* observes, the process of dressing jade entails cutting and splitting the stone, as well as bringing out its luster through polishing. There is an immediate analogy here with the manner in which language is perceived to "dress" the world, both cutting it up and arranging it (Hall and Ames 1995, 212–13; emphasis in original).

For more about this character see chapter 2, especially section 2.5.

Li 禮 "rites," "ritual," proper conduct, norms of propriety, appropriate (ritual) behavior, ritualized roles and responsibilities, *ritual propriety*. In R. P. Peerenboom's words, "The *li*—conventionally translated as rites—may be understood more broadly to include the full range of social customs, ethical norms, and political principles embodied in the complex relations, organizations, and institutions of society. They are culture-specific norms, the contingent, ever-changing values of a particular society" (1993, 45). Similarly, Ames and Rosemont write, "*Li* are those meaning-invested roles, relationships, and institutions which facilitate communication, and which foster a sense of community. . . . They are a social grammar that provides each member with a defined place and status within the family, community, and polity. *Li* are life forms transmitted from generation to generation as repositories of meaning, enabling the youth to appropriate persisting values and to make them appropriate to their own situations" (1998, 51). Nicholas F. Gier notes, "A standard translation of *li* as 'propriety' takes on deeper meaning when we are reminded that the English word comes from the Latin *propius*—'making something one's own'" (2001, 289, citing Ames and Rosemont 1998, 51–52). In the *Xunzi*, *li* is often paired with *yi*, appropriateness (see *liyi* below).

Liyi 禮義 *Ritual propriety combined with a sense of appropriateness.* Consider Kwong-loi Shun's description of the relation between *li* and *yi*. He writes, "A person with *li* is not only skilled in and disposed to follow the rules of *li* but is also prepared to depart from such rules when appropriate. This preparedness involves the operation of *yi*, and commitment to propriety. Even when a rule of *li* should be followed, *yi* still has a role to play in that one should ideally follow the rule with an awareness of its appropriateness to the situation and, in that sense, *make the observance of the rule not a mechanical action but a display of one's own assessment of the situation*" (1997, 65; emphasis added). *Yi* is necessary for each and every performance of *li*, the degree of leeway, however, will depend on the particular case.

Liyi may be thought of as one idea with two sides, summed up in an ode quoted by Xunzi twice: "Ritual ceremony, completely according to the standard; laughter and speech, completely appropriate."[14] One side

---

14. 詩曰。禮儀卒度。笑語卒獲。此之謂也。 (72/19/42; K: 19.3; W 96; H 268).

emphasizes the formal aspect, the other side emphasizes the informal and personal. Paired together they represent the interdependence of the two sides. A performance of *li* without *yi* is no performance of *li* at all. Xunzi writes, "If it is not timely and fitting (*yi* 宜), if it is not respectfully sociable, if it is not cheerfully enjoyed, although it may be beautiful, it is not ritual propriety."[15] On the other hand, one cannot put *yi* into practice in a social vacuum. *Yi* requires *li* as a medium in which to operate. *Liyi*, then, is a sense of appropriateness informed by established rules of proper conduct, and vice versa.

Ming 名 "Names," *name-concepts*. *Ming* means name or term, but it also means something like concept, or meanings associated with a name. In the Chinese and Japanese literature on Xunzi, *ming* is often interpreted as 概念 (*gainian*, J: *gainen*) meaning concept, conception, notion, or idea. For example, Zhang Pei states plainly, "What Xunzi called '*ming*' is equivalent to 'concept.'"[16] In a Japanese dictionary of Chinese thought, Kaji Nobuyuki writes: "A name first of all means a term, it is the resultant auditory or visual symbol which names certain objects. At the same time, because it also includes the concept of these objects, '*ming*' indicates both the concept and its symbol."[17] In other words, *ming* is a vague concept in the sense that includes both what we would distinguish as a label, on the one hand, and the idea it signifies, on the other. Though one or the other may be more prominent depending on the context, *ming* as name-concept is one idea always carrying both connotations. It has other senses as well, such as rank and fame. These too are conceptually related. To have a rank is to have a degree of fame. Even one's personal name, which is added to as one's accomplishments grow, becomes a kind of indicator of fame. Moral terms indicate levels of honor and disgrace and thus a kind of moral rank, and when such terms attach to a person, they contribute to his or her fame or infamy.

   Ming can also be used as a verb meaning "to name." According to A. C. Graham, "Etymologically *ming*/*MIENG* 'name' is related to falling-tone *ming*/*MIANG* 命 'to ordain' which is to name either something to be brought about (a sense distinguished by another cognate word, *ling*/*LIENG* 令 'command') or an already existing thing" (1978, 196). In a world where the concept of "concept" and that of "ordaining" are both implicit in the same word, it would be difficult not to understand concepts as established—at least in part—by stipulation, and thus as contingent historical products.

---

15. 不時宜。不敬交。不驩欣。雖指。非禮也。 (96/27/9–10; K: 27.11).
16. 荀況的所謂「名」, 相當於概念。 (Zhang 1978, 32). Cf. Wei 1974, 162.
17. 名はまず名称を意味し、ある対象に対して名づけた結果の音声的視覚的符号である。同時に、その対象の概念をも含むので、概念とその符号との両者を指して名という。 (Hihara, p. 397). This entry is on names and actualities (*mingshi*, J: *meijitsu* 名実).

Ming 命 "Fate," decree, *the forces of circumstance*. Unlike the regularities of *tian* and *di*, *ming* takes into account the more random forces of circumstance, in this it is like *fortuna*. For example, Xunzi writes, "The circumstances one encounters are called *ming*."[18] The *Shuowen* defines *ming* as *shi* 使 "to cause to happen" (see Ames and Hall 2001, 71). Nagao Ryūichi likens the distinction between nature (J: *shizen* 自然) and artifice (J: *jin'i* 人為) in Xunzi to that between *ming* 命 and *dao* 道 in Confucius. The suggestion that *dao* is like artifice is consistent with the idea expressed in *Analects* 15.29: "People are able to broaden the way, it is not the way which broadens people."[19] Also, the idea that *ming* 命 is like *shizen* (nature) suggests a reading of *ming* closer to "the forces of circumstances" than the usual "fate."

   Tianming 天命 is a term which indicates a ruler has the moral authority to rule. While this can be thought of as "the decree of *tian*," it is so in a metaphorical sense of decree, and, at least for Xunzi, a naturalistic understanding of *tian*. Thus, *tianming* is that which is so by virtue of the propensities of things, and what is dictated by the forces of circumstance.

Qi 期 *Specify*. This character typically has to do with time. It can mean "a period of time," or "time limit." Significantly, it is often a stipulated period of time. The usage of *qi* at issue here, however, is technical (see section 3.3 for the relevant passages). Yang Liang's commentary identifies *qi* with *hui*, to combine (期，會也; Wang 1988, 422). Commenting on another passage Yang writes: "*Qi* is that which combines (*hui* 會) things and events (*wu* 物)" (期，物之所會也。 Wang 1988, 342). That is, *qi* indicates the combining of terms to clarify one's meaning. He gives the example of a white bird. If the object is not clear when one merely says "bird," one combines "bird" with "white." As an interpretation of *qi* for the relevant passages, this theory is somewhat persuasive—largely because it fits so nicely as a stage between names and phrases in the progression described in one of the passages. But this is only part of the story.

   Knoblock, along with Duyvendak and Mei, translates *qi* as "define," whereas Dubs and Goldin opt for versions of "designate." Morohashi offers support for this line of interpretation, so long the idea of a "definition" is not taken to indicate that things are fixed or "definite" in some absolute sense, but rather the practical activity of constructive stipulation. Morohashi lists twenty definitions for *qi* 期, the first of which is "To meet, meet by agreement" (あう。約束してであう。).[20] The third definition is "to contract, or make an agreement" (ちぎる。約束する。). The passages he cites for the first definition all equate *qi* with *hui* 會. *Hui* means "to gather," or "to join or bring together" in the sense of collect and unite, that is, to

---

18. 節遇謂之命。 (83/22/6; K: 22.1b; W 140; H 279).
19. 子曰：人能弘道，非道弘人。
20. I have updated the hiragana to conform to modern conventions.

assemble. It also means "opportunity or chance" (*jihui* 機會), and as an adjective, "by chance, fortunately" (*qiaqiao* 恰巧), thus: a chance opportunity. Contingency is written all over this character, and yet, at the same time, it also means "specified and definite" (*yiding* 一定). *Qi* also means specified and definite. Indeed, Morohashi's second definition of *qi* is *kimeru*, "to fix firmly." Expressing all this as a single concept, we could say that *qi* means "opportune assembly of contingent elements into a relatively stable standard, or convention." The word "specify" has been chosen as an attempt to include this meaning as well as that suggested by Yang. It means, on the one hand, to give more information to make one's meaning clearer, and, on the other hand, to stipulate what something is to mean. It is making a detailed description/prescription.[21]

Ren 仁 Along with *tian*, this is a term for which a suitable English equivalent has thus far proved elusive. Possible glosses and close associations include: "humanity," kindness, sensitivity, human connectedness, *comprehensive virtue*, *consummate person* (*ren ren* 仁人). Mencius defines *ren* as "to be human" or "to be a person." *Mencius* 7B16 states, "To be *ren* is to be a person. *Dao* is the doctrine which puts these two together."[22] Mencius also says that *ren* grows out of a sense of compassion, without which we would not be human (*ren* 人) (*Mencius* 2A6).

Confucius is responsible for this concept as we know it, and—along with the concept of *li* 禮 (ritual propriety)—it could be considered his most central idea. It plays a more minor role in Xunzi, but it is still a term of considerable moral weight. Confucius's understanding of *ren* can be thought of as being composed of *zhong* and *shu*. *Shu*, conveniently, has the sense of putting oneself in another person's *shoes*. And, *zhong* is doing one's utmost. Thus, to be *ren* is to try to see things from other people's perspectives, and then to do one's best for them with that in mind (*Analects* 6.30).

Also, *ren* is often paired with *ai* (愛 love)—as in *Analects* 12.22 and *Xunzi* K: 29.7. So the connotations associated with love are likewise to be included in our understanding or *ren*, while not limiting it to a psychological feeling. *Ren* is also homophonous with *ren* 任 meaning burden.[23] In the *Analects*, Zengzi says, "Scholar-officials must be strong and determined, for their burden (*ren* 任) is heavy and their way (*dao*) is long. They take *ren* 仁 as their own responsibility (*ren* 任). Is this not heavy? And they carry it until their dying day. Is this not long?"[24] Thus *ren* may be thought of as taking

---

21. For an alternative view, see Cua 1985, 47–51. Cua hypothesizes that "While *ming* fits a term to actuality, *qi* fits the term to the understanding of the hearer" (51).

22. 仁也者，人也。合而言之，道也。(*Mencius* 7B16).

23. Irene Bloom's note (Bloom 1996, 150 n30) called this to my attention.

24. 曾子曰：「士不可以不弘毅，任重而道遠。仁以為己任，不亦重乎？死而後已，不亦遠乎？」(*Analects* 8.7).

on a burden on behalf of those loved. As Chen Jingpan puts it, "[*Ren*] is an earnest desire and beneficent action, both active and passive, for the well-being of the one loved" (1990, 252).

Ren is also defined in terms of virtues, such as "Deference, tolerance, making good on one's word, diligence, and generosity" (*Analects* 17.6, Ames and Rosemont's translation). Being *ren* can indeed be thought of as exhibiting the full range of Confucian virtues. Thus, "comprehensive virtue."

Considering the Confucian conception of the social self, and the form of the character *ren* 仁—that is, 人 (person) plus 二 (two)—it makes sense to think of a *ren* person as someone who has developed these virtues through appropriate social engagements, and has thus increased the scope of his or her relations and influence. In Peerenboom's words: "the Confucian concept of *ren* is a duty to act appropriately in relation to others," it is "excellence in interpersonal relations" (1993, 44, 42). Capturing this sense of the term, James Behuniak, in his *Mencius on Becoming Human*, consistently glosses *ren* as "associated humanity." Further, *ren ren* 仁人 can be rendered "consummate person," or "authoritative social person." It can be thought of as: those of comprehensive virtue who do their utmost in the service of others.

Shi 實 object, *actuality*, the actual thing, concrete particulars. "*Shi* is the thing or affair which is indicated by the name" (Chen 1990, 124).[25] It is not the concept indicated by the name. *Ming* covers both label and concept. *Shi*, on the other hand, refers to the actual and particular things or events in the world that count as instances of a name-concept.[26]

Tiandi 天地 "What Xunzi calls '*tian*' means *tian* as nature."[27] *Tian* refers to the propensities associated with the sky,[28] for example, the progression of the seasons. *Di* refers to those characteristics of nature associated with the earth, such as natural resources and plant growth. Sometimes *tian* alone stands for the combination *tiandi*, the propensities of the heavens and the earth, that is, nature. A third factor is required in order to make the most of these natural propensities: *ren* 人 (people). Through the judicious use of available resources, people bring to completion what is made possible by *tian* and *di* (see 62/17/7; K: 17.2a; W 80).

---

25. 實是名所的指事物。

26. See Graham 1978, 196–97, 325.

27. 荀子所言之天，則為自然之天。 (Feng 1961, 355; cf. Fung 1952, 284). Kakimura and Azuma's Japanese translation reads: 荀子のいう「天」は自然としての天を意味する。 (1995, 421).

28. Consider Ogyū Sorai's comments on *tian*. "*Tian* needs no explanation. Everybody knows where it is. Gazing at its vast and hazy blueness, it seems dusky dim, far and high. We cannot fully fathom it. The heavenly bodies are fastened to it. Wind and rain, cold and heat, travel through it." 天不待解。人所皆知也。望之蒼蒼然。冥冥乎不可得而測之。日月星辰繫焉。風雨寒暑行焉。 (Inoue and Kanie 1970, 79; cf. Najita 1998, 114) Sorai was an influential Tokugawa Confucian thinker who was strongly influenced by Xunzi.

Wei 偽 "Conscious activity," deliberative effort, *constructive activity* and its resulting *constructs*, artifice. *Li* 禮 (ritual propriety) is an example of *wei* as constructive artifice. However, *wei* is also—indeed it is *especially—acquired character* in contrast to original character (*xing* 性). That is, it is one's developed and refined qualities and values, as well as those constructs that facilitate the development of such characteristics. See chapter 5, especially section 5.2.

Xin 心 Heart-mind. For *xin* I have succumb to the usage of a dash separating the words "heart" and "mind." If one were forced to choose, in the case of Xunzi, the choice would have to be "mind." However, the character *xin* has a strong association with the region of the heart, and is more embodied then the modern concept of mind. While Xunzi concerns himself with the activities of the calm (unified, empty and still)—and thus reasonable—mind, *xin* is nevertheless something potentially susceptible to influence from emotions, and is at the same time integrated with the sense organs.

Xing 性 "Human nature," original (human) nature, original desires. Xunzi defines *xing* as follows: "*Xing* is something given by nature (*tian*). It cannot be learned nor acquired through work."[29] "What is so by virtue of birth is called *xing*."[30] Xunzi is most famous for his statement *xing e* 性惡, original human nature is crude/detestable (see *e* 惡 above, and section 5.1). Xunzi finds our original desires highly problematic and our original nature crude and unadorned. "Human nature" is somewhat problematic as a translation of *xing* because it may be taken to imply how we are fated to be. According to Xunzi's philosophy, however, while our initial dispositions are base, we can and should transform ourselves. Through the practice of ritual propriety, we can develop an admirable character. This second nature is not included under Xunzi's definitions of *xing*, rather he characterizes it as *wei* 偽 (manmade).

Yi 義 "Righteousness," "rightness," *appropriate, sense of appropriateness*. Cua, who translates *yi* as "rightness," explains: "*Yi* focuses principally on what is right or fitting. The equation of *yi* with its homophone meaning 'appropriateness' [宜] is explicit in *Zhongyong*, Section 20, and generally accepted by Confucianists, e.g., Xunzi, Li Gou, and Zhu Xi. However, what is right or fitting depends on reasoned judgment. As Xunzi puts it: 'The person concerned with *yi* follows reason.' Thus, *yi* may be construed as reasoned judgment concerning the right thing to do in particular exigencies. Recall Li Gou's plausible statement that what is *yi* is 'decisive judgment' that is appropriate to the situation at hand" (Cua 1998, 277).

---

29. 凡性者。天之就也。不可學不可事。 (87/23/11; K: 23.1c; W 158; H 285).
30. 生之所以然者謂之性。 (83/22/2; K: 22.1b; W 139; H 278).

Gier maintains, "'Right' rather than the traditional 'righteousness' is a much better translation of *yi*, as long as we realize that this would always mean what is right for us or right for our condition" (2001, 287). And, Huang Chung-chieh submits, "In China, *yi* has never been a universal rule of conduct eternally fixed in the cognitive heavens, but instead has always been a matter of flexible judgment rendered to make ourselves fit for ever-changing situations" (1993, 60). Since there is no presumption of a *single* "right answer," I prefer some variation on the word "appropriate." Also, for Xunzi, *yi* can mean a faculty, or an ability, so sometimes it may be rendered "a sense of appropriateness." There are also instances where Xunzi uses *yi* to mean merely that which makes such a sophisticated sense possible; in such cases it is the *potential* for practical wisdom. Nevertheless, generally, *yi* indicates a *developed* sense of appropriateness.

Zhi 知 "To know," intelligence, *to grasp the significance of*, *to appreciate* (in the senses of perceiving the value of something and acknowledging its legitimacy). *Zhi* can be understood as a highly developed understanding of the relatedness of phenomena. Graham states that for Xunzi, "intelligence is what Anglo-Saxons call 'common sense,' the sort which values a synthesizing grasp of how things hang together above analysis, and which prefers not to push analysis further than needed to resolve issues arising in controversy" (1989, 254). In addition, *zhi* can mean "to realize," in the sense of having a robust kind of appreciation for the significance of something as a result of putting it into practice (*xing* 行). In this respect, it is like *tihui* 體會, to learn through experience and embody. This should be contrasted with the idea of knowing something abstractly and *then* putting it into practice. Knowledge (*zhi*), on Xunzi's view, is inseparable from practice.

Highlighting a different aspect of *zhi*, Yearley offers a helpful contrast between a common Western understanding of knowledge and one assumed by ancient Chinese philosophers:

Unlike most traditional Western thinkers who argue that immutable truths exist and that people's knowledge can correspond to them—a correspondence theory of truth—most classical Chinese thinkers see knowledge in a different way. For them, to know is to follow out a learned system of naming and evaluating, to be guided by a learned process of construing what we are taught when we learn a language. . . . Human beings are controlled by the language they use; they depend on what their language allows them to do. *To know*, then, *is to make distinctions that engender attitudes that cause actions*. What we seek, what we fear, and what we hope for arise from the language that our culture gives us. No objective truths exist to which one language can correspond; what exists are those ways in which particular groups use a language to divide up the world. . . . What we say, think, and do depends on the discourse of the particular group or culture we live in. Such a perspective severs any simple correspondence between language and the world, any simple relationship between things out there and our talk about those things. (1983, 126; emphasis added)

Putting Graham's and Yearley's insights together, we can say that *zhi* entails both a "synthesizing grasp of how things hang together" as well as a constructive stipulation of distinctions. Rather than the synthesizing grasp serving as a foundation for a determinate analysis, the two sides of knowledge inform each other in the ongoing process of learning, as we play out the roles that we both inherit and create in a world we are both grasping and constructing.

References

Abe Yoshio 阿部吉雄. 1964. *Chūgoku no Tetsugaku* 中国の哲学 [Chinese philosophy]. Tokyo: University of Tokyo Press.

Ames, Roger T., and David L. Hall 2001. *Focusing the Familiar: A Translation and Philosophical Interpretation of the* Zhongyong. Honolulu: University of Hawaii Press.

Ames, Roger T., and Henry Rosemont, Jr. 1998. *The Analects of Confucius: A Philosophical Translation*. New York: Ballantine Books.

Behuniak, James Jr. 2005. *Mencius on Becoming Human*. Albany: SUNY.

Bell, Catherine. 1992. *Ritual Theory, Ritual Practice*. New York: Oxford University Press.

Bloom, Irene. 1996. "Confucian Perspectives on the Individual and the Collectivity." In *Religious Diversity and Human Rights*, ed. Irene Bloom, J. Paul Martin, and Wayne L. Proudfoot, 114–51. New York: Columbia University Press.

Bodde, Derk. 1953. "Harmony and Conflict in Chinese Philosophy." In *Studies in Chinese Thought*, ed. Arthur F. Wright, 19–80. Chicago: University of Chicago Press.

Campany, Robert F. 1992. "Xunzi and Durkheim as Theorists of Ritual Practice." In *Discourse and Practice*, ed. Frank Reynolds and David Tracy, 197–231. Albany: SUNY.

Chan, Wing-tsit. 1963. *A Source Book in Chinese Philosophy*. Princeton: Princeton University Press.

——. 1964. "The Evolution of the Neo-Confucian Concept of *Li* as Principle." *Tsinghua Journal of Chinese Studies* 4 (2): 123–49.

Chen Daqi 陳大齊. 1954. *Xunzi xueshuo* 荀子學說 [Xunzi's theory]. Taipei: Chung-hua wen-hua Publication Committee.

Chen Jingpan. 1990. *Confucius as a Teacher*. Beijing: Foreign Languages Press.

Cheng Chung-ying. 1969. *Tai Chen's Inquiry into Goodness*. Hong Kong: South Sky Book Company.

Chong, Kim-Chong. 2003. "Xunzi's Systematic Critique of Mencius." *Philosophy East and West* 53 (2): 215–33.

Cook, Scott. 1997. "Xun Zi on Ritual and Music." *Monumenta Serica* 45: 1–38.

Creel, Herrlee G. 1974 . *Shen Pu-Hai: A Chinese Political Philosopher of the Fourth Century B. C.* Chicago: University of Chicago Press.

Cua, A. S. 1979. "Dimensions of *Li* (Propriety): Reflections on an Aspect of Hsün Tzu's Ethics." *Philosophy East and West* 29 (4): 373–94.

——. 1985. *Ethical Argumentation: A Study in Hsün Tzu's Moral Epistemology*. Honolulu: University of Hawaii Press.

——. 1989. "The Concept of *Li* in Confucian Moral Theory." In *Understanding the Chinese Mind: The Philosophical Roots*, ed. Robert E. Allinson, 209–35. New York: Oxford University Press.

——. 1993. "The Possibility of Ethical Knowledge: Reflections on a Theme in the Hsün Tzu." In *Epistemological Issues in Classical Chinese Philosophy*, ed. Hans Lenk and Gregor Paul, 159–79. Albany: SUNY.

——. 1997. "Reason and Principle in Chinese Philosophy: An Interpretation of *Li*." In *A Companion to World Philosophies*, ed. E. Deutsch and R. Bontekoe, 201–13. Malden: Blackwell.

——. 1998. *Moral Vision and Tradition: Essays in Chinese Ethics*. Washington: Catholic University of America Press.

——. 2003. "The Ethical Significance of Shame: Insights of Aristotle and Xunzi." *Philosophy East and West* 53 (2): 147–202.

——. 2005. *Human Nature, Ritual, and History: Studies in Xunzi and Chinese Philosophy*. Washington: Catholic University of America Press.

Downes, Stephen M. 1998. "Constructivism" In *Routledge Encyclopedia of Philosophy*, vol. 2, ed. Edward Craig. New York: Routledge.

Dubs, Homer. 1966a. *Hsüntze: The Moulder of Ancient Confucianism*. Taipei: Ch'eng-Wen Publishing Company.

——, trans. 1966b. *The Works of Hsüntze*. Taipei: Ch'eng-Wen Publishing Company.

Duyvendak, J. J. L. 1924. "Hsün-tzu on the Rectification of Names." *Toung Pao* 2 (23): 221–54.

Ebrey, Patricia Buckley. 1991. *Confucianism and Family Rituals in Imperial China: A Social History of Writings about Rites*. Princeton: Princeton University Press.

Eno, Robert. 1990. *The Confucian Creation of Heaven: Philosophy and the Defense of Ritual Mastery*. Albany: SUNY.

Feng Youlan [Fung Yu-lan] 馮友蘭. 1961. *Zhongguo zhexueshi* 中國哲學史 [A history of Chinese philosophy]. Hong Kong: Taiping Yang Tushu.

Fu Yunlong and He Zuokang, trans. 1996. 大學 中庸 *The Great Learning—The Doctrine of the Mean*. Beijing: Sinolingua. (Fu provides a modern Chinese translation, and He provides an English translation).

Fung Yu-lan [Feng Youlan]. 1952. *A History of Chinese Philosophy*. Vol. 1, *The Period of the Philosophers*. Translated by Derk Bodde. Princeton: Princeton University Press.

——. 1953. *A History of Chinese Philosophy*. Vol. 2, *The Period of Classical Learning from the Second Century B.C. to the Twentieth Century A.D.* Translated by Derk Bodde. Princeton: Princeton University Press.

Giddens, Anthony. 1981. "Agency, institution, and time-space analysis." In *Advances in Social Theory and Methodology*, ed. K. Knorr-Cetina and A. V. Cicourel, 161–74. Boston: Routledge and Kegan Paul.

Gier, Nicholas F. 2001. "The Dancing *Ru*: A Confucian Aesthetics of Virtue." *Philosophy East and West* 51 (2): 280–305.

Gill, Sam. 1998. "No Place to Stand: Jonathan Z. Smith as *Homo Ludens*, The Academic

Study of Religion *Sub Specie Ludi.*" *Journal of the American Academy of Religion* 66 (2): 283–312.

Goldin, Paul Rakita. 1999. *Rituals of the Way: The Philosophy of Xunzi*. Chicago: Open Court.

Gould, Stephen Jay. 1983. "What, If Anything, Is a Zebra?" In *Hen's Teeth and Horses's Toes*, 355–65. New York: Norton.

Graham, A. C. 1978. *Later Mohist Logic, Ethics and Science*. Hong Kong: Chinese University Press.

———. 1989. *Disputers of the Tao: Philosophical Argument in Ancient China*. La Salle, IL: Open Court.

———. 1990. *Studies in Chinese Philosophy and Philosophical Literature*. Albany: SUNY.

———. 1991. "Reflections and Replies." In *Chinese Texts and Philosophical Contexts: Essays Dedicated to Angus C. Graham*, ed. Henry Rosemont, Jr. Chicago: Open Court.

Hagen, Kurtis. 2000. "A Critical Review of Ivanhoe on Xunzi." *Journal of Chinese Philosophy* 27 (3): 361–73.

———. 2001a. Review of *Virtue, Nature, and Moral Agency in the* Xunzi. *Philosophy East and West* 51 (3): 434–40.

———. 2001b. "The Concepts of *Li* and *Lei* in the *Xunzi*: Constructive Patterning of Categories." *International Philosophical Quarterly* 41 (2): 183–97.

———. 2002. "Xunzi's Use of *Zhengming*: Naming as a Constructive Project." *Asian Philosophy* 12 (1): 35–51.

———. 2003a. "Artifice and Virtue in the Xunzi." *Dao: A Journal of Comparative Philosophy* 3 (1): 85–107.

———. 2003b. "Xunzi and the Nature of Confucian Ritual." *Journal of the American Academy of Religion* 71 (2): 371–403.

———. 2005. "Junshi ni oite no 'ri', 'rui' soshite 'na' ni tsuite: Junshi ni kansuru eigo bunken no kentō" 荀子においての「理」、「類」そして「名」について：荀子に関する英語文献の検討 [Patterns, categories and names in the *Xunzi*: A critical review of the English language literature on Xunzi]. *Studies in Humanities and Social Sciences* (Nihon University) 69: 9–27.

Hall, David L., and Roger T. Ames. 1987. *Thinking through Confucius*. Albany: SUNY.

———. 1995. *Anticipating China: Thinking through the Narratives of Chinese and Western Culture*. Albany: SUNY.

———. 1999. *The Democracy of the Dead: Dewey, Confucius, and the Hope for Democracy in China*. Chicago: Open Court.

Hansen, Chad. 1983. *Language and Logic in Ancient China*. Ann Arbour: University of Michigan Press.

———. 1992. *A Daoist Theory of Chinese Thought: A Philosophical Interpretation*. New York: Oxford University Press.

Heritage, John. 1984. *Garfinkel and Ethnomethodology*. Cambridge: Polity Press.

Hihara Toshikuni, ed. 日原利国. 1984. *Chūgoku shisō jiten* 中国思想辞典 [Dictionary of Chinese thought]. Tokyo: Kenbun Shuppan.

Hu Shih. 1963. *The Development of the Logical Method in Ancient China*. New York: Paragon Reprint Co.

Huang Chun-chieh. 1993. "'Rightness' (*i*) versus 'Profit' (*li*) in Ancient China: The Polemics between Mencius and Yang Chu, Mo Tzu, and Hsün Tzu." *Proceedings of the National Science Council, Part C: Humanities and Social Sciences* 3 (1): 59–72.

Hutton, Eric L. 2001. "Xunzi." In *Readings in Classical Chinese Philosophy*, ed. Philip J. Ivanhoe and Bryan W. Van Norden. New York: Seven Bridges Press.

———. 2002. "Moral Reasoning in Aristotle and Xunzi." *Journal of Chinese Philosophy* 29 (3): 355–84.

———. 2003. "On Nature and Ethics in the Philosophy of Xunzi." Unpublished manuscript.

Ikeda Tomohisa 池田知久. 1996. "Juka no 'sansai' to Rōshi no 'shidai'" 儒家の「三才」と『老子』の「四大」[Confucianism's "trinity" and the *Laozi*'s "four great elements"]. In *Nakamura Shōhachi hakushi koki kinen tōyōgaku ronshū* 中村璋八博士古稀記念東洋学論集. Tokyo: Kyūko shoin.

Inoue Tetsujirū and Kanie Yoshimaru, eds. 井上哲次郎, 蟹江義丸共編. 1970. *Nihon Rinri Ihen* 日本倫理彙編 Vol. 6. Kyoto: Rinsen Book Co.

Itano Chōhachi 板野長八. 1995. *Jukyō seiritsu shi no kenkyū* 儒教成立史の研究 [A study of the historical formation of Confucianism]. Tokyo: Iwanami shoten.

Ivanhoe, Philip J. 1991. "A Happy Symmetry: Xunzi's Ethical Thought." *Journal of the American Academy of Religion* 59 (2): 309–22.

———. 2000. "Human Nature and Moral Understanding in the *Xunzi*." In Kline and Ivanhoe, *Virtue, Nature, and Moral Agency in the* Xunzi, 237–49.

Jiang Shangxian 姜尚賢. 1966. *Xunzi sixiang tixi* 荀子思想體系 [Xunzi's Ideology]. Tainan: Xie yi yinshua ju.

Kaizuka Shigeki 貝塚茂樹. 1961. *Shoshi hyakka: Chūgoku kodai shisōkatachi* 諸子百家：中国古代思想家たち [The various masters of the 100 schools: thinkers of ancient China]. Tokyo: Iwanami shoten.

Kaji Nobuyuki 加地伸行. 1971. "Chūgoku kodai ronrigakushi ni okeru Junshi" 中国古代論理学史における荀子 [On Hsün-tzu in the history of logic in ancient China]. *Tōhōgaku* 41: 32–47.

Kakimura Takashi and Azuma Jūji 柿村峻、吾妻重二. 1995. *Chūgoku Tetsugakushi* 中国哲学史 [History of Chinese philosophy]. Tokyo: Fuzanbo.

Kanaya Osamu 金谷治. 1970. "Junshi no tenjin no bun ni tsuite" 荀子の天人の分について [Xunzi's distinction between *tian* and people]. *Shūkan tōyōgaku* 24: 1–14.

Karlgren, Bernhard. 1957. *Grammata Serica Recensa. Bulletin of the Museum of Far Eastern Antiquities* 29: 1–332.

Kasoff, Ira E. 1984. *The Thought of Chang Tsai (1020–1077)*. New York: Cambridge University Press.

Kline T. C., III. 2000. "Moral Agency and Motivation in the *Xunzi*." In Kline and Ivanhoe, *Virtue, Nature, and Moral Agency in the* Xunzi, 155–75.

———, ed. 2004. *Ritual and Religion in the Xunzi*. Chatham, NJ: Chatham House Publishers.

Kline, T. C., III, and Philip J. Ivanhoe, eds. 2000. *Virtue, Nature, and Moral Agency in the* Xunzi. Indianapolis: Hackett Publishing Company.

Knoblock, John. 1988–1994. *Xunzi: A Translation and Study of the Complete Works.* 3 vols. Stanford: Stanford University Press.

Kodama Rokurō 兒玉六郎. 1973. "Junshi no 'ren zhi xing e, qi shan zhe wei ye' no kaisyaku" 荀子の「人之性惡，其善者偽也」の解釈 [An interpretation of Xunzi's 'Human nature is crude, its goodness is artifice']. *Kagoshima kōgyō kōtō senmon gakkō kenkyū hōkoku* 8: 79–89.

———. 1992. *Junshi no shisō* 荀子の思想 [Xunzi's thought]. Tokyo: Kozama shobō.

Lakoff, George. 1987. *Women, Fire and Dangerous Things: What Categories Reveal about the Mind.* Chicago: University of Chicago Press.

Lao Siguang [Lao Sze-kwang] 勞思光. 1968. *Zhongguo Zhexueshi* 中國哲學史 [A history of Chinese philosophy]. Vol. 1. Hong Kong: The Chinese University of Hong Kong.

Lau, D. C., trans. 1979. *Confucius: The Analects.* Harmondsworth: Penguin Books.

———, ed. 1996. *A Concordance to the Xunzi* [*Xunzi zhuzi suoyin* 荀子逐字索引]. Hong Kong: The Commercial Press.

———. 2000. "Theories of Human Nature in Mencius and Xunzi," In Kline and Ivanhoe, *Virtue, Nature, and Moral Agency in the* Xunzi, 188–219.

Lee, Janghee. 2004. *Xunzi and Early Chinese Naturalism.* Albany: SUNY.

Li, Chenyang. 1999. *The Tao Encounters the West.* Albany: SUNY.

Lin Lizhen 林麗真. 1978. "Xunzi" 荀子 in *Zhongguo lidai sixiangjia* 中國歷代思想家, ed. Wang Shounan 王壽南. Vol. 1. Taipei: Taiwan Shangwu yin shu guan.

Machle, Edward J. 1976. "Hsün Tzu as a Religious Philosopher." *Philosophy East and West* 26 (4): 443–61.

———. 1993. *Nature and Heaven in the Xunzi: A Study of the Tian Lun.* Albany: SUNY.

Makeham, John. 1994. *Name and Actuality in Early Chinese Thought.* Albany: SUNY.

Maspero, Henri. 1978. *China in Antiquity.* Translated by Frank A. Kierman, Jr. Amherst: University of Massachusetts Press.

Mei, Y. P. 1951. "Hsün-tzu on Terminology." *Philosophy East and West* 1 (2): 51–66.

Morohashi Tetsuji 諸橋轍次, ed. 1957. *Daikanwa jiten* 大漢和辭典 [Great Chinese–Japanese dictionary]. Tokyo: Taishūgan.

Munro, Donald J. 1969. *The Concept of Man in Early China.* Stanford: Stanford University Press.

Murase Hiroya 村瀬裕也. 1986. *Junshi no sekai* 荀子の世界 [The world of Xunzi]. Tokyo: Nichū shuppan.

Nagao Ryūichi 長尾龍一. 1999. *Kodai Chūgoku shisō nōto* 古代中国思想ノート [Ancient Chinese thought notebook]. Tokyo: Shinzansha shuppan.

Najita, Tetsuo, ed. 1998. *Tokugawa Political Writings.* New York: Cambridge University Press.

Nishi Junzō 西順蔵. 1969. *Chūgoku shisō ronshū* 中国思想論集 [Collected essays on Chinese thought]. Tokyo: Chikuma.

Nivison, David S. 1996a. "Replies and Comments." In *Chinese Language, Thought, and Culture: Nivison and His Critics*, ed. Philip J. Ivanhoe. Chicago: Open Court.

———. 1996b. *The Ways of Confucianism: Investigations in Chinese Philosophy*. Edited by Bryan W. Van Norden. Chicago: Open Court.

———. 2000. "Xunzi and Zhuangzi." In Kline and Ivanhoe, *Virtue, Nature, and Moral Agency in the* Xunzi, 176–87.

Okamoto Tetsuharu 岡本哲治. 1986. *Ten to Jin to Koku: Junshi no shisō to keisei no ronri* 天と人と国：荀子の思想と経世の倫理 [Heaven, people and country: Xunzi's thought and the ethics of government]. Tokyo: Geiritsu Shuppan.

Ōmuro Mikio 大室幹雄. 1967. "Junshi no rekishi ishiki" 荀子の歴史意識 [Historical sense of Hsün-tzu]. *The Tokyo Shinagaku-hō: Bulletin of the Tokyo Sinological Society* 13: 113–34.

O'Neill, Onora. 1998. "Constructivism in Ethics." In *Routledge Encyclopedia of Philosophy*, ed. Edward Craig. Vol. 2. New York: Routledge.

Peerenboom, R. P. 1993. "What's Wrong with Chinese Rights? Toward a Theory of Rights with Chinese Characteristics." *Harvard Human Rights Journal* 6: 29–57.

Perrett, Roy. 2002. "Evil and Human Nature." *Monist* 85 (2): 304–19.

Puett, Michael. 2001. *The Ambivalence of Creation: Debates Concerning Innovation and Artifice in Early China*. Stanford: Stanford University Press. An earlier version of this essay can be found in: Michael Puett (1997), "Nature and Artifice: Debates in Late Warring States China concerning the Creation of Culture," *Harvard Journal of Asiatic Studies* 57 (2): 471–518.

Radcliffe-Brown, A. R. 1952. *Structure and Function in Primitive Society: Essays and Addresses*. London: Cohen & West.

Rawls, John. 1999. "Kantian Constructivism in Moral Theory." In *John Rawls: Collected Papers*, ed. Samuel Freeman. Cambridge, MA: Harvard University Press.

Rosemont, Henry Jr. 1971. "On Reappraising Ancient Chinese Philosophy." *Philosophy East and West* 21 (2): 203–17, and the public correspondence between Rosemont and Donald Munro in *Philosophy East and West* 21 (3): 351–57.

———. 1976. Review of *Confucius—The Secular as Sacred* by Herbert Fingarette. *Philosophy East and West* 26 (4): 463–77.

———. 2000. "State and Society in the *Xunzi*." In Kline and Ivanhoe, *Virtue, Nature, and Moral Agency in the* Xunzi, 1–38.

Sato, Masayuki. 2000. "The Development of pre-Qin Conceptual Terms and their Incorporation into Xunzi's Thought." In *Linked Faiths: Essays on Chinese Religions and Traditional Culture in Honour of Kristofer Schipper*, ed. Jan A. M. De Meyer and Peter M. Engelfriet. Boston: Brill.

———. 2003. *The Confucian Quest for Order: The Origin and Formation of the Political Thought of Xun Zi*. Boston: Brill.

Schofer, Jonathan. 2000. "Virtues in Xunzi's Thought." In Kline and Ivanhoe, *Virtue, Nature, and Moral Agency in the* Xunzi, 69–88.

Schwartz, Benjamin I. 1985. *The World of Thought in Ancient China*. Cambridge: Harvard University Press.

Searle, John R. 1995. *The Construction of Social Reality.* New York: The Free Press.

Shun, Kwong-loi. 1997. *Mencius and Early Chinese Thought.* Stanford: Stanford University Press.

Singer, Marcus G. 1995. "Moral Epistemology." In *The Cambridge Dictionary of Philosophy*, ed. Robert Audi. New York: Cambridge University Press.

Smith, Jonathan Z. 1978. "Map Is Not Territory." In *Map Is Not Territory: Studies in the History of Religions*, 289–309. Leiden: E. J. Brill.

———. 1987. *To Take Place: Toward Theory in Ritual.* Chicago: University of Chicago Press.

Stalnaker, Aaron. 2002. Review of *Virtue, Nature, and Moral Agency in the* Xunzi. *Journal of Chinese Philosophy* 29 (2): 293–96.

Stevenson, Charles L. 1963. *Facts and Values: Studies in Ethical Analysis.* New Haven: Yale University Press.

Sugimoto Tatsuo 杉本達夫. 1996. *Junshi* 荀子 [Xunzi]. Tokyo: Tokuma shoten.

Takeuchi Yoshio 武内義雄. 1936. *Chūgoku shisōshi* 中国思想史 [History of Chinese thought]. Tokyo: Iwanami, reprint 1965.

Tillman, Hoyt Cleveland. 1994. *Ch'en Liang on Public Interest and the Law.* Honolulu: University of Hawaii Press.

Timmons, Mark. 1996. "Constructivism." In *The Encyclopedia of Philosophy Supplement*, ed. Donald M. Borchert. New York: Macmillan.

Tversky. Amos. 1977. "Features of Similarity." *Psychological Review* 84 (4): 327–52.

Van Norden, Bryan W. 1993. "Hansen on Hsün-Tzu." *Journal of Chinese Philosophy* 20: 365–82.

———. 1996. Introduction to *The Ways of Confucianism: Investigations in Chinese Philosophy*, by David Nivison, 1–13. Chicago: Open Court.

———. 2000. "Mengzi and Xunzi: Two Views of Human Agency." In Kline and Ivanhoe, *Virtue, Nature, and Moral Agency in the* Xunzi, 103–34.

Waley, Arthur. 1938. *The Analects of Confucius.* London: George Allen & Unwin.

Wang Xianqian 王先謙. 1988. *Xunzi Jijie* 荀子集解 [Collected commentaries on the *Xunzi*]. 2 vols. Beijing: Zhonghua Shuju.

Watanabe Takashi 渡邊卓. 1973. *Kodai Chūgoku shisō no kenkyū* 古代中国思想の研究 [A Study of ancient Chinese thoughts. Tokyo: Sōbunsha.

Watson, Burton. 1963. *Hsün-tzu: Basic Writings.* New York: Columbia University Press.

Wei Zhengtong 韋政通. 1974. *Xunzi yu gudai zhexue* 荀子與古代哲學 [Xunzi and ancient philosophy]. Taipei: Commercial Press.

Xu Fuguan [Hsü Fu-kuan] 徐復觀. 1963. *Zhongguo renxing lun shi* 中國人性論史 [The history of the Chinese philosophy of human nature]. Taizhong: Sili Donghai Daxue.

Xunzi yinde 荀子引得 [Concordance to the Hsün Tzu]. 1966. Harvard-Yenching Institute Sinological Index Series, suppl. 22. Taipei: Chinese Materials and Research Aids Service Center. (References to the Chinese text for the *Xunzi* are to this concordance.)

Yearley, Lee. 1980. "Hsün Tzu on the Mind: His Attempted Synthesis of Confucianism and Taoism." *Journal of Asian Studies* 39: 465–80.

——. 1983. "The Perfected Person in the Radical Chuang-tzu." In *Experimental Essays on Chuang-tzu*, ed.Victor H. Mair, 125–39. Honolulu: University of Hawaii Press.

Zhang Bei 章沛. 1978. "Guanyu Xun Kuang de luoji sixiang de tantao" 關於荀況的邏輯思想的探討 [Exploring Xun Kuang's logical thought]. *Zhexue yanjiu*. 6: 32–39. An English translation of this article by Morimasa Kushihara can be found in *Chinese Studies in Philosophy* 10, no. 3 (1979): 28–40.

Index